# Fun with the Family™ Florida

Praise for previous editions:

"Thankfully, it's not all just Disney."

—*Rocky Mountain News* (Denver, Colo.)

"[The] emphasis on wilderness, educational, and kitschy attractions is a refreshing alternative to theme park overkill."

—*Prodigy Travel Newsletter*

"Designed to keep vacationing parents and kids happy."

—*Tennessean* (Nashville, Tenn.)

"Thinking like a parent with one hand on her purse, Walton alerts her readers to 'Florida's excellent and extensive state park system.' I've learned to rely on the 'best of' lists that appear in each chapter."

—*Times* (St. Petersburg, Fla.)

D1509207

# Help Us Keep This Guide Up to Date

Every effort has been made by the author and editors to make this guide as accurate and useful as possible. However, many changes can occur after a guide is published—establishments close, phone numbers change, hiking trails are rerouted, facilities come under new management, etc.

We would love to hear from you concerning your experiences with this guide and how you feel it could be improved and be kept up to date. While we may not be able to respond to all comments and suggestions, we'll take them to heart, and we'll make certain to share them with the author. Please send your comments and suggestions to the following address:

The Globe Pequot Press
Reader Response/Editorial Department
P.O. Box 480
Guilford, CT 06437
Or you may e-mail us at: editorial@GlobePequot.com

Thanks for your input, and happy travels!

INSIDERS' GUIDE®

FUN WITH THE FAMILY™ SERIES

# fun WITH the Family™
## FLORIDA

HUNDREDS OF IDEAS FOR DAY TRIPS WITH THE KIDS

CHELLE KOSTER WALTON AND SARA KENNEDY

REVISED AND UPDATED BY

STEPHEN MORRILL AND ADELE WOODYARD

SIXTH EDITION

INSIDERS' GUIDE®

GUILFORD, CONNECTICUT
AN IMPRINT OF THE GLOBE PEQUOT PRESS

The prices, rates, and hours listed in this guidebook were confirmed at press time. We recommend, however, that you call establishments to obtain current information before traveling.

To buy books in quantity for corporate use or incentives, call **(800) 962-0973** or e-mail **premiums@GlobePequot.com.**

# INSIDERS' GUIDE®

Text design by Nancy Freeborn and Linda R. Loiewski
Maps by Rusty Nelson © Morris Book Publishing, LLC
Spot photography throughout © Photodisc and © RubberBall Productions

ISSN 1537-0518
ISBN 978-0-7627-4545-6

Manufactured in the United States of America
10 9 8 7 6 5 4 3 2 1

To Aaron, who has helped me love Florida like a kid.
—Chelle Koster Walton

To my husband, Robert Morris Kennedy,
whose love of his home state has been an inspiration;
and to my spritely daughters, Clare and Kate.
—Sara Kennedy

# FLORIDA

# Contents

# Acknowledgments

Thanks and hugs to my family, Rob and Aaron Walton, for their help and understanding. Thank God they love to travel! Special thanks to my research assistant, Amy Ligon.

Verbal bouquets of gratitude also to the following, who assisted me in my research: Amanda Clements, Leon Corbett, Brandy Henley, Wit Tuttell, Kelly Yatcko, Kelly Earnest, Dawn Chesko-Grisby, Cindy Cockburn, Julie Root, Susan McLain, Dan Ryan, Dave Herbst, Cozy Montgomery, Linn Burnaw, Kjerstin Dillon, Mandy Fillenwarth, Claudia L'Engle Hafling, Michelle Revuelta, Rhonda Murphy, Cindy Malin, Rick Gregory, Beth Preddy, and all the people who endured my questions.

—Chelle Koster Walton

Thanks to Chelle Koster Walton for her energy and bright, readable style. My gratitude also goes to the patient marketing types at the Orlando theme parks, Dave Herbst, Rick Sylvain, Rhonda Murphy, and Susan Flower, who fielded my interminable questions with grace; and to my *Weekly Planet* editor, Susan Edwards, who provided some breathing room so I could juggle this book into my crazy schedule.

—Sara Kennedy

# Introduction

Florida is a natural for families, and not only because of the universal attraction of Disney World and the countless theme parks that have cropped up in its wake. In the Orlando area alone, there are kid attractions enough to delight families for days. Many concentrate on pure showbiz or get-wet entertainment; others enrich with lessons on nature, science, history, and outer space. The Disney influence has spread throughout Florida, and here you'll find the widest assortment of twisting, twirling, often enlightening, sometimes frightening diversions in any one state.

On the quieter side of things, however, visitors are often surprised to discover all that Florida has to offer in terms of wilderness and adventure experiences that the whole family can enjoy. Below the surface of glossy brochure items dwells another Florida for families to discover, one that outweighs in sheer volume and enrichment value the artificial high-dollar-ticket Florida.

Of course your children will insist on visiting the artificial attractions; my son does, anyway. One day at an amusement park can easily be balanced with something more physically and mentally challenging, however. This book, a result of my many years as a mother doing the balancing act, takes you to both extremes, but with emphasis on discovery opportunities.

Fortunately for everyone, government agencies at all levels have worked to preserve Florida's special spectrum of fragile environments. City, county, state, and national parks and preserves strive to ensure that our children and theirs will know the teeming wildlife and habitat that once dominated the state—the rare panthers, alligators, manatees, roseate spoonbills, torreya trees, mangroves, and coral reefs. Many of the parks provide recreational opportunities that allow families to play while immersing themselves ecologically. Florida's excellent and extensive state park system is a good place to begin your adventures. If you plan on exploring these parks to any extent, consider purchasing an annual family pass for $80 ($40 for individuals).

Some of Chelle's fondest memories reflect family forays into the wilderness preserved at Florida's state parks. Her favorite mental snapshot: Aaron's shrieks of "Mom, look!" as, at age four, he chased giant ghost crabs—the "most biggest" he'd ever seen—into their sandy foxholes among the glare-white sand dunes of St. Joseph Peninsula State Park in the Panhandle.

Sara remembers a day in a canoe atop the bracing, perfectly clear, and cold river at Alexander Springs, in the Ocala National Forest, where her family paddled past gaudy flora and among dense greenery, while birds of every hue careened and called around them.

## Lodging and Restaurant Rates

In the "Where to Eat" section and for other stand-out family restaurant listings, prices are indicated by dollar signs. The range is figured per adult meal of one typically priced dinner (unless dinner is not served, then lunch) entree, beverage (nonalcoholic), and dessert or appetizer:

### Rates for Restaurants

| | |
|---|---|
| $ | under $10 |
| $$ | $10 to $20 |
| $$$ | $21 to $30 |
| $$$$ | over $30 |

Dining recommendations usually avoid the family and fast-food chains, which are in abundance throughout most of Florida. Instead we concentrate on restaurants that can be enjoyed by the entire family. (Mom and Dad shouldn't be subjected to burger-doodle boredom just because they're on a family vacation.)

Under the "Where to Stay" section and for other lodging recommendations, room rates are based on double occupancy of a typically priced room, per night, before tax or service charge. The range covers the lowest rates during off-peak season to the highest rates in peak season. Many large resorts offer family packages throughout the year and have a "kids stay free" policy. Where rates include meals, it is so indicated in the lodging description.

### Rates for Lodging

| | |
|---|---|
| $ | under $90 |
| $$ | $90 to $150 |
| $$$ | $151 to $200 |
| $$$$ | over $200 |

Again, we generally leave out the less expensive chain motels and hotels that travelers find along highways, although these are great for overnight stops and tight budgets. Included are most of Florida's great family destination resorts, which offer kids programs and often some kitchen facilities. Florida is known for these, but they can be pricey.

# Attractions Key

The following is a key to the icons found throughout the text.

| | |
|---|---|
| **SWIMMING** | **FOOD** |
| **BOATING / BOAT TOUR** | **LODGING** |
| **HISTORIC SITE** | **CAMPING** |
| **HIKING / WALKING** | **MUSEUM** |
| **FISHING** | **PERFORMING ARTS** |
| **BIKING** | **SPORTS/ATHLETICS** |
| **AMUSEMENT PARK** | **PICNICKING** |
| **HORSEBACK RIDING** | **PLAYGROUND** |
| **SKIING/WINTER SPORTS** | **SHOPPING** |
| **PARK** | **PLANTS/GARDENS/NATURE TRAILS** |
| **ANIMAL VIEWING** | **FARM** |

# Northwest
# Florida

Northwest Florida folks talk with a twang and invite you in with Dixie hospitality. Oaks and pines, not palms and orange trees, grace roadsides brightened by magnolia, camellia, and azalea blossoms. Restaurants serve fried catfish and hush puppies. This may be northern Florida, but it's still the Deep South, sure as neighboring Alabama—and much surer than Florida's southern reaches, where influences from the Yankee states hold sway.

## TopPicks for Family Fun in Northwest Florida

1. Beaching and ruins-ruminating at Fort Pickens National Park, Pensacola Beach

2. Spotting animals in the wilds and watching nineteenth-century farmers at Tallahassee Museum of History and Natural Science, Tallahassee

3. Going underground at Florida Caverns State Park, Marianna

4. Swimming and boat touring at Wakulla Springs State Park, Wakulla Springs

5. Taking cockpit controls at the National Museum of Naval Aviation, Pensacola

6. Tubing at Ichetucknee Springs State Park, Fort White

7. Sunday-driving the canopy roads of Tallahassee

8. Seeing trees and bushes aflutter with monarch butterflies in migration, St. Marks National Wildlife Refuge, St. Marks

9. Strolling through time at Pensacola Historic Village, Pensacola

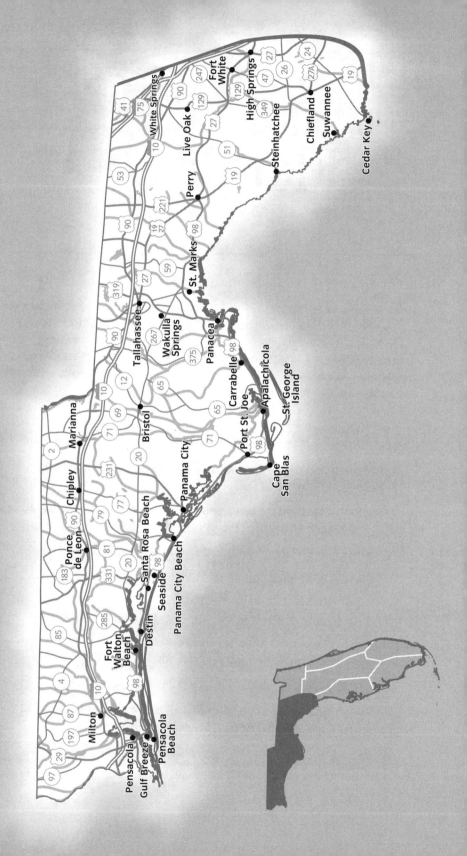

NORTHWEST FLORIDA

Sometimes known as the Redneck Riviera, Florida's Panhandle holds the most prideful beaches in the entire state. Created over the centuries from quartz rock flushed westward from the Appalachian Mountains, these sandy beaches sparkle the whitest, feel the softest, and drift the most mountainous of any in Florida. Trouble is, winters are too cold to fully enjoy them year-round, as you can in southern regions. The tourist season here begins at spring break, then slacks off until summer, when families converge on resorts known for their value.

Of the seven sections of Florida covered in this book, the Northwest boasts the most state parks, recreation areas, historic sites, and national wildlife refuges, affording the adventurous family endless latitude for fun and meaningful vacations.

# Tallahassee and Area

On Interstate 10.

Home of Florida State University, Tallahassee boasts fine museums and well-dressed streets, all decked in enough trees to earn the city a listing among the Top Ten Scenic Byways in America. At its southern doorstep, Florida reverts to its natural tendencies and holds some secrets of times past.

### Downtown Historic District (ages 4 to 13)

**A brochure for a self-guided walking tour of downtown is available through the Tallahassee Area Convention and Visitors Bureau; (850) 413-9200 or (800) 628-2866.**

The 10-block area contains two districts listed on the National Register of Historic Places: Calhoun Street and Park Avenue. Following are some highlights.

### New Capitol (ages 4 to 12)

**South Monroe and Apalachee Parkway; 400 South Monroe Street, Tallahassee; (850) 488-6167. Open 8:00 a.m. to 5:00 p.m. Monday through Friday. Forty-five-minute guided tours must be booked in advance; call ahead for times. Admission is free.**

The centerpiece of the historic section is the Capitol Complex, which juxtaposes the classic domed structure of 1845 against the sleek new high-rise built in the late 1970s. Begin at the New Capitol, where you can tour the town in a few steps by circling the gallery on the twenty-second floor, or sit in on legislative sessions. Stop at the Visitor Information Center to learn more about what the city has to offer.

### Old Capitol (ages 8 to 12)

**South Monroe Street and Apalachee Parkway; 400 South Monroe Street, Tallahassee; (850) 487-1902. Open 9:00 a.m. to 4:30 p.m. Monday through Friday, 10:00 a.m. to 4:30 p.m. Saturday, and noon to 4:30 p.m. Sunday. Admission is free.**

You can tour the restored legislative chambers and view exhibits on the state's political history.

## Amazing
# Tallahassee Facts

- Tallahassee is closer to Alabama, Louisiana, Georgia, Kentucky, Tennessee, Mississippi, Texas, Arkansas, North Carolina, and South Carolina than it is to Key West, Florida.
- America's largest concentration of original plantations—seventy-one plantations comprising 300,000 acres—exists between Tallahassee and Thomasville, Georgia, 28 miles away.

### Museum of Florida History (ages 5 to 12)

**500 South Bronough Street, Tallahassee; (850) 488-1484. Open 9:00 a.m. to 4:30 p.m. Monday through Friday, 10:00 a.m. to 4:30 p.m. Saturday, and noon to 4:30 p.m. Sunday. Free.**

The kids will marvel at the 12,000-year-old skeleton of the 9-foot-tall mastodon affectionately known as Herman and a display of Spanish doubloons. The comprehensive museum chronicles the state's bygones from the days of prehistoric settlement and European invasion to more modern eras of pioneer settlement and the "Tin Can Tourist" (trailer traveler) invasion.

### Mary Brogan Museum of Art and Science (ages 5 to 12)

**Kleman Plaza, 350 South Duval Street, Tallahassee; (850) 513-0700; www.thebrogan .org. Open 10:00 a.m. to 5:00 p.m. Monday through Saturday, 1:00 to 5:00 p.m. Sunday. Admission is $6.00 for adults, $3.50 for seniors, college students, and children ages 3 through 17. From 4:00 to 5:00 p.m., admission is free.**

This three-story family attraction has interactive exhibits on the second floor and an art gallery on the third. Changing exhibits feature art collections and themed hands-on experiences.

### Civic Center (ages 5 to 12)

**505 West Pensacola Street, Tallahassee; (850) 487-1691 or (800) 322-3602; www.tlccc.org.**

Check out ice shows, concerts, sports events such as Florida State University basketball games, and Broadway musicals at this modern, multipurpose convention and entertainment center.

### Springtime Tallahassee Parade and Jubilee (ages 4 to 12)

(850) 224-5012 or (800) 628-2866; www.springtimetallahassee.com.

The town's big event each year begins in late March or early April, an extravaganza of parades, a kids park, and fairs that runs for three weeks during prime azalea-blooming time.

### Goodwood Plantation (ages 9 to 12)

1600 Miccosukee Road, Tallahassee; (850) 877-4202; www.goodwoodmuseum.org. Open 10:00 a.m. to 4:00 p.m. Monday through Friday and 10:00 a.m. to 2:00 p.m. Saturday. Admission is $5 for ages 3 and older. The gardens are open 9:00 a.m. to 5:00 p.m. Monday through Friday and 10:00 a.m. to 2:00 p.m. Saturday; free.

The gardened grounds and restored nineteenth- and early-twentieth-century buildings are open for touring.

### Bradley's Country Store (all ages)

10655 Centerville Road, Tallahassee; (850) 893-1647. Open 8:30 a.m. to 6:00 p.m. Monday through Friday and 8:30 a.m. to 5:00 p.m. Saturday.

Homemade sausage is the claim to fame at this circa-1920 vestige of yesteryear. It holds all the sweetness of childhood days, moon pies, and old-time sugarmaking.

### Alfred B. Maclay State Gardens (ages 8 to 12)

3540 Thomasville Road, Tallahassee; (850) 487-4556. Gardens open from sunrise to sunset daily, state park open 8:00 a.m. to sunset daily, house open 9:00 a.m. to 5:00 p.m. from January through April, when entrance to the gardens, house, and park is $4 for adults, $2 for children under 12. Park entrance is $4 per car year-round.

One of Quail Trail's most important sites bursts into bloom December through April with camellias and azaleas. It's a lovely place for a stretch of the legs anytime. The state park, which contains the gardens, offers swimming, nature trails, canoe rentals, fishing, and boating. You can tour the gardens' historic home and botanical exhibits in season.

## Florida **Trivia**

**Sand Facts** Why are Panhandle beaches so blindingly white? Unlike other Gulf Coast beaches, which are coral based—made from pulverized shell matter—Panhandle beaches are quartz based.

Why does Panhandle sand crunch when you walk on it? During its centuries-long journey from the Appalachian Mountains, the quartz sand was buffeted smooth, whereas most other sand has rough edges. That's what makes it sound as if you're walking on fresh, cold snow.

# Canopy **Roads**

For detailed directions to trails and their attractions, obtain a copy of the *Driving Guide to Scenic Leon County* from the Tallahassee Area Convention and Visitors Bureau; (850) 413-9200 or (800) 628-2866. Among arboresque Tallahassee's best features are the five oak-tunnel routes once followed by Native Americans and Spanish conquistadors. They are Old St. Augustine, Miccosukee, Meridian, Centerville, and Old Bainbridge Roads. Many of the area's most worthwhile sites lie along these routes. Four peaceful trails to the past have been devised to incorporate the sites along these routes.

**The Cotton Trail** A 50-mile eastward loop visits the *Gone with the Wind* era of plantations. It begins on lovely Miccosukee Road (Route 0347), where red earth and live oaks draped dreamily with ghostlike Spanish moss create an antebellum mood. The trail turns north onto Crump Road, then left onto Roberts Road and follows Centerville Road (Route 151) to Moccasin Gap Road.

**The Quail Trail** This northern loop of about 50 miles leaves town via Thomasville Road (Highway 319) and takes in Meridian Road.

**The Native Trail** Beginning downtown, it leads to archaeological sites of ancient civilizations along both Old Bainbridge and Old St. Augustine Roads.

**Old St. Augustine Road** A designated canopy road, it dates back to the 1600s, when it linked the colonial settlements of Tallahassee and the earlier Florida capital of St. Augustine.

## Tallahassee Antique Automobile Museum (all ages)

**3550 Mahan Drive, Tallahassee; (850) 942-0137; www.tacm.com. Open 10:00 a.m. to 5:00 p.m. Monday through Saturday and noon to 5:00 p.m. Sunday. Admission is $7.50 for adults, $5.00 for children 11 to 15, and $4.00 for children under 11.**

Vehicles from Abraham Lincoln's 1860s hearse to Hollywood's Batmobiles, a Bat Boat, and the Penguin's Duck join rooms crammed with collectibles of every description that will fascinate young and old.

### Challenger Learning Center and IMAX Theatre (ages 5 to 12) 🎵

Kleman Plaza, South Duval Street and College Avenue; (850) 695-7827. IMAX: $7.00 for adults, $6.50 for seniors, $5.50 for children 5 to 12; planetarium: $5.00 for adults, $4.50 for seniors, $4.00 for children 5 to 12.

With its K through 12 outreach program, the simulated "Mission Control" requires groups of fourteen or more, but the 50-foot planetarium and IMAX theater bring space adventures to all.

### Mission San Luis Archaeological and Historic Site (ages 7 to 12) 🏛

2021 West Mission Road, Tallahassee (near the intersection of Tennessee Street and White Drive); (850) 487-3711; www.missionsanluis.org. Open 10:00 a.m. to 4:00 p.m. Tuesday through Sunday. Living history program available daily. Admission is free.

As in California, Catholic Spanish missions once spread across the northern part of Florida. San Luis survives as the only reconstructed Spanish mission in the state. Living history re-creates the days when the mission was built in the mid-seventeenth century to convert the Apalachees to Christianity. Archaeological digs are ongoing here, and you can watch and question archaeologists at work. The kids will enjoy seeing the Apalachees' ball game plaza, where Indians played a competitive, ritualistic sport that combined elements of soccer and handball.

### Tallahassee Museum of History and Natural Science (ages 4 to 12) 🐾🐘

Near the airport off Route 371 at 3945 Museum Drive, Tallahassee; (850) 576-1636. Open 9:00 a.m. to 5:00 p.m. Monday through Saturday and 12:30 to 5:00 p.m. Sunday. Admission is $8.00 for adults, $7.50 for seniors, and $5.50 for children ages 4 to 15, and free to those 3 and under.

If you do nothing else in the capital city, you must make it to this attraction. Part zoo, part hands-on museum and living history arena, it gives you fifty-two acres and a half-day's worth of activities, including a re-created nineteenth-century farm, boardwalks through panther and red wolf habitat, historical buildings, and a Discovery Center. The animal exhibits are conscientious in the way they allow Florida's native critters to roam freely within low-impact barriers. Kids love the indoor Discovery Center—especially the feel-and-identify box and crawl-through tree—and the old schoolhouse once attended by the children of former slaves. Go when guides dress and act the part of nineteenth-century settlers, usually every day but Monday, but for sure on weekends.

# Florida **Trivia**

**How Tallahassee Became Capital** Before Florida became a U.S. territory, it was split in two parts. St. Augustine served as East Florida's governmental seat, while Pensacola ruled West Florida. When the two became one, a new centrally located capital was needed. Legend says envoys were sent by horseback from St. Augustine and by boat and foot from Pensacola to see where they'd meet. And so backwoods Tallyhassee, as it was known, became capital of Florida.

### Natural Bridge Battlefield Reenactment (ages 7 to 12)
**Natural Bridge Battlefield State Historic Site, 15 miles southeast of Tallahassee off Route 363; 1022 DeSoto Park Drive, Tallahassee; (850) 922-6007. Open 8:00 a.m. to sunset daily. Admission is free.**

Relive one of Florida's most important Civil War battles, where Confederate troops kept Union soldiers at bay and prevented the capture of Tallahassee in 1865. Thus Tallahassee remained the only uncaptured Confederate capital east of the Mississippi. The battle comes to life each March with a staged reenactment. The park is open for picnicking year-round.

### Tallahassee–St. Marks Historic Railroad State Trail
(ages 7 to 12)
**Along Route 363; same address and phone as Natural Bridge, above.**

Follow the 20 miles of paved and unpaved trail from Tallahassee to St. Marks by foot, horseback, bike, or in-line skates.

## Where to Eat

Eating and lodging are inexpensive in and around Tallahassee.

**Andrew's Capital Grill and Bar.** 228 South Adams Street, Tallahassee; (850) 222-3444. Popular with state politicians and university sports fans. Sandwiches and casual entrees for lunch Monday through Saturday, dinner daily, Sunday brunch. $$

**Barnacle Bill's.** 1830 North Monroe Street, Tallahassee; (850) 385-8734. Florida seafood raw, grilled, steamed, smoked, or fried; casual atmosphere. Big-screen and cable TVs. Lunch and dinner daily. $$

## Where to Stay

Most of the lodging choices in town are of the chain variety.

**DoubleTree Hotel.** 101 South Adams Street, Tallahassee; (850) 224-5000 or (800) 222-TREE; www.doubletree.com. An old downtown hotel luxuriously renovated with 242 well-appointed units, restaurant, pool, and **free** chocolate chip cookies upon check-in. $

## For More Information

**Tallahassee Area Convention and Visitors Bureau.** 106 East Jefferson Street, Tallahassee 32301; (850) 413-9200 or (800) 628-2866; www.seetallahassee .com.

# Nature Attractions along I-10

The Panhandle's main northern route, I-10, strings together natural wonder gems with tons of recreational adventures for families.

### Torreya State Park (ages 6 to 12)

**Route C1641 off Route 12; 2576 Northwest Torreya Park Road, Bristol; (850) 643-2674. Open 8:00 a.m. (Eastern Standard Time) to sundown daily. Park entrance is $2 per vehicle; admission to the Gregory House is $2 for adults, $1 for children 12 and under.**

Named for a rare species of evergreen that grows in abundance here, the 12,000-acre park is also unusual for its towering bluff formations along the Apalachicola River. Yew and winged elm trees and other vegetation reminiscent of the Appalachian Mountains add to the park's mystique. Avid hikers take to the 15 miles of Florida's most strenuous (read: *hilly*) trail. History lovers tour the antebellum Gregory House.

### Florida Caverns State Park (ages 5 to 12)

**Off Highway 167; 3345 Caverns Road, Marianna; (850) 482-9598 (recorded message) or 482-1228. Open 8:00 a.m. (Central Standard Time) to sunset daily (you must buy tour tickets before 1:00 p.m.). Tour hours are 9:00 a.m. to 4:00 p.m. Park entrance is $4 per car of eight persons or fewer, $1 per extra passenger, cyclist, or pedestrian. Guided one-hour cave tours cost $8 for visitors age 13 or older and $5 for children 3 to 12.**

Take your explorations 50 feet underground at an unusual network of classic limestone formations. Spelunking tours are ranger guided. Aboveground you can hike, camp, fish, swim, golf, and canoe.

## Florida **Trivia**

**Clock Watch** Just west of Bristol, across the Apalachicola River, time seems to stand still. Actually, it reverses as you leave behind Eastern Standard Time (EST) and cross into the Central Standard Time (CST) zone. Don't forget to set your watch back an hour.

### Falling Waters State Park (ages 7 to 12)

**1130 State Park Road, Chipley; (850) 638-6130. Open 8:00 a.m. to sunset daily. Park entrance is $4 per vehicle of eight persons or fewer, $1 per extra passenger, cyclist, or pedestrian.**

A dramatic, 67-foot waterfall tumbles over the edge of a 100-foot stovepipe sinkhole. Explore it and other sinks along 945 feet of boardwalks. Have a swim and a picnic while you're there.

### Ponce de Leon Springs State Park (ages 5 to 12)

**Off Highway 98, 12 miles north of de Funiak Springs; 2860 Ponce de Leon Springs Road, Ponce de Leon; (850) 836-4281; ranger station, (850) 638-6130. Open 8:00 a.m. to sunset daily. Park entrance is $3 per vehicle, $1 per cyclist or pedestrian.**

Hot with irritable kids? Take a quick detour off Interstate 4 for a cool plunge into the clear springs pool. Have a picnic and a nature hike while you're at it.

### Adventures Unlimited (ages 8 to 12) 🔺 Ⓐ ⊖

**Off Highway 87, 12 miles north of Milton; 8974 Tomahawk Landings, Milton; (850) 623-6197 or (800) 239-6864; www.adventuresunlimited.com. Open daily; hours vary according to the season. Prices vary according to length of trip.**

The town of Milton is the self-proclaimed Canoe Capital of Florida. Adventures Unlimited, an eighty-eight-acre privately owned park, launches canoeing, kayaking, rafting, paddleboating, and tubing expeditions into the spring-fed wilderness streams of Coldwater, Blackwater, Sweetwater, and Juniper Creeks. It also provides cabins and campsites.

### Blackwater River State Park (ages 8 to 12)

**15 miles northeast of Milton off Highway 90; 7720 Deaton Bridge Road, Holt; (850) 983-5363. Open 8:00 a.m. to sunset daily. Park entrance is $3 per vehicle of eight persons or fewer, $1 per extra passenger, cyclist, or pedestrian.**

Named for one of the Panhandle's great natural rivers, it gives outdoor types the opportunity to revel in canoeing, hiking, camping, and biking opportunities.

## Road **Markers**

This Panhandle Express begins in Tallahassee, capital of Florida and its Southern culture. From there it follows scenic and brisk I-10 westward to the Alabama border, where it drops south to Pensacola, western gateway to the shimmering emerald coastline.

Here begins the most scenic portion of the trip—along Highway 98 and its offshoots—to Florida's top-shelf beaches. The route rounds the so-called Big Bend, where Highways 98 and 19 merge, and ends at the pristine shores of historic Cedar Key. Highway 98 becomes congested in places, especially in the summer and especially where it narrows to two lanes.

# Pensacola Area

From I-10, Interstate 110's exit 4 will drop you into Pensacola.

I-10 forms the northern border of Pensacola, where Florida history takes a turn toward salt and swashbuckling as wilderness meets the sea. This is the very brink of Florida, and Pensacola's close proximity to Alabama has a decided effect upon the temperament and tradition of the city. Things move at the pace of a southern drawl, music goes country, and hospitality is steeped in the graciousness of eras past.

This route takes you first into Pensacola's historic downtown district, so prettily restored and valuable for its history lessons and antiques shopping. Three oak-lined districts hold the town's treasures: Seville, Palafox, and North Hill.

Pensacola and much of the Panhandle coastline have been pervaded by military history since the days when the Spaniards first arrived and built forts to protect the deep harbor. More recently, Pensacola is home to the Pensacola Naval Air Station and its Blue Angel daredevil flyers.

In the westernmost part of town, off the beaten path, lies an island whose name means "lost," which is what you'll be if you don't get good directions. Perdido Key is situated on a quiet, little-known island that is partly the property of Alabama and a part of the Gulf Islands National Seashore system. The beaches here present lightly developed dunescapes, where a peculiar sort of maritime ecology persists despite the effects of salt-battering waves and hurricane winds.

To the east, looping back along the coast, a bridge crosses from downtown Pensacola to the community of Gulf Breeze, then another takes you to Pensacola Beach.

Historic attractions aside, the best part of Pensacola lies there, on Santa Rosa Island, with its 22 miles of brilliant, fluffy, dunes-drifted sand. Most of these beaches are protected also by the U.S. government under the auspices of the Gulf Islands National Seashore.

### Sam's Fun City (all ages)

**Just south of I-10 on Route 29; 6709 Pensacola Boulevard, Pensacola; (850) 505-0800; www.samsfuncity.com. Open 10:00 a.m. to 10:00 p.m. Sunday through Thursday; 9:00 a.m. to midnight Friday and Saturday. General admission free. Multiple-ride wristbands available from $6 to $33; combos extra.**

Cartoon characters Dudley Do-Right, Underdog, and Rocky and Bullwinkle provide the theme for this park. Amusements include an eighteen-hole mountain minigolf course, a Ferris wheel, go-kart and antique-car tracks, amusement park rides, laser tag, a video arcade with simulators, and Surf City Water Park.

### Pensacola Historic Village (ages 6 to 13)

**320 South Jefferson Street, Pensacola; (850) 595-5985; www.historicpensacola.org. The parking lot for the village is located at the intersection of South Tarragona Street and Zaragoza Street. All attractions open 10:00 a.m. to 4:00 p.m. Monday through Saturday. Admission is $6.00 for adults, $5.00 for seniors, and $2.50 for children ages 4 to 16.**

This 4-block complex contains several museums and historic sites, all of which you can enter for one admission fee. Daily guided tours are held at 11:00 a.m., 1:00 p.m., and 2:30 p.m.

### T. T. Wentworth Jr. Florida State Museum (ages 3 to 9)

**320 South Jefferson Street, Pensacola; (850) 595-5990. Open 10:00 a.m. to 4:00 p.m. Monday through Saturday. Admission is included in Pensacola Historic Village fees.**

Here's where your Pensacola Historic Village tour begins. Outside, you'll see a colonial archaeological dig in progress. Inside, you can purchase tickets and pick up a tour map and other local information. A beautiful keepsake of local neo-Mediterranean-style architecture, the museum once served as city hall. Its first floor is devoted to the slightly oddball collection of Mr. Wentworth. Among the artifacts are a petrified cat and the world's largest pair of shoes. Exhibits on the second floor rotate, except for a permanent Coca-Cola nostalgia collection. The Discovery Gallery on the third floor lets kids experience real-life situations on their scale. They can "pretend work" at a radio station, grocery store, post office, and city hall.

### Fiesta of Five Flags (all ages)

An annual celebration in Pensacola each June, it includes activities for all ages and ranks as one of the oldest and largest festivals in the state. It commemorates Pensacola's rich history and culture under five governmental powers—Spain, France, England, the United States, and the Confederacy. It is celebrated throughout the community, including Pensacola Beach, with costumed revelry, parades, music, antiques shows, and sports activities. For a detailed calendar of events, visit its Web site, www.fiestaoffiveflags.org, or call the Pensacola Convention and Visitors Bureau, 1401 East Gregory Street, Pensacola 32501; (850) 434-1234 or (800) 874-1234; www.visitpensacola.com.

### The National Museum of Naval Aviation (ages 6 to 12)

**Pensacola Naval Air Station, off Route 292A on Blue Angel Parkway; 1750 Radford Boulevard, NAS Pensacola; (850) 452-3604 or (800) 327-5002. Open 9:00 a.m. to 5:00 p.m. daily. Admission to museum is free. Admission to simulator is $5.00 per person; IMAX costs $8.00 for adults, $7.50 for seniors and ages 5 through 12.**

This immense facility preserves the history of military aircraft. It contains more than 150 specialized aircraft in all, including the A-4 Skyhawks once used by the world-famous Blue Angels. Kids can manipulate controls in a test cockpit trainer and antiaircraft gun battery. A motion-based, fifteen-seat flight simulator ride re-creates a Desert Storm aircraft engagement and barnstorming flight. In the IMAX theater, you feel as though you're flying an F-18 fighter jet. Guided tours of the museum run four times daily. The Blue Angels Air Show highlights a November visit.

## Some Pensacola **Historic Village Sites**

**The Museum of Industry.** 200 East Zaragoza Street. It exhibits old sawmill machinery from the area's lumber boom.

**The Museum of Commerce.** 201 East Zaragoza Street. Static displays depict an 1890s streetscape, complete with trolley car, barbershop, print shop, hardware store, leather shop, toy store, and early-1900s newsroom and pressroom.

**Julee Cottage.** 210 East Zaragoza Street. This circa-1804 home of a free African-American woman houses a museum on local black history.

**1810 Lavalle House.** Behind Julee Cottage. Here you find a prime example of old Pensacola's French-Creole architecture.

**Manuel Barrios Cottage.** East Zaragoza Street, in front of the Museum of Industry. Exhibits depict the 1920s lifestyle.

**Dorr House.** This beautifully ornate home is filled with Victorian antiques.

**The Barkley House.** Florida Blanca Street. Another fine example of French-Creole architecture.

# Seashore **Pristine**

**Gulf Islands National Seashore,** 1801 Gulf Breeze Parkway, Gulf Breeze (850-934-2600; www.nps.gov/guis), holds in its protective embrace a total of 52 miles of Florida Panhandle barrier islands. Most of it lies in and around Pensacola, on Perdido Key and Santa Rosa Island (Pensacola Beach). Birdwatchers have counted more than 280 different species of birds in these areas. Another small section of the Seashore is found on Okaloosa Island, home of Fort Walton Beach.

## Fort Barrancas (ages 5 to 10) 🏛

Pensacola Naval Air Station, off Route 292A on Blue Angel Parkway; 3822 Taylor Road, Pensacola; (850) 455-5167. Open 9:30 a.m. to 4:45 p.m. daily from March 1 to October 1; and 8:30 a.m. to 3:45 p.m. daily from November through February. Daily tours at 2:00 p.m.; lighthouse tour on Sunday. Admission is **free.**

The Naval Station also preserves the city's military past at Fort Barrancas, built between 1839 and 1844 to protect Pensacola Harbor and once a Confederacy stronghold. Bring a picnic lunch and spend some time exploring the fort ruins at its elevated site (*barranca* means "bluff" in Spanish). Self-guided tours are available; daily guided tours at 2:00 p.m.

## Big Lagoon State Park (ages 5 to 12) 🅰 🏕

12301 Gulf Beach Highway, Pensacola (at the intersection of Bauer Road); (850) 492-1595. Open 8:00 a.m. to sunset daily. Park entrance is $4 per vehicle of eight persons or fewer, $1 per extra passenger, cyclist, or pedestrian.

Camp, hike, fish, and commune with nature. Gray foxes, cardinals, and nuthatches inhabit this 698-acre world of coastal ecology. Nature study programs familiarize you with life on the bay beach and along the trails.

## Perdido Key Gulf Islands National Seashore Day Use Area
(ages 4 to 12) 🌊 🤾

Route 292/Johnson Beach Road; (850) 934-2600. Open 8:00 a.m. to sunset daily. Park entrance is $8 per car, $1 per bike or hiker for a seven-day pass, good also at Fort Pickens National Park and Santa Rosa Day Use Area.

Beachgoers can park and take advantage of sugar-fine sands, clear aquamarine waters, well-maintained picnic shelters, and other facilities. You can continue to walk along the beach where the road ends—undisturbed by modern conveyances—for 6 miles. During the summer, you'll find food concessions and lifeguards.

## Perdido Key State Park (all ages)

**15301 Perdido Key Drive; (850) 492-1595. Open 8:00 a.m. to sunset daily. Park entrance is $2 per car.**

Less out of the way than the national seashore, this 247-acre beach park lies in the midst of the island's condominium community. There are picnic facilities but no lifeguards. Shops and water-sports concessions are nearby.

## Fort Pickens National Park (ages 4 to 12)

**West end of Fort Pickens Road; 1400 Fort Pickens Road, Pensacola Beach; (850) 934-2635 or (850) 934-2622. Park is open 7:00 a.m. to 10:00 p.m. daily. Fort is open 8:00 a.m. to sunset daily. Park entrance is $8 per car for a seven-day permit into the park, good also for Perdido Key National Seashore and Santa Rosa Day Use Area.**

Part of the above-mentioned Seashore system, these extensive fort ruins, circa 1830, add to the attraction of the pristine beachfront. The park is a definite must-see because of the variety of activities offered within its vast acreage. The drive through the park is sheer entrancement with its otherworldly terrain of undulating sand dunes and salt-dwarfed maritime vegetation. Adjuncts to the fort pop up around this corner and that and at beach recreational areas, where you can camp, hike, fish, or bike. The main fort complex occupies the island's west end with a natural history museum, terrific book and gift shop, fishing pier, and administration buildings. You can see the fort, which operated during the Civil War (it was held by Yankee troops while Fort Barrancas, across the bay, was occupied by Confederates) and once imprisoned Apache chief Geronimo and his tribe, by a self-guided or guided tour (offered summers at 2:00 p.m. seven days a week, except Christmas Day). As of press time, the park is closed for repair and is open to foot traffic only. Call for information.

## Florida **Trivia**

**In the First Place** En route to Fort Pickens, you may notice a white cross perched atop one of the dunes. It marks the location of the first religious service held in Pensacola, in August 1559—a reminder that colonists attempted to build a settlement here four years before St. Augustine, "The Oldest City," was settled. Pensacola claims its place in history as "America's First Place City."

**Gulf Breeze X-Files** Gulf Breeze, which occupies the peninsula between Pensacola and Pensacola Beach, has the dubious distinction of being the world's UFO sighting capital. Most explain this away by the presence of air force bases and their wacky experiments. In any case, you may want to keep an eye to the sky while you are thereabouts.

### Bike Path

Seven miles of bike path travel along Fort Pickens Road and Via de Luna, plus Fort Pickens National Seashore holds miles of unpaved bike trails through ruins and natural flora.

### Main Beach (ages 8 to 12)

**On Via de Luna near the Bob Sikes Bridge.**

Look for the beachball water tower. Sometimes still referred to by locals as Casino Beach, this was renovated with new, expanded facilities and restaurants at the center of town. It appeals to water-sports enthusiasts, fun lovers, and older children.

### Quietwater Beach (all ages)

**Quietwater Beach Road.**

At the island's doorstep, this protected bay beach in the crook of the causeway greets you with shopping, restaurants, and calm, tot-friendly waters. In this area and around the main beach to the west, you will find all manner of water-sports facilities. Fishing is popular at the Bob Sikes Fishing Pier, which parallels the causeway.

### Key Sailing (ages 9 to 12)

**500 Quietwater Beach Road, Suite 14, Pensacola Beach; (850) 932-5520. Open usually 9:00 a.m. to 6:00 p.m. daily.**

Rents pontoons, catamarans, and parasail equipment.

### Santa Rosa National Seashore Day Use Area (ages 6 to 12)

**Via de Luna; (850) 934-2600. Open 8:00 a.m. to sunset daily. Park entrance is $8 per car, $3 per bike or hiker for a seven-day pass to all Florida Gulf Islands National Seashore accesses.**

Past the business and resort district of Pensacola Beach, and then past its residential neighborhoods, you come to a desolate stretch of beach, a day-use segment of Gulf Islands National Seashore. Here, you can lose yourself among the dunes, have a beach-blanket picnic, and snooze on some of the world's softest sands. Facilities were totally destroyed in 1995 by Hurricane Opal but have been rebuilt.

### Naval Live Oaks (ages 5 to 12)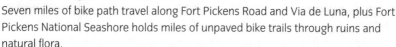

**East of the Three-Mile Bridge at 1801 Gulf Breeze Parkway, Gulf Breeze; (850) 934-2600. Open 8:00 a.m. to 5:30 p.m. year-round. Free.**

Gulf Islands National Seashore has its local headquarters here, along with an informative visitor center and 5 miles of nature trails. Bobcats and red foxes survive among nearly 1,400 acres of live oaks, Southern magnolia, and sand pines.

## The Zoo (all ages)

**5701 Gulf Breeze Parkway, Gulf Breeze; 10 miles east of Gulf Breeze on Highway 98; (850) 932-2229; www.the-zoo.com. Open 9:00 a.m. to 5:00 p.m. (6:00 p.m. in summer) daily. Admission is $11.50 plus tax for adults, $10.50 for seniors, and $8.25 for children ages 3 to 11. Under 3 free.**

In wide open spaces, 900 animals—everything from pygmy hippos to black rhinos—forage and go about life. You can see them all aboard the Safari Line minitrain ($3 plus tax) or take part in feeding giraffes. Other attractions include a petting farm of domestic animals, a nursery and incubator room, wildlife demonstrations on weekends, food concessions, and a great wildlife gift shop.

## Where to Eat

**Flounder's Chowder House.** 800 Quietwater Beach Road, Pensacola Beach; (850) 932-2003; www.flounderschowderhouse.com. You can't miss the landlocked thirty-ton shrimp boat. Open daily for lunch and dinner. $$

**Peg Leg Pete's Oyster Bar.** 1010 Fort Pickens Road, Pensacola Beach; (850) 932-4139. Little buccaneers receive their meals in a beach sand bucket. Oysters and affordable Cajun dishes. Daily lunch and dinner. $–$$

## Where to Stay

Best place for families to stay is on Pensacola Beach.

**Pensacola Beach Resort.** 16 Via de Luna Drive, Pensacola Beach; (850) 934-3300 or (800) 934-3001; www.pensacolabeachresort.net. Offers a Gulf beach, two pools, and continental breakfast; pet friendly. $–$$$

**Bay Beach Inn.** 51 Gulf Breeze Parkway, Gulf Breeze; (850) 932-2214 or (866) 932-2214; www.baybeachinn.com. Two outdoor pools and boat, kayak, and Jet Ski rentals keep guests hopping. Pet friendly. $–$$

**Holiday Inn Express Pensacola Beach.** 333 Fort Pickens Road, Pensacola Beach; (805) 932-3536 or (800) HOLIDAY. Formerly the Dunes, this Gulf-front resort has a heated pool, continental breakfast, golf and recreational packages. $$–$$$$

## For More Information

**Pensacola Convention and Visitors Information Center.** 1401 East Gregory Street, Pensacola 32501; (850) 434-1234 or (800) 874-1234; www.visitpensacola.com.

# Smart **Travel**

- The Panhandle's extra-white sand extra-magnifies the sun's intensity. One-up your family's normal SPF and don't forget sunglasses for everyone. This stuff is like looking at the sun's glare reflected off snow drifts. It can fry your eyeballs.

- Walking in the Panhandle's brand of superfine sand puts a strain on the legs—1 mile of beach walking bears little resemblance to 1 mile on hard surfaces. Go easy and take plenty of water.

- Most beaches post flags to alert bathers about sea conditions. Purple means dangerous marine life, green means low hazard/calm condition, yellow means medium hazard/moderate surf or currents, red means high hazard/high surf or currents, and double red, with a no-swimming symbol, means the water is closed to the public. If a red or a double red flag is flying on the beach, do something else that day. The danger, even for strong swimmers, is real.

- Thorny, scrubby sandspurs arm coastal regions throughout Florida. Stay on pathways when walking to and from the beach, and make sure everyone wears shoes. To remove the prickly burrs from bare feet or shoe soles, lick your fingers before lightly grasping the pests. Check shoes before going inside. They like to grab on to carpeting and attack when least expected.

- Panama City Beach, Fort Walton Beach, and, to a lesser extent, Pensacola Beach are spring break magnets. College students pour in by the thousands. Resorts become all-night party spots, and streets fill with beer hounds. Not a pretty picture for the family. Avoid these towns at all costs, during March and early April.

# Emerald Coast

About a half-hour east of Gulf Breeze on Highway 98.

East of the Navarre Beach bridge, the road leads to Fort Walton Beach and Destin, a stretch of seashore known as the Emerald Coast. It marks the onset of coastal Highway 98. What was one of Florida's most scenic drives is fast becoming a peek-a-boo game between emerald green water and the condos, hotels, and seaside cottages that line the shore.

Fort Walton Beach begins on the mainland and spills onto Okaloosa Island, where the gorgeous white beaches have attracted sun-seekers for decades. In years past, this resort town had become a tacky haven for students on spring break. However, it has spruced up its image with a more modern look that enhances its appeal and affordability for families. The attractions are small, a couple of hours' worth of entertainment, which works well for fitting in beach time—a must in this land of dunes and shimmering green water.

Besides fun-time diversions, the Fort Walton Beach area offers some nice, small learning experiences that won't tax the kids' attention spans.

Just a bridge away from Fort Walton Beach's east end, Destin is a newer version of a seaside resort. Its amusement parks are on a grander scale, and the town in general is better thought out. It has a reputation as the World's Luckiest Fishing Village and maintains an extensive fleet of fishing charters, tournaments, and seafood restaurants to prove it.

Amberjack, triggerfish, snapper, and grunts are common catches. Billfishing for sailfish and marlin is good from summer through fall. The town promotes its good fortune with shark, king mackerel, billfish, and cobia tournaments throughout the year and features an October-long Fishing Rodeo (800-322-3319).

## Seafood **Satiation**

The **Destin Seafood Festival** takes place each year during the first week of October, and 30,000 people turn up to partake of its goodies. About twenty restaurants sell samples of their best dishes from booths, and festivalgoers can nosh while they tour arts and crafts displays or listen to bands. For the younger set, from toddlers to teens, there's Tadpole Town, with rides and a kids' activity tent. Festival admission is **free.**

### Air Force Armament Museum (ages 6 to 12)

100 Museum Drive, Eglin Air Force Base; (850) 882-4062. Open 9:30 a.m. to 4:30 p.m. daily; closed federal holidays. Admission is **free.**

Warplane hounds can whet their appetites on indoor and outdoor aircraft, and missile, bomb, and weapon exhibits. The park outside is literally cluttered with monster fighter craft (including one called "Warthog") and their artillery. There's also a picnic grounds. Inside, a thirty-two-minute movie explains the history of the Eglin base and its role in the development of armament, and two cockpits give kids a hands-on experience.

### The Emerald Coast Science Center (ages 3 to 10)

139 Brooks Street, off Highway 98 west of the bridge to Okaloosa Island, Fort Walton Beach; (850) 664-1261; www.ecscience.org. Open 9:00 a.m. to 4:00 p.m. Monday through Friday; 11:00 a.m. to 4:00 p.m. Saturday and Sunday. Admission is $5.00 for adults, $4.00 for seniors, and $3.50 for children ages 4 to 17.

Make a 4-foot bubble, play on the computer, and experience a wind tunnel among the 250 interactive displays. There are critters, like geckos and snakes, and science experimentation that intrigues all ages.

### Indian Temple Mound Museum (ages 4 to 10)

139 Miracle Strip Parkway (Highway 98), just west of the bridge to Okaloosa Island, Fort Walton Beach; (850) 833-9595. Open 10:00 a.m. to 4:00 p.m. Monday through Friday and 9:00 a.m. to 4:00 p.m. Saturday from September to May; closed Sunday. From June to August, open 9:00 a.m. to 4:30 p.m. Monday through Saturday. Open noon to 4:30 p.m. Sunday in June and July. Admission is $5.00 for adults, $4.50 for seniors, and $3.00 for children ages 4 to 17.

The centerpiece of the attraction, an 800-year-old, 17-foot-tall mound, took 100,000 cubic feet of soil to build—an estimated 500,000 basketsful carried by natives to the site. The mound was used for worship and held the home of the tribe's political and religious leader. The museum showcases the largest collection of native Indian ceramic artifacts in the United States. Admission includes entry to the Camp Walton Schoolhouse and the Garnier Post Office Museum.

### Gulfarium (all ages)

1010 Highway 98 East, Fort Walton Beach; (850) 244-5169; www.gulfarium.com. Opens at 9:00 a.m.; shows begin at 10:00 a.m., noon, 2:00 and 4:00 p.m., and a summer 6:00 p.m. show. Admission is $17.50 for adults, $15.50 for seniors, and $10.50 for children ages 4 to 11. **Free** for ages 3 and under (tax not included).

At Fort Walton Beach's premier attraction, dolphins and seals perform acts and scuba divers demonstrate. The state's second oldest such facility, it also does rehabilitation and educational work. Gulfarium has a beach setting, which makes it feel more natural to see dolphins leaping into the air.

## Okaloosa Island Park
**Highway 98, Fort Walton Beach.**

Boardwalk complex offers access to the beach's amazingly white sands and the Okaloosa Fishing Pier, as well as shopping and dining.

## Beasley County Park
**East of Fort Walton Beach on Highway 98 East.**

One of the nicest Fort Walton Beach public access points, it frames a bed of Okaloosa's famous fluffy sands between huge dunes and that indescribable green sea. It is well maintained with a Florida-style shelter, picnic facilities, and lifeguards.

## *The American Spirit*
**194 Highway 98 East, just east of the Destin Bridge; P.O. Box 68, Destin 32540; (850) 837-1293. Fare is $45 per person for a half-day excursion (plus tax); half price for kids ages 8 to 12.**

One of the best fishing party boats on the scene. The crew is helpful with reeling in and cleaning your catch.

## Kokomo Snorkeling Headquarters
**400 Harbor Boulevard, behind Marina Cafe, Destin; (850) 837-9029; www.kokomo snorkeling.com. Fares are $25 for adults, $20 for children 12 and under, and $10 for nonsnorkelers for a two-hour trip.**

Snorkeling excursions take you to live shell and fish finds in clear waters. Open April through October. Reservations suggested.

## Big Kahuna's (all ages)
**1007 Highway 98 East, Destin; (850) 837-4061. Seasonal hours—during summer, it opens at 10:00 a.m. and closes according to demand; it's closed during winter. Call park in advance before you go, or visit its Web site, www.bigkahunas.com. Water park admission is $34.99 for those 48 inches or taller; $28.99 for seniors and those under 48 inches tall and 3 years or older; 2 and younger are free. Golf, go-kart, and adrenaline ride fees range from $4.29 to $45.99 for combinations.**

The grandest of Destin's kid parks, it brags up its water park for "the world's longest tube river," and the Bombs Away Bay with Mayan ruins and a real B-25 bomber. On the dry side, it has carnival games, fifty-four holes of miniature golf, go-karts, kiddie land, a Vertical Accelerator that drops ten stories and two other "adrenaline attractions," an ice cream parlor, and other junk food concessions. Activities are limited in the winter months.

# On a **Budget**

- **Old Town Trolley,** Tallahassee, **free** transportation through downtown
- **Capitol Complex,** Tallahassee, **free** admission
- **Museum of Florida History,** Tallahassee, **free** admission
- **Mission San Luis Archaeological and Historic Site,** Tallahassee, **free** admission
- **National Museum of Naval Aviation,** Pensacola, **free** admission to most parts
- **Naval Live Oaks,** Gulf Breeze, **free** admission
- **Air Force Armament Museum,** Fort Walton Beach, **free** admission
- **Alvin's Island-Magic Mountain Store,** Panama City Beach, **free** admission
- **Junior Museum of Bay County,** Panama City, **free** admission

### The Track Family Recreation Center (all ages)

1125 Highway 98, Destin; (850) 654-4668; www.funatthetrack.com. Open in the summer from 9:00 a.m. to midnight. Off-season hours vary. Closing hours may vary according to attendance. Admission is charged per activity.

Go-karts, miniature golf, bungee jumping, kiddie rides, video arcade.

### Henderson Beach State Park

17000 Emerald Coast Parkway, Destin; (850) 837-7550. Open 8:00 a.m. to sunset daily. Park entrance is $4 per vehicle, $3 for single occupant.

Destin's premier beach, it spans a beautiful dunesy stretch east of town, away from the crowds. The park recently added sixty campsites to its facilities.

### James W. Lee Park

Scenic Highway 98.

It lets you park for **free** (but the lot fills quickly on sunny days) and has a popular seafood restaurant and picnic shelters.

## Where to Eat

**A.J.'s Seafood and Oyster Bar.** 116 Highway 98 East, just east of the Destin Bridge, Destin; (850) 837-1913; ajs@ ajs-destin.com. Serves the best of local seafood daily for lunch and dinner. $$–$$$

**Fudpucker's.** 20001-A Emerald Coast Highway, Destin; (850) 654-4200. Shipwreck motif, casual, with a comprehensive menu of faddish munchies, burgers, and seafood. Lunch and dinner daily. Menu for "little puckers." Gator show **(free)** on the hour from noon to 4:00 p.m. $$

## Where to Stay

**Marina Bay Resort.** 80 Miracle Strip Parkway, Fort Walton Beach; (850) 244-5132; www.marinabayfla.com. On Intra-coastal Waterway. Boat dock. Amenities include full kitchen, heated pool, sauna, and bicycles. $–$$$

**SunDestin Beach Resort.** 1040 Highway 98 East, Destin; (850) 837-7093 or (800) 336-4853. One- to three-bedroom modern apartments with indoor and outdoor pools, health club, shuffleboard, and kids' recreational program in season. $$–$$$$

## For More Information

**Emerald Coast Convention and Visitors Bureau.** 1540 Miracle Strip Parkway, Fort Walton Beach 32549; (850) 651-7131 or (800) 322-3319; www.destin-fwb.com.

# South Walton County

South Walton County begins on Highway 98 East where Destin leaves off.

Destin encroaches upon what is known as South Walton County, a natural, well-planned stretch of eighteen quaint to upscale beach communities. Scenic Route C-30A takes a back-road look at the quiet, away-from-it-all neighborhood off Highway 98. At various tucks in the road, beach communities have gathered, each exerting its own character. Grayton Beach, the first beach community between Pensacola and Apalachicola to develop, circa 1920, is most appealing. Get there via Route 283. Historically it attracted surfers, artisans, and free spirits. More recently, yuppies have discovered the town. As a result, Grayton Beach is experiencing a nudge in growth off its traditional path of renovated historic cottages and artsy, humble beach abodes.

An overnight success begun in the early 1980s, Seaside was conceived as the embodiment of beach-town memories—a place where people rocked on front porches and children played carefree in the surf. It grew quickly as an award-winning community model in shades of pastel and Florida-style Victorian chic. One of the Panhandle's most upscale resort options, it embraces families and encourages old-fashioned values, despite its new veneer.

### Sandestin Golf and Beach Resort (all ages)

**9300 Emerald Coast Parkway West, Sandestin; (850) 267-8150 or (866) 293-4816; www.sandestin.com.**

If you're looking for a full-service family resort in this vicinity, look no further than Sandestin. Within this 2,400-acre community, you'll find accommodations from hotel rooms to family villas, a beach, seventy-three holes of golf, tennis, bike rentals, Kid Zone summer programs, a pirate's playground, a nature park, and a marina that rents boats and organizes fishing charters. For older kids, the sailing school is super. $$$

### Topsail Hill State Park (ages 6 to 13)

**7525 West Scenic Highway 30A, Santa Rosa Beach; (877) 232-2478. Open 8:00 a.m. to sunset. Admission is $2 per vehicle of eight persons or fewer, $1 per extra passenger, cyclist, or pedestrian.**

Its undeveloped beachfront serves as a nature conservatory and is touted as the most pristine, primitive coastal stretch in Florida. Unregimented sand trails take you through cypress swamp, pine forest, sand scrub, and heaving dunes beach with few souls in sight. An RV resort has been added in recent years, and bungalows are available for rent.

### Blue Sky Kayak (ages 5 to 12)

**Matt Labo, (850) 368-3150; www.blueskykayak.com. Two-hour tours are $55 for adults and $30 for children under 10.**

Families will enjoy the Western Lake Discovery Expedition, an easy guided paddle in shallow waters. Follow in the footsteps of Indians, early settlers, Spanish conquistadors, and others as you look for bobcat, deer, birds, and other wildlife. Their tracks may be spotted on a short stop in their natural habitat.

### Grayton Beach State Park (all ages)

**Route C-30A, 357 Main Park Road, Santa Rosa Beach; (850) 231-4210. Open 8:00 a.m. to sunset daily. Park entrance is $4 per vehicle of eight persons or fewer, $1 per extra passenger, cyclist, or pedestrian.**

One reason Grayton Beach has been "discovered" is the high national beach rating accorded this park by Dr. Stephen Leatherman, a coastal geographer more commonly known as Dr. Beach. Here, snow white sand dips into spring-clear, aqua waters and builds mounds of grass-tufted dunes. Not far off the beach, forests of pines and fresh- and saltwater lakes make you feel like you've suddenly arrived in the mountains. The juxtaposition of the two contrasting terrains provides a pleasant disarray in your sense of place. There's lake and Gulf fishing, with a boat ramp onto the brackish lake. A nature trail tours inland areas. Camping is allowed in thirty-seven wooded sites that have grills, picnic tables, water, and electricity. The park also offers rental cabins. (Reservations are recommended, 800-326-3521.)

## Eden Gardens State Park (ages 8 to 13) 🏛️ ⊛

1 mile north of Highway 98 on Route 395; P.O. Box 26, Point Washington 32454; (850) 231-4214. Gardens are open 8:00 a.m. to sundown. Guided mansion tours are offered on the hour from 10:00 a.m. to 3:00 p.m. Thursday through Monday. Admission to the park is $3 per vehicle. Mansion tour is $3 for adults, $1 for children ages 12 and younger.

A remnant of the region's lumbering era, this neoclassic plantation-style manor is the centerpiece for gracious gardens of ancient moss-dripping live oaks and blossoming camellias and azaleas. Peak blooming period is mid-March. Bring a picnic lunch, tour the house, and revel in the peace and Old South beauty.

## Seaside Kids Programs

Each summer, Camp Seaside (850-231-2246) keeps the children of resort guests productively occupied with recreational and crafts projects. The resort also sponsors special enrichment programs throughout the year, such as a children's architectural camp. Ruskin Place, the community's artist colony, offers workshops for both children and adults. One shop lets them paint their own pottery pieces. Storytelling takes place at the town's outdoor amphitheater.

## Where to Eat

**Bud & Alley's.** Route 30A, Seaside; (850) 231-5900. The place to go for a family splurge. Creative, cutting-edge dishes, kids' menu, seaside atmosphere. Open daily for lunch and dinner March through October; closed Tuesday, September through May. $$$

**Gilligan's.** 530 Highway 98E, Destin; (850) 650-4400. Not his island, but casual dining for lunch and dinner on a deck overlooking water and beach. Kids' menu. $–$$$

**Goatfeathers.** Route 30A, Dune Allen; (850) 267-3342. Family favorite with seafood sandwiches and po'boys, Louisiana specialties, and fun finger foods. Lunch and dinner seven days a week. $$$

**Pompano Joe's Seafood House.** Miramar Beach; 2237 Old Highway 98, Destin; (850) 837-2224. On the beach and replete with colorful seaside character and great food. Lunch and dinner daily. $$$

## Where to Stay

(See also Sandestin Resort, page 24.)

**Sandestin Beach Hilton.** Sandestin; (850) 267-9500 or (800) 367-1271. Four hundred of the 600 suites have bunk beds for the kids. Kitchenettes, a well-planned kids program, and use of Sandestin Resort facilities. $$$

**Seaside Cottages.** P.O. Box 4730, Seaside 32459; (850) 231-2222 or (888) SEASIDE; www.seasidefl.com. More than 270 cottages—from one- to six-bedroom, fully furnished and character replete—are perfect for family seaside vacations. Swimming pools, tennis courts, playground, croquet, shuffleboard, recreational rentals. Three-day minimum in summer and over holidays in some cottages. (Prices are per unit.) $$$–$$$$

## For More Information

**South Walton Tourist Development Council.** P.O. Box 1248, Santa Rosa Beach 32459; (850) 267-1216; www.beachesof southwalton.com.

# Panama City Beach and Panama City

About a half mile east of Seaside on Highway 98 and Alternate Highway 98.

The Disney World of the Panhandle, Panama City Beach brims with attractions and activities tailored to families. It wins awards for its good value, but avoid it at spring break.

Most of the community's attractions lie on Highway 98 (Panama City Beach Parkway) and Alternate 98 (Front Beach Road/Thomas Drive). That makes them the most-traveled routes, ones you want to avoid in the middle of the day during peak spring break and summer periods. The gorgeous beach and Gulf waters focus vacationer attention on water sports, from diving and snorkeling to Jet Skiing and fishing.

### Museum of Man in the Sea (ages 6 to 12)

**17314 Panama City Beach Parkway, Panama City Beach; (850) 235-4101. Open 10:00 a.m. to 4:00 p.m. daily. Admission is $5.00 for adults, $2.50 for children ages 6 to 16.**

This unusual museum underscores the area's reputation for great diving. It traces the history of underwater adventure from its humble beginnings and diving bells to modern times and recreational scuba equipment. Kids gravitate to the exhibits of treasures from Florida shipwrecks.

### Gulf World Marine Park (ages 4 to 12)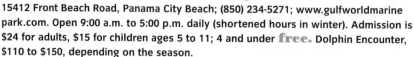

**15412 Front Beach Road, Panama City Beach; (850) 234-5271; www.gulfworldmarine park.com. Open 9:00 a.m. to 5:00 p.m. daily (shortened hours in winter). Admission is $24 for adults, $15 for children ages 5 to 11; 4 and under free. Dolphin Encounter, $110 to $150, depending on the season.**

Besides the usual marine-park attractions, it offers scuba demonstrations and educational dolphin and sea lion shows. Kids can touch a stingray and watch a shark feeding. The attraction also has tropical gardens graced by flamingos, parrots, and a loggerhead turtle and shark channel, plus a dolphin encounter program.

### Ripley's Believe It Or Not! Museum (all ages)

9907 Front Beach Road, Panama City Beach; (850) 230-6113; www.ripleyspanamacity beach.com. Opens at 10:00 a.m. daily. Museum admission is $14.95 for adults, $11.95 for children ages 6 to 12; under 6 **free.** Combo tickets available.

This brand new museum, built to resemble a luxury liner run aground, houses hundreds of strange and unusual exhibits. The bizarre gives way to the unique in a stretch limo plated with gold coins worth $1.3 million. For an additional fee, you can take a ride in a moving theater.

### Shipwreck Island (ages 3 to 12)

12000 Front Beach Road, Panama City Beach; (850) 234-0368; www.shipwreckisland .com. Open generally 10:30 a.m. to 5:30 p.m., but the schedule varies. Closed after Labor Day until April. Admission is $29 for persons taller than 50 inches, $24 for persons between 35 and 50 inches tall, $18 for seniors. **Free** for those under 35 inches tall.

This attraction offers rides the likes of Tadpole Hole, Elephant Slide (all for tot-types), and the thrilling Raging Rapids, Pirate's Plunge, and the six-story White Knuckle River tube ride. Lifeguards supervise. No food or coolers can be brought into the park.

### Alvin's Island-Magic Mountain Store (ages 2 to 6)

12010 Front Beach Road, Panama City Beach; (850) 234-3048 or (888) 4-ALVINS; www .alvinsisland.com. Open 8:00 a.m. to midnight daily.

Across the side street from the amusement parks, it is part souvenir mart, part **free** sightseeing attraction, with aquariums, alligator-feeding shows, and tropical birds to entertain the kids while you pick up inexpensive T-shirts, shells, toys, and Florida souvenirs.

### Zoo World (ages 2 to 10)

9008 Front Beach Road, Panama City Beach; (850) 230-1243 or (850) 230-4839. Open 9:00 a.m. to 5:30 p.m. daily (seasonal changes). Admission is $16.50 for adults, $14.50 for seniors, $10.50 for children ages 4 to 11 (plus tax); 3 and under, **Free.**

Endangered animals and other rare creatures are among the inhabitants here. A petting zoo and infant care facility are prime attractions. You can buy a bucket of feed for $5 and even pet a giraffe.

### St. Andrews State Park/Shell Island (all ages)

East end of Thomas Drive, 4607 State Park Lane, Panama City Beach; (850) 233-5140. Park entrance is $5 per vehicle with up to eight passengers, $2 for a single passenger, and $3 for extra passengers, bicyclists, and pedestrians. The shuttle to Shell Island costs $9.50 for adults, $5.50 for children ages 6 to 12. Snorkel equipment rentals available. Shuttle is closed during the off-season and runs every hour or half hour, 10:00 a.m. to 4:00 p.m., March to October.

When you're ready to get away from the Ferris wheels and racetracks, this is your place. Set up camp and bask on the glorious white beach, or follow nature trails into pine forest and have a picnic. Fishing enthusiasts can cast from its gulfside pier, bayside pier, or from the rock jetty at the pass between the park and Shell Island. The park also sponsors trips to unbridged Shell Island for shelling, beaching, and snorkeling.

### Sea Dragon Pirate Cruise (all ages)

**5325 North Lagoon Drive, Panama City Beach; (850) 234-7400 or (866) 964-6461; www .piratecruise.net. Fares are $19 for adults, $17 for seniors, $15 for children ages 3 to 14, $9 for children ages 1 and 2; babies free. From 10:00 a.m. daily, weather permitting. Call for schedule.**

Heave-ho mateys for a two-hour cruise on a pirate ship within cannon range of Shell Island. Pirate hats are the headgear of the day for little privateers hunting for treasure.

### Junior Museum of Bay County (ages 4 to 12)

**1731 Jenks Avenue, Panama City; (850) 769-6128; www.jrmuseum.org. Open 9:00 a.m. to 4:30 p.m. Monday through Friday and 10:00 a.m. to 4:00 p.m. Saturday. Suggested donations are $3 for adults, $2 for children ages 2 to 14.**

Nature trails, a train engine, a pioneer village, and live chickens and ducks make learning fun. Indoor exhibits teach about the body, nature, and other scientific elements with games and interactivities.

## Where to Eat

**Capt. Anderson's Restaurant.** 5551 North Lagoon Drive, Panama City Beach; (850) 234-2225 or (888) US-TOP-50; www .captandersons.com. A Panama City Beach institution, it specializes in seafood and steaks, prepared by classic methodology and dependably well executed. Expect a wait. Open daily for dinner except Sunday and November through January. $$–$$$$

**Pineapple Willy's Beachside Restaurant and Sports Bar.** 9875 South Thomas Drive, Panama City Beach; (850) 235-0928 (recorded message) or 235-1225. Outdoor deck and indoor dining room seating overlook the beach. Specialty is Jack Daniel's barbecue ribs served in a plastic souvenir bucket. Sandwiches, salads, seafood, and kids' menu. Lunch and dinner daily. $–$$$

**Treasure Ship.** 3605 Thomas Drive, Panama City Beach; (850) 234-8881; www.thetreasureship.com. What could be more exciting than dinner on a treasure ship? This ship-shaped restaurant overlooks bay waters. The staff, dressed like pirates, serve seafood and steaks. The main dining room serves dinner only, but the waterfront Hook's Grille and Grog is open for lunch and dinner. $–$$$

**Uncle Ernie's Bayfront Grill and Brew House.** 1151 Bayview Avenue, Panama City; (850) 763-8427. Dine overlooking St. Andrews Bay in a late-1800s restored home and enjoy some of the best seafood, salads, and sandwiches around. Open daily for lunch and dinner. $$–$$$

## Where to Stay

**The Boardwalk Beach Resort.** 9450 South Thomas Drive, Panama City Beach; (850) 234-3484 or (800) 224-GULF; www.boardwalkbeachresort.com. Actually two hotels in one, with 320 rooms in a variety of styles and ranges, interconnected by a beachfront boardwalk. Restaurants (kids eat **free**), beach bars, kids' club, and playgrounds. $–$$$$

**Edgewater Beach Resort.** 11212 Front Beach Road, Panama City Beach; (800) 874-8686; www.edgewaterbeachresort.com. A step above most other resorts on the beach, this condominium resort features well-equipped luxury one- to three-bedroom accommodations, a fetching lagoon pool area, a restaurant, tennis, golf, and organized kids' activities. $–$$$$

**Flamingo Motel.** 15525 Front Beach Road, Panama City Beach; (850) 234-2232; www.flamingomotel.com. Family oriented, lush, and beachfront. Rooms and efficiencies sleep up to eight. Refrigerators in all rooms, full kitchens in others. Two swimming pools and hot tub. Ask about special family rates. $–$$

**Marriott Bay Point Resort Village.** 4200 Marriott Drive off Thomas Drive, Panama City Beach; (850) 234-3307 or (800) 874-7105. A destination golf resort away from the beach, it offers full services, including kids' program, biking, exercise room, marina, and pools. $$–$$$$

## For More Information

**Panama City Beach Convention and Visitors Bureau.** 17001 Panama City Beach Parkway (mailing address: P.O. Box 9473, Panama City Beach 32417), Panama City Beach; (850) 234-6575 or (800) PC-BEACH; www.panamacitybeachfl.com.

# Apalachicola Area

Continue along Highway 98 for about an hour's drive.

East of Panama City, the Panhandle pace bogs. Nature and hometowns dictate a tempo that seems worlds away from the airbrushed T-shirt and body piercing shops to the west. Mexico Beach presents a laid-back strip of sand not yet infected by high-rises or high prices. The distinctive odor of pulp mills greets you as you cross the bridge to Port St. Joe, but past that, the gulfside town offers superb scalloping, fishing, and diving, plus a historic site or two.

Continue along Route C-30 east of Port St. Joe about 40 miles to find a secluded sliver of Gulf Coast shoreline, a land of minimal development and beach wilderness known as Cape San Blas, and its offshore loner island, St. Vincent. Cape San Blas juts from Panhandle Gulf shores like the prong of a sprung safety pin. Long and lanky, the peninsula, with its tenuous grasp to mainland, is more like an island in its isolation.

Apalachicola, which shares its name with a river and a species of local oyster, is one of Florida's prettiest old towns. Developed in the early 1800s as a cotton port, its waterfront warehouses and other historic buildings have been restored to preserve fifty-some sites—more pre–Civil War structures than anywhere else in Florida. Many of the old buildings hold galleries and charming boutiques that beg to be browsed. Stop in at the local chamber of commerce for a historic-district walking tour.

A trip across the 5-mile-long Bryant Patton Bridge to St. George Island is a must. The bridge crosses Apalachicola Bay at Eastpoint. Watch for the signs. Only recently discovered as a summer beach refuge and fishing hot spot, St. George Island offers overnighters an inn, a motel, state park camping, and house rentals. This is a good place to journey for lunch, where something with oysters is de rigueur.

East of Apalachicola in Carrabelle, you'll see the world's smallest police station on Highway 98.

### The Constitution Convention State Museum (ages 6 to 12)
**200 Allen Memorial Way, Port St. Joe; off Highway 98 east of Port St. Joe; (850) 229-8029. Tours are given 9:00 a.m. to noon and 1:00 to 5:00 p.m. Thursday through Monday. Admission is $1 for visitors age 7 or older.**

Talking mannequins reenact Florida's first state Constitution Convention and the history of a long-gone town named St. Joseph, which was decimated by hurricane and yellow fever in the mid-1800s.

### Salinas Park (ages 2 to 10)
**On Route C-30E, near the intersection of Route C-30, Cape San Blas.**

This roadside park embraces a beautiful white beach, shady picnic areas, a playground, and a dunes-top gazebo. When the weather is warm, the biting insects are horrendous, so come prepared. Also beware of sandspurs when you step off the boardwalk.

### St. Joseph Peninsula State Park (ages 3 to 12)
**8899 Cape San Blas Road, Port St. Joe; north of Cape San Blas; (850) 227-1327. Open 8:00 a.m. to sunset daily. Park entrance is $4 per vehicle of eight persons or fewer, $1 per extra passenger, cyclist, or pedestrian.**

The ultimate beach lies at the end of the road, where civilization meets utter wilderness, at the tip of the cape. Tall dunes sequester the beach from the road and leave you in a still world of ghost crabs and shorebirds. Across the road, a boat ramp and a picnic shelter bring you back in touch with reality. Camp and cabin sites, canoe and nature trails, and a 1,650-acre wilderness preserve occupy the park's 2,500 acres. It's a good place to see migratory birds and monarch butterflies.

## Florida **Trivia**

**Time to . . .** Set your watches ahead an hour per Eastern Standard Time. The Apalachicola River is the dividing line between Central Standard Time (CST) and Eastern Standard Time (EST).

# Other Panama City Beach
# **Amusement Parks and Attractions**

**Super Speed Fun Park** (ages 4 to 12) 9523 Front Beach Road; (850) 234-1588. A haunted house and 3-D black-light minigolf add extra fun to the go-kart and bumper boat rides. Open daily 10:00 a.m. to midnight (summer); price depends on activity but starts at $5.63 (plus tax).

**Airboat Adventures** (ages 4 to 12) Beside West Bay Bridge, Highway 79, 14852 Bayview Circle; (850) 230-3822; www.swampvette.com. Look for wildlife in a boat powered by a huge fan. Half-hour ride $18.95 adults, $11.95 children.

**Barnacle Bay** (ages 4 to 12) 11209 Front Beach Road; (850) 234-7792. Generally open 10:00 a.m. to midnight in spring/summer, 10:00 a.m. to 8:00 p.m. in winter. Charge for eighteen holes is $8.50 for golfers ages 8 and older and $7.00 for children ages 4 to 7 (plus tax). Miniature golf.

**Coconut Creek Mini Golf and Gran Maze** (ages 4 to 12) 9807 Front Beach Road; (850) 234-2625. Opens daily at 9:00 a.m. Admission is $16.00 for unlimited use of facilities, $9.50 for eighteen holes of golf or maze play.

**Rock It Lanes** (ages 7 to 12) 513 Beckrich Road; (850) 249-2695; www.rockitlanes.com. Open 10:00 a.m. to 2:00 a.m. Monday through Saturday and noon to 2:00 a.m. Sunday. $5 skating rink; call for information on bowling, billiards, and a mega arcade with 130 games.

**Capt. Anderson's Marina** (ages 4 to 12) 5550 North Lagoon Drive; (850) 234-3435; www.captain andersonsmarina.com. Open daily 9:00 a.m. to noon and 1:00 to 4:00 p.m. $18 adults, $10 children 2 to 11. Watch dolphins and other sea life on a glass-bottom boat cruise to Shell Island where you can add to your shell collection.

## St. Vincent National Wildlife Refuge (ages 8 to 12)

**For permits and information contact the refuge manager at P.O. Box 447, Apalachicola 32329; (850) 653-8808. Visitor center open 8:00 a.m. to 4:00 p.m. Monday through Friday.**

One of the area's most acclaimed destinations is accessible by charter or private boat only. (Call the Apalachicola Bay Chamber of Commerce, 850-653-9419, for information.) Once a private hunting preserve, it holds a diverse selection of native and exotic wildlife: Asian sambar deer, white-tailed deer, red wolves, and bald eagles. The island's small lakes, ponds, and creeks are open for fishing May through September. Freshwater fish include bream, shellcracker, speckled perch, catfish, and bass. To manage the populations of deer and feral hogs, controlled annual hunts are held. Camping is allowed in conjunction with the hunts. All participants must be approved by the refuge manager.

## John Gorrie State Museum (ages 8 to 12)

**1 block off Highway 98 on Sixth Street (P.O. Box 267, Apalachicola 32320) Apalachicola; (850) 653-9347. Open 9:00 a.m. to 5:00 p.m. Thursday through Monday. Admission is $1 for visitors ages 6 and older.**

It pays tribute to Apalachicola's most important historical figure, a nineteenth-century physician who, in trying to develop a method for making yellow fever sufferers more comfortable, invented a forerunner of today's ice-making machine and air conditioner.

# A Walton **Adventure**

Aaron was only four when he and I made our first Panhandle trip. Actually, it was our first long trip together, alone. It's tough to say who was more awed by the dramatic terrain of it all. We stayed in a cabin on Cape San Blas. While I walked around, mouth agape at the sheer beauty and quiet of the place, he chased ghost crabs. He loved that name— "ghost" crabs (it was right before Halloween). I did too because Cape San Blas, at that time of the year, was ghostly silent, except for the occasional Air Force jet scrambling the air waves. Close enough to the family-frantic pace of Panama City Beach, but blissfully far enough away, it provided a peaceful, satisfying outcome to our mother-son travel experiment. Since then, we've made our twosome road trip an annual tradition.    —C.K.W.

# Florida **Trivia**

**Amazing Scallop Facts** What has one hundred blue eyes and can swim sideways? A Florida sea scallop. Once common throughout the state, its populations have suffered from pollution and other factors. Today, recreational scalloping is allowed only north of the Suwannee River between July 1 and September 10. Limits apply. Commercial scalloping has been banned statewide. Most popular scalloping locales are around Port St. Joe near Apalachicola and at Steinhatchee on the Nature Coast.

### St. George Island State Park (all ages)

1900 East Gulf Beach Drive, St. George Island; (850) 927-2111. Open 8:00 a.m. to sunset daily. Park entrance is $5 per vehicle with up to eight passengers, $3 for a single passenger, and $1 per extra passenger, bicyclist, and pedestrian. East end access is $6 for adults, and **free** for children under 12.

St. George Island is one long stretch of sand, but the best of its beach lies beyond state park gates, where the dunes tower and the birds come to stay warm and nest. Go there to camp, canoe, and hike inland trails along rush-fringed marshes and freshwater ponds.

### Journeys of St. George Island

240 East Third Street, St. George Island; (850) 927-3259; www.sgislandjourneys.com.

To get out on the water and take advantage of the great fishing and rich wildlife, you can arrange a fishing charter, barrier island tour, oysters and sunset cruise, kayak and scallop snorkeling adventure, canoe trip, or kids-only trips.

## Where to Eat

**Boss Oyster Restaurant.** 125 Water Street, Apalachicola; (850) 653-9364; www.apalachicolariverinn.com/boss.html. Oysters right from the bay prepared seventeen different ways, plus other seafood specialties (including seafood pizza) in a casual atmosphere. $$–$$$

**Gibson Inn.** 51 Avenue C, Apalachicola; (850) 653-2191; www.gibsoninn.com. This is the most formal Apalachicola has to offer, but it's fine for kids, especially for lunch. Seafood is done Florida and Cajun style. $$$

**Sisters Restaurant.** 236 Reid Avenue, Port St. Joe; (850) 229-7121. Lunch on home-cooked specials, salads, and sandwiches at this quaint restaurant. Open daily 11:00 a.m. to 2:00 p.m. $–$$

## Where to Stay

Rental homes and rustic cabins are your primary option on Cape San Blas and St. George Island. Elsewhere you'll find inns and B&Bs.

**Gibson Inn.** 51 Avenue C, Apalachicola; (850) 653-2191; www.gibsoninn.com. Built in 1907 and restored in 1983; each of its thirty-one rooms is individually furnished Victorian style. $–$$

**Old Salt Works Cabins.** Route 30E, Cape San Blas; 1085 Cape San Blas Road, Port St. Joe; (850) 229-6097. One of several cabin resorts on Cape San Blas, it offers a taste of history and entertainment for the kids. It spreads from Gulf to bay with pleasantly modern cabins, a historic museum that remembers the site's former life as a Civil War salt plant, and Fort Crooked Tree, where kids can intermingle their imaginations with mannequins in Civil War dress. $

## For More Information

**Apalachicola Bay Chamber of Commerce.** 122 Commerce Street, Apalachicola 32320; (850) 653-9419; www.apalachicolabay.org.

**Gulf County Chamber of Commerce.** P.O. Box 964, Port St. Joe 32457; (850) 227-1223; www.gulfcountybusiness.com.

# The Big Bend

Continuing along Highway 98.

This marshy stretch of shoreline, sometimes disparagingly referred to as Florida's Armpit, holds a subtle intrigue. Its lack of spectacular sand beaches leaves it forgotten by most tourists, other than those looking for plentiful wildlife, fishing towns, and water sports. Some of Florida's earliest Indian and European colonial settlements took advantage of the strategic location at this crossroads between peninsula and panhandle.

This drive skirts a rare stretch of wilderness: the immense, more than half-million-acre Apalachicola National Forest, Wakulla Springs State Park, St. Marks National Wildlife Refuge, and the Aucilla Wildlife Management Area.

## Florida **Trivia**

**Oyster Facts in a Shell** On the average, an annual commercial harvest of Apalachicola Bay oysters produces enough meat to cover a football field three deep. Franklin County produces 90 percent of Florida's oysters and 10 percent of the nation's supply. Oyster lovers are still advised to eat raw oysters only in months with an "R" in the name. The young, the old, and those with certain health problems should avoid eating raw oysters altogether.

### Gulf Specimen Marine Laboratories Aquarium (ages 4 to 12)

222 Clark Drive at Palm Street south of Highway 98 (P.O. Box 237, Panacea 32346), Panacea; (850) 984-5297; www.gulfspecimen.org. Open 9:00 a.m. to 5:00 p.m. Monday through Friday, 10:00 a.m. to 4:00 p.m. Saturday, noon to 4:00 p.m. Sunday. Admission is $6 for adults and $4 for children 3 to 11.

Jack Rudloe, author of *Living Dock at Panacea* and other Florida-related naturalist books, operates this nonprofit organization, which stocks schools with sea-life specimens and conducts research. You can visit the lab—unsophisticated but full of great surprises, such as an electric fish. A touch tank and aquariums fill several rooms and hold sharks, stingrays, moray eels, and other unusual creatures that are native to Florida waters.

### San Marcos de Apalache Historic Site (ages 7 to 12)

South end of Route 363; 148 Old Fort Road, St. Marks; (850) 922-6007. Open 9:00 a.m. to 5:00 p.m. Thursday through Monday. Admission is $1 for visitors ages 6 and older.

St. Marks began its life as an important center, first for the Apalachee Indians and later, circa 1679, for Spanish explorers, who named it San Marcos de Apalachee. Today the remains of the Spanish fort and a museum bear witness to the early importance of the strategically placed town, now a humble fishing village.

### St. Marks National Wildlife Refuge (ages 5 to 12)

Off Highway 98; 1255 Lighthouse Road (P.O. Box 68, St. Marks 32355), St. Marks; (850) 925-6121. Visitor center open 8:15 a.m. to 4:00 p.m. Monday through Friday and 10:00 a.m. to 5:00 p.m. weekends. Park entrance is $4 per car.

A historic lighthouse and monarch butterflies draw most visitors to this vast 65,000 acres of marsh and woodlands. The butterflies arrive in thick, colorful swarms every fall, making trees seem to blossom in orange and black. The best place to find the butterflies is at the refuge's lighthouse on the bay. St. Marks also offers biking, hiking, and canoeing opportunities.

### The Wilderness Way (ages 7 to 12)

4901 Woodville Highway, Tallahassee; (850) 877-7200; www.thewildernessway.net.

For a guided introduction into the region's wilderness, join a paddling or hiking trip with the history and wildlife experts at the Wilderness Way. Canoeing and kayaking clinics; bird-watching; paddling trips on the St. Marks, Wacissa, Aucilla, or Wakulla Rivers; and specialty trips are also available.

### Wakulla Springs State Park (ages 3 to 12)

North of Highway 98, west of St. Marks; 550 Wakulla Park Drive, Wakulla Springs; (850) 224-5950. Open 8:00 a.m. to sunset daily. Park entrance is $4 per vehicle of eight persons or fewer, $1 per extra passenger, cyclist, or pedestrian. Boat tour fares are $6 for adults and $3 for children ages 12 and under for a forty-five-minute tour.

Swim in one of the world's deepest and largest freshwater springs. Take a glass-bottom boat or jungle cruise into the realm of alligators and anhingas. One of the park's highlights is its 1937 marble-floored Wakulla Springs Lodge, where you can get a room, an ice-cream cone, some lunch, or a T-shirt.

## Where to Eat

**Wakulla Springs Lodge.** Wakulla Springs State Park, 550 Wakulla Park Drive, Wakulla Springs; (850) 224-5950. A grand lodge built in 1937, it's a great place for a Southern-style breakfast, lunch, or dinner any day of the week. Kids' menu and soda fountain. $$

## Where to Stay

**Wakulla Springs Lodge.** Wakulla Springs State Park, 550 Wakulla Park Drive, Wakulla Springs; (850) 224-5950. A historic lodge set on the banks of a sparkling, wildlife-rich spring. $

# Weekend Jaunt: Northern Springlands

Head east off Highway 98/19. For information contact Original Florida, P.O. Box 1300, Lake City 32056-1300, (877) 746-4778, www.originalflorida.org; or Florida Nature and Heritage Tourism Center, P.O. Box 849, White Springs 32096, (386) 397-4461.

Wakulla Springs heads Florida's springlands, a concentration of more than one hundred inland limestone springs that spreads to the south as far as Orlando. Before beaches became a magnet, these warm, windowpane springs and their resultant health resorts attracted Florida's earliest tourists. The roads that head east off Highway 98/19 lead to these springs, as well as to their state parks and a wealth of wildlife, oak canopies, diving caves, and canoeing outposts. Many of the springs are

## Florida **Trivia**

**Fluttering By** The Panhandle is a major hatching locale for monarchs as they make their annual 5,000-mile journey from northern Canada to Mexico. It takes five generations of butterflies to complete the trip. From late October through November, the region dances with the orange and black flutter of swarming wings. Prime monarch rest stops include St. Marks National Wildlife Refuge and St. Joseph Peninsula State Park.

# A Walton **Adventure**

We expected to see wildlife at Wakulla Springs State Park. They practically guarantee it on their boat tours. However, we didn't expect it the minute we drove into the park, which is when a doe and her fawn leaped across the road right in front of our car. Aaron insisted we return to the ranger station and tell them they should erect a DEER CROSSING sign.

—*C.K.W.*

part of the Suwannee River basin. Most of the attraction is natural, but you may enjoy exploring some of the quiet old towns, such as High Springs, where you can stroll through antiques shops, arts and crafts boutiques, a museum, and historic bed-and-breakfast inns in vintage buildings.

## Suwannee River State Park (ages 6 to 12)

**15 miles west of Live Oak off Highway 90; 20185 County Road 132, Live Oak; (386) 362-2746. Open 8:00 a.m. to sunset daily. Park entrance is $4 per vehicle of eight passengers or fewer, $1 for a single passenger.**

If you're hooked on canoeing, this is the place to head in these parts. The canoe trail that goes through the park actually begins in Georgia. Take a short hike along a cliff overlooking the historic Suwanee River to Balance Rock, or go for a dip in a secluded sinkhole. There's also picnicking, a boat ramp, a playground, and thirty campsites.

## Suwannee Canoe Outpost (all ages)

**Spirit of the Suwannee Music Park on Highway 129; 2461 Ninety-fifth Drive, Live Oak; (386) 364-4991 or (800) 428-4147; www.canoeoutpost.com. Canoe rentals are $12 to $26 per adult for day trips, depending upon the trip's duration. Children ages 3 to 12 pay half price.**

Canoe rentals and shuttle outside the park for day and overnight trips.

## The Suwannee County Historical Museum
(ages 8 to 12)

**208 North Ohio Avenue, Live Oak; (386) 362-1776. Open 9:30 a.m. to noon and 1:00 to 4:30 p.m. Monday through Friday. Donations requested.**

The museum glorifies the Cracker way of life at its railway station home. Remnants of the pioneer era include a copper moonshine still, cornhusk chairs, a butter churn, and old school books.

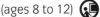

## Way Down upon **the Suwannee River**

The historic Suwannee River originates in Georgia's Okefenokee Swamp and runs along eleven Florida counties for 235 miles. It holds more than seventy springs and was a center of ancient Timucuan Indian civilization. Composer Stephen Foster, who wrote "Old Folks at Home," Florida's state song, never even saw the Suwannee River, nor did he step foot in Florida.

**Stephen Foster Folk Culture Center State Park** (ages 6 to 12)
**Highway 41 North Park (P.O. Drawer G, White Springs 32096), White Springs; (386) 397-4331; www.stephenfostercenter.com. Open 8:00 a.m. to sunset daily; carillon tower, craft shops, and museum open 9:00 a.m. to 5:00 p.m. Park entrance is $4 per vehicle of eight persons or fewer, $1 per extra passenger, cyclist, or pedestrian.**

In addition to its history museum and memorial to Florida's favorite composer, this popular attraction lets you experience "way down upon the Suwannee River." At Craft Square, demonstrators practice old-time craftsmanship and artisans sell their wares while a carillon tower chimes the well-loved tunes of Stephen Foster. The gift shop sells old-fashioned toys and stick candy. At the annual Florida Folk Festival in May, musicians of various genres join artisans and crafters for a three-day tribute to the old arts. Campsites and picnicking facilities are also available.

Other Folk Culture Center events include:

• Stephen Foster Day, January

• Antique Tractor and Gas Engine Show, April

• Quilt Show and Sale, October

• Rural Folklife Days, November

• Christmas Festival of Lights, December

## Florida **Trivia**

**Springs Trivia** Florida counts more than 300 natural springs. They are a product of Florida's honeycombed limestone foundation and hydrostatic pressure. About thirty of Florida's springs qualify as first magnitude, meaning they have an average flow of greater than one hundred cubic feet per second. Most of the northland springs maintain a cool 72 degrees year-round.

## Panhandle **Climes**

The four seasons perform more dramatically in the Panhandle than elsewhere in Florida. Temperatures range from an average of 83 degrees in summer to 50 degrees in winter. Snow does occasionally fall at these latitudes. If visiting in late fall, winter, or early spring, pack to dress in layers. Summer and early fall, temperatures stay warm day and night.

The Panhandle sees its share of tropical storm and hurricane warnings June through October. Plenty of advance warning allows time to evacuate.

### Ichetucknee Springs State Park (ages 6 to 12)

**Route 2, Box 5355, Fort White 32038; (386) 497-2511 (recorded message) or 497-4690. Two entrances are located off Highway 27 between Fort White and Branford, with tram transportation between the two entrances. (Admission at the north entrance is limited.) Open 8:00 a.m. to sunset daily. Park entrance is $5 per vehicle of eight persons or fewer, $3 for a single passenger. Additional fees for canoeing and tubing apply.**

The preferred activity in the 72-degree waters of this designated National Natural Landmark is inner-tubing. Canoeing, swimming, snorkeling, hiking, and camping are also pursued. Use is limited to 2,000 visitors a day to protect the natural environs. Canoe, raft, and tube rentals are available inside and outside the park.

### O'Leno State Park (ages 7 to 12)

**6 miles north of High Springs on Highway 441, High Springs; (386) 454-1853. Open 8:00 a.m. to sunset daily. Park entrance is $4 per vehicle of eight persons or fewer, $1 per extra passenger, cyclist, or pedestrian.**

Hikers especially love it here! Its 15 miles of nature trails explore an old limestone quarry, underground river, and natural bridge.

# The Nature Coast: Cedar Key

Follow Highway 98 and take designated side roads. To get to Cedar Key, head south on Route 345 out of Chiefland, then west on Route 24.

What's south of Florida's Big Bend has been termed "The Nature Coast" in recognition of its flourishing wildlife. Highway 98 skirts this area, but you really must side-trip off to see what's so real about Florida in these parts. West of the main highway, the Gulf coastland exudes a quiet, marshy temperament more conducive to thriving fishing villages than resort enclaves. Towns with names such as Keaton Beach and Horseshoe Beach retain the atmosphere of eras past, while Steinhatchee has evolved into a low-key resort devoted to fishing and canoeing. Don't forget to sample the oysters, scallops, blue crabs, and other local delectables.

The best the coast has to offer is Cedar Key, one of Florida's earliest flourishing towns. Pencil manufacturing and lumbering enabled it to prosper in the mid-1800s, but it later died back to its current 700-something population of clammers and fishermen. It occupies one of a cluster of out-of-the-way islands, many of which have been designated as part of Cedar Keys National Wildlife Refuge.

At this unpretentious preserved relic of yesteryear, take a self-guided tour around the historic district; you can get a map from the local chamber of commerce. Cedar Key's waterfront along Dock Street holds what's best loved about the quaint little town—art galleries, artisan shops, and seafood restaurants.

### Weekender: Miller's Marine and Suwannee Houseboats
(ages 5 to 12)

**Route 349 south of Highway 19/98; end of Highway 349 South, Suwannee; (352) 542-7349 or (800) 458-BOAT. Rates start at $495 during off-season, from December to February; and from $575 during the busy season, from March to November. Canoe rental available.**

Your family can penetrate the past and present of the historic Suwannee River on a leisurely cruise. The vessels can accommodate up to eight. The river is wide enough that kids can drive the boat. See gorgeous scenery, manatees, and prehistoric fish (gulf sturgeon).

### Manatee Springs State Park (ages 6 to 12)

**End of Route 320 off Highway 98, 6 miles west of Chiefland; 11650 Northwest 115th Street, Chiefland; (352) 493-6072. Open 8:00 a.m. to sunset daily. Park entrance is $4 per vehicle of eight persons or fewer, $1 per extra passenger, cyclist, or pedestrian.**

Named for the lovable Florida critter that favors it, the park encompasses a spring-head that pumps out 116.9 million gallons of crystalline water daily. Activities include swimming in spring-cooled water, canoeing, kayaking, picnicking, fishing, biking, camping, and hiking the boardwalk through ancient cypress wetlands and into the Suwannee River.

## Top Family **Resorts**

1. **Old Salt Works Cabins,** Cape San Blas
2. **Seaside Resort,** Seaside
3. **Sandestin Resort,** Sandestin
4. **St. Joseph Peninsula State Park,** Cape San Blas

## Top Family **Beaches and Parks**

1. **Fort Pickens National Park,** Pensacola Beach
2. **Wakulla Springs State Park,** Wakulla Springs
3. **Grayton Beach State Recreation Area,** Grayton Beach
4. **St. Joseph Peninsula State Park,** Cape San Blas
5. **St. George Island State Park,** St. George Island

### Cedar Key Historical Society Museum (ages 5 to 12)
**Second Street at Route 24; 609 Second Street; (352) 543-5549. Open 1:00 to 4:00 p.m. Sunday through Friday, and 11:00 a.m. to 5:00 p.m. Saturday. Admission is $1 for adults and 50 cents for children.**

A small, homey facility in a circa-1870 building, it tells the story—with artifacts, photos, and newspaper clippings—of Cedar Key's past, throughout its various occupations of turtling, sponging, fishing, and pencil-making.

### Cedar Key Seafood Festival; Cedar Key Sidewalk Arts Festival (ages 9 to 12)
**(352) 543-5600.**

These two events take place along Second Avenue between Route 24 and the downtown city park, and tens of thousands of visitors join town residents each year to celebrate both. The Cedar Key Seafood Festival takes place annually during the third week of October, attracting 30,000 to 40,000 people. In addition to the food, it features arts and crafts, food concessions in the park, and all manner of seafood, from smoked mullet to crab cakes and fresh clams. The arts festival is smaller and occurs in April. Along with the artists exhibiting their wares, there's food, entertainment, live bands, and lots of fun for kids.

### The Cedar Key Museum State Park (ages 8 to 12)
**Hodges Avenue and Whitman Drive; 12231 Southwest 166 Court; (352) 543-5350. Open 9:00 a.m. to 5:00 p.m. Thursday through Monday. Admission is $1 for those 6 and older; 5 and under, free.**

Tucked away in a residential section, the modern museum documents island bygones, from its earliest inhabitants through its various phases of war, lumbering, fiber manufacturing, shipbuilding, and fishing. Its shell collection, donated by an early settler, is a highlight.

# More Things to See and Do in Northwest Florida

- **Old City Cemetery,** Tallahassee
- **Governor's Mansion,** Tallahassee; (850) 488-4661
- **Tallahassee Antique Car Museum,** Tallahassee; (850) 894-9656
- **PJC Planetarium and Theatre,** Pensacola; (850) 484-1150
- **Apalachicola River Tours,** Apalachicola; (850) 653-2593
- **Forest Capital State Museum,** Perry; (850) 584-3227

## Out-Islands

For transportation to the outer keys, contact Island Hopper at the City Marina Basin; P.O. Box 106, Cedar Key 32625; (352) 543-5904; www.cedarkeyislandhopper.com. It makes daily excursions beginning at 11:00 a.m. and also rents boats. Fares are $20 for adults and $15 for children under age 12. Boat rentals range from $90 for a four-person boat for four hours to $210 for a nine-person boat for eight hours.

Cedar Key itself has no beach to speak of, but a couple of the outer islands do, along with historic remnants hidden among the overgrowth. Seahorse Key is the most interesting island to visit, with its 52-foot ridge (Florida's highest coastal elevation), sand beach, and defunct lighthouse now used by the University of Florida. The island is an important nesting area for pelicans, egrets, ibises, herons, and ospreys. In bird-nesting season (March through June), you are not allowed on the island. Snake Key has a nice beach. It once held a quarantine hospital. Atsena Otie, nearest to Cedar Key, held the original town of Cedar Key. Remnants of its early settlements remain.

## Where to Eat

**Akins Bar-B-Q & Grill.** Highway 129 (P.O. Box 267, Bell 32619), Bell; (352) 463-6859. The tops in ribs, baked beans, and potato salad. Breakfast, lunch, and dinner daily. $

**Captain's Table.** 590 Dock Street, Cedar Key; (352) 543-5441. Captain Don makes the special hearts of palm salad and Key lime pie himself in this seafood and steak restaurant. Lunch and dinner Wednesday through Sunday. Kids' menu. $–$$

**Fiddler's Restaurant.** Highway 51 North, Steinhatchee; (352) 498-7427. Order seafood, and you won't find it any fresher than here in the scalloping-fishing capital of the coast. Expect forthright service and genuine sweet tea (according to a sweet-tea critic I know). Kids' menu. $$–$$$

# Where to Stay

**Beach Front Motel.** 873 West First Street (P.O. Box 38, Cedar Key 32625), Cedar Key; (352) 543-5113. Unpretentious with swimming pool, rooms, and efficiencies. Kids under age 6 stay **free.** $

**Cedar Key Bed and Breakfast.** 810 Third Street; (352) 543-9000 or (877) 543-5051; www.cedarkeybandb.com. Built in 1880 by the Eagle Cedar Mill as a guest house for its employees, it is a quiet spot, shaded by massive oaks, within walking distance of Cedar Key's most interesting places to visit. Though the owners discourage bringing babies and toddlers, well-mannered teens will enjoy its peaceful, gracious charm and a hearty, hot breakfast in the sunny porch dining room. $$

**Holiday Inn.** Highway 90 at Interstate 75, Lake City; (386) 752-3901 or (800) HOLIDAY. Your gateway to the springs and other natural resources of north central Florida. Swimming pool, playground, restaurant, and lounge. Kids ages 10 and younger stay and eat **free** at the buffet only. $

**The Island Place.** First and C Streets (P.O. Box 687, Cedar Key 32625), Cedar Key; (352) 543-5307. One of Cedar Key's modern lodging options, it offers thirty waterfront condominiums with one or two bedrooms. Kids under age 6 stay **free.** $–$$

**Mermaid's Landing.** 12685 Route 24, Cedar Key; (877) 543-5949; www.mermaids landing.com. A touch of Old Florida in nine one- to four-room cottages with painted wood floors and pine paneling. Watch the sunset, feed the birds, or kayak on the shallow bay. $–$$

**Steinhatchee Landing.** Highway 51 North, Steinhatchee; (352) 498-3513 or (800) 584-1709. Vernacular-style luxury Florida cottages and homes off the beaten path in a fishing village setting. For families: swimming pool, playground, petting zoo, and canoes rented for a nominal fee. $$$–$$$$

# For More Information

**Cedar Key Area Chamber of Commerce.** P.O. Box 610, Cedar Key 32625; (352) 543-5600; www.cedarkey.org.

**Columbia County Tourist Development Council/Florida Welcome Center.** 263 Northwest Lake City Avenue, Lake City 32055; (386) 758-1397 or 758-1312; www.springs-r-us.com.

# Annual Events

**Civil War Reenactment.** Eden State Gardens, Point Washington; (850) 231-4214. In late January, the gardens host a reenactment of the Seventh Vermont Volunteer Infantry, Company "A" Encampment.

**Olustee Battle Festival and Reenactment.** Lake City; (386) 752-2031 or (386) 758-0400. Actors recall the Confederates' six-hour battle and victory over Union troops during the Civil War in the middle of February. The largest Civil War reenactment in the South. **Free.**

**Springtime Tallahassee.** Tallahassee; (850) 224-5012 or (800) 628-2866. Tallahassee's big annual event is an extravaganza of parades and fairs that runs for three weeks in April during prime azalea-blooming time. **Free.**

**Seaside Easter Egg Hunt.** Seaside; (850) 231-5424. An Easter Sunday visit from the Easter Bunny. **Free.**

**Suwannee Bicycle Festival.** Live Oak; (386) 397-2347. Biking, canoeing, snorkeling, tubing, and kayaking in springs country, early May.

**ArtsQuest.** South Walton County; (850) 237-0885. A weeklong cultural fair that culminates with an art fair at Eden State Gardens early in May.

**Billy Bowlegs Festival.** Fort Walton Beach; (850) 244-8191 or (800) 322-3319. Starting early June, it's a week of pirate revelry, seafood, and entertainment. **Free.**

**Destin Fishing Rodeo.** Destin; (850) 837-6734 or (800) 322-3319. A month of fishing tournaments and events in October.

**Indian Summer Seafood Festival.** Panama City Beach; (800) PC-BEACH. A weekend of country music, seafood, exhibits, and fireworks in October.

**Monarch Butterfly Festival.** St. Marks National Wildlife Refuge; (850) 925-6121. A celebration of the annual monarch migration in October.

**Spooky Springs.** Wakulla Springs State Park; (850) 561-7217. Early in November, a night cruise, tricks, and treats.

**Blue Angels Homecoming Air Show.** Pensacola; (850) 434-1234 or (800) 874-1234. Daredevil stunt-flying by the world-famous team at their home station in July and November. **Free.**

# Northeast Florida

J ust imagine! History was being made in Florida fifty years before the Pilgrims landed at Plymouth Rock—history of the most raucous, adventuresome sort! The city of St. Augustine, hub of the so-called First Coast, safeguards 400 years of history behind fortress walls and city gates. From St. Augustine north to Amelia Island's Fernandina Beach, from the sixteenth century to the twentieth, a colorful cast of historic characters included youth-seeking Juan Ponce de León, French conquistador Jean Ribault, privateer Francis Drake, French Huguenots, Spanish Minorcans, Civil War heroes, President Ulysses S. Grant, and railroad magnate Henry Flagler. Relics of the long years have been preserved despite Florida's architecture-devastating humidity, termites, and hurricanes.

## TopPicks for Family Fun in Northeast Florida

1. Going back in time at the Colonial Spanish Quarter Museum, St. Augustine

2. Listening to whale and manatee calls at the Museum of Science & History, Jacksonville

3. Talking to Yankee soldiers at Fort Clinch State Park, Fernandina Beach

4. Counting teeth at St. Augustine Alligator Farm and Zoological Park, St. Augustine

5. Going all-aboard at Jacksonville Zoo and Gardens, Jacksonville

6. Playing soggy pirate at Adventure Landing, Jacksonville Beach

7. Taking a sunset drive or walk along the hard-packed sands of Anastasia Island, St. Augustine

8. Exploring the children's gallery at Cummer Museum of Art and Gardens, Jacksonville

# NORTHEAST FLORIDA

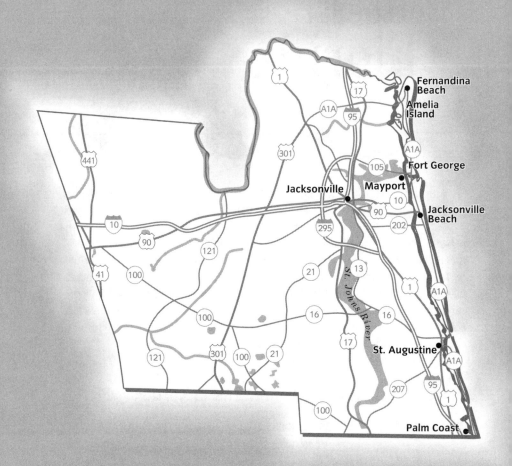

Besides some of America's oldest structures, northeast Florida boasts a cache of untouted beaches and haunting wildlands of marsh, hardwood forest, and sandhill terrain. Big-city Jacksonville spills out to the Atlantic Ocean, along with the St. Johns River that runs through it. It is the coast's center of culture, commerce, and festivities, which cluster around downtown's riverfront.

The St. Johns, Florida's longest navigable inland waterway, with a length of 342 miles, has played a crucial role in the social history of Jacksonville and the towns along it to the south, from steamboat days to now.

# Amelia Island and Fernandina Beach

Take the Route A1A exit off Interstate 95 and head east for about twenty minutes.

What are your kids going to love most about Amelia Island? Its great beaches, no doubt. Yet even those who are blasé about history can't help but be intrigued by this island's past. A narrated tour of Amelia's cemeteries or a candlelit walk through an old fort will surely pique their interest. The historic district lies in the Italian Victorian port town of Fernandina Beach. For a walking or driving tour of the area, pick up a copy of *Amelia Now,* available **free** in many stores.

### Centre Street (ages 4 to 13)
**Follow Route A1A as it becomes South Eighth Street to Centre Street.**

At the heart of Fernandina Beach's 50-block historic district, nearly fifty of its structures predate the twentieth century. Classic buildings house shops great for browsing, antiques marts, restaurants specializing in the local white shrimp, and Florida's oldest surviving tavern. Frilly Victorian Italianate architecture embellishes the residential Silk Stocking District that emanates from Centre Street. Many vintage homes open their doors to guests as charming inns and bed-and-breakfasts, just as they did in the days of Ulysses S. Grant, when the town became Florida's first island resort.

### On the Water Adventures (all ages)
**Egan's Creek Marina, Fernandina Beach; (904) 206-1762.**

Birds, dolphins, and even wild horses may be seen on guided nature tours on this 26-foot ponga boat. Call to arrange times as brief as two hours to a full-day jaunt. Summer rates (subject to change) from one to six people start at $200 for two hours; a full day starts at $500.

# Who are the **Minorcans?**

In 1767 a Scottish physician named Dr. Andrew Turnbull brought 14,000 indentured servants and other recruits from Italy, Greece, and Minorca (a Spanish island) to build a brave new settlement around New Smyrna. His experiment failed, and most of the Minorcans fled to St. Augustine ten years later. Their influence is felt most potently in their unique datil pepper, which flavors local sauces, desserts, and pilaus with fire. The chile is grown only in St. Augustine and vicinity, from seeds passed from generation to generation.

### Victorian Seaside Christmas (all ages)
**Throughout Amelia Island; (904) 261-3248.**

Downtown is where most of the action for the island's annual holiday festival takes place, beginning the Saturday after Thanksgiving and continuing through the holidays. Highlights include beach rides on a horse-drawn sleigh at the Ritz-Carlton, holiday parade and tree-lighting, children's tea with Santa, and a Civil War soldiers' Christmas reenactment.

### Isle of Eight Flags Shrimp Festival (all ages)
**(904) 261-3248.**

In early May, this big event celebrates Amelia's history of eight sovereign rulers (France, Spain, England, the "Patriots of Amelia Island," the Green Cross of Florida, Mexican rebels, the United States, and the Confederacy) as well as its seafood reputation, all to the tune of a pirate's lusty "yo-ho-ho." Sometimes the pirates even invade the harbor!

# Towering **Timucuans?**

Early explorers depicted the Timucuans as 7-foot giants who never cut their straight, black hair. In truth, the natives averaged slightly over 6 feet (still gigantic compared with the small-statured Spaniards), and widowed Timucua women did cut their hair. (They were not allowed to remarry until their hair grew back to its original length.) Men wore their hair in top knots to keep cool and thwart scalpers.

### Amelia Island Museum of History (ages 8 to 13)

**233 South Third Street, Fernandina Beach; (904) 261-7378; www.ameliamuseum.org. Open 10:00 a.m. to 4:00 p.m. Monday through Saturday and 1:00 to 4:00 p.m. Sunday. Admission is $7 for adults, $4 for students. Museum tours Monday through Saturday at 11:00 a.m. and 2:00 p.m. and Sunday at 2:00 p.m. Ghost tours Friday at 6:00 p.m.; $10 adults, $5 students. Special walking tours (reservations required) are $10 per person, groups of four or more.**

Learn about the legends and deep history connected with Amelia Island: why some Timucua Indians didn't cut their hair, why the natives got along with the French and not the Spanish, and the haunting story of the island's namesake. The museum occupies the old county jailhouse and conducts living history tours of its 400 years' worth of artifacts. The ninety-minute tour may get long for younger children, but it is the only way to see the bulk of the exhibits downstairs. The museum also conducts specialty tours of the town's cemetery, lovely old churches, and other themed sights.

### Florida House Inn (all ages)

**22 South Third Street, Fernandina Beach; (904) 261-3300.**

You may as well go gung-ho on this history thing and take the kids to eat in a historic setting, where dining is boardinghouse style. Built in 1857 as one of Florida's first hostelries, Florida House Inn still provides rooms with antebellum simplicity and meals with down-home Southern goodness. Breakfast, lunch, and dinner daily. $–$$$$

### Amelia Island Charter Boat Association (ages 5 to 13)

**1 North Front Street, Fernandina Harbour Marina, Fernandina Beach; (904) 261-2870; www.ameliaislandcharterboatassociation.com.**

To arrange a fishing, sightseeing, sailing, or any type of water excursion, contact the association. Largemouth bass fishing is a specialty in local rivers.

### Fort Clinch State Park (all ages)

**2601 Atlantic Avenue, Fernandina Beach; (904) 277-7274. Entrance is on Atlantic Avenue, which is a continuation of Centre Street to the east. Open 8:00 a.m. to sunset (later for candlelight tours) daily. Park entrance is $5 per vehicle of eight persons or fewer, $1 per extra passenger, cyclist, or pedestrian. Fort is open 9:00 a.m. to 5:00 p.m.; admission is an additional $2 per person ages 6 and older; $3 each for weekend candlelight tours (by reservation only, May through Labor Day), which begin forty-five minutes after sunset and last about seventy-five minutes.**

The town's proudest pre–Civil War relic stands at this state park. The well-preserved bastion is staffed with park rangers in Union dress, who relive the life of a Fort Clinch soldier. Kids are urged to ask them questions about their life in 1864. The view from the embankments is well worth the climb. Also demanding a visit within the 1,086-acre park are a 1,500-foot fishing pier, 4,000 feet of wide beach facing Georgia's Cumberland Island, picnic grounds, camping, towering dunes, and moss-shawled oaks. Candlelight tours (reservations required) inside the fort are held each Friday and Saturday night from early May through Labor Day to re-create how the soldiers saw it at night.

### Main Beach (all ages)

**Route A1A (Fletcher Avenue) and Trout Street.**

A more popular beach with families, it prohibits surfing. Families will find many other activities to keep them busy, however, including volleyball, a playground, miniature golf, and a game room.

### Island Falls Adventure Golf (ages 4 to 12)

**1550 Sadler Road, Fernandina Beach; (904) 261-7881. Open summers 10:00 a.m. to 11:00 p.m. daily; in winter (October through February), 2:00 to 10:00 p.m. Friday, 10:00 a.m. to 10:00 p.m. Saturday, and 11:00 a.m. to 9:00 p.m. Sunday. Admission is $6.78 for persons ages 13 and older, $5.85 for children ages 4 to 12, $2.00 for children 3 and under. Seniors and military, $6.31.**

Streams and a waterfall provide a challenge at this eighteen-hole miniature golf course.

### Kayak Amelia (ages 8 to 13)

**13030 Heckscher Drive, Jacksonville; (904) 251-0016 or (888) 30-KAYAK; www.kayak amelia.com. Rates are $55 for a half-day guided trip; or rent equipment and $35 for a single kayak or $45 for a double kayak or canoe.**

Experienced guides instruct novice kayakers and lead them on a guided nature and history tour of the island's creeks, rivers, marshes, and other backwaters.

# Northeastern **Climes**

The average annual temperature in the coast's northernmost reaches is 69.9 degrees; in winter, 67; in summer, 91. High season hits in summer in this part of Florida, when rates are higher, crowds more crowded, and hours extended at many attractions. Winter weather is normally pleasant, typically requiring long sleeves by day and more layers by night. Snow does fall in these latitudes, albeit rarely.

## Where to Eat

Look along Sadler Road for chain-style fast-food and family restaurants. For something with more atmosphere, refer to the other listings in this section.

**Brett's Waterway Cafe.** 1 South Front Street, Fernandina Beach; (904) 261-2660. View of Cumberland Sound; shrimp, other seafood. Lunch and dinner daily. $$–$$$$

## Where to Stay

**Amelia Island Plantation.** Route A1A, Amelia Island; (904) 261-6161 or (800) 874-6878; www.aipfl.com. Family-friendly, woodsy, and beachy destination resort with tram service, restaurants, kids' program, spa, nature center, and golf courses. $$–$$$$

**Florida House.** 22 South Third Street, Fernandina Beach, Amelia Island; (904) 261-3300 or (800) 258-3301; www.florida houseinn.com. One of the few local B&Bs that accepts children and pets, it is also historic (Florida's first guest accommodations, circa 1857) and Southern-style friendly. $$–$$$$

**Ritz-Carlton, Amelia Island.** 4750 Amelia Island Parkway, Amelia Island; (904) 277-1100 or (800) 241-3333. Luxury beach resort with kids' programs. $$$$

## For More Information

**Amelia Island Tourist Development Council.** 961687 Gateway Boulevard, Suite G, Amelia Island 32034; (800) 2AMELIA; fax (904) 261-2440; www.amelia island.org.

# Fort George

Continue south of Amelia Island on Route A1A, also known as the Buccaneer Trail.

## Little Talbot Island State Park (all ages)

**Route A1A/12157 Heckscher Drive, Jacksonville; (904) 251-2320. Open 8:00 a.m. to sunset daily. Park entrance is $4 per vehicle of eight persons or fewer, $1 per extra passenger, cyclist, or pedestrian.**

Little Talbot Island's coastline is distinguished on one side by vegetated dunes and gorgeous, empty beach, while the other side is given over to salt marshlands. Bird-watchers find lots to enjoy. Anglers can cast in salt or fresh water. Make yourself at home in the picnic or camp area. Hiking trails follow the path of early missionaries, conquerors, and plantation owners. The beach at Big Talbot Island, to the north, is even less populated and edged by sand bluffs. It is part of the state park, but admission is only $1 for parking there (no facilities). Call Kayak Amelia at (888) 305-2925 for guided paddle tours and/or rentals.

### Kingsley Plantation Historic Site (ages 5 to 13)

**Fort George, Jacksonville (mailing address: 11676 Palmetto Avenue, Jacksonville 32226); (904) 251-3537. Open 9:00 a.m. to 5:00 p.m. daily. Admission is free or by donation.**

The intriguing tale of one slave owner, his African wife, and his slaves unfolds. The long, haunting, unpaved drive to the plantation passes slave hut ruins and ends at the sea, where the manor and other outbuildings are preserved. Kids can learn from exhibits how tabby and cotton were made in plantation times. Ranger tours are offered at 2:00 p.m. daily.

### Huguenot Memorial Park (all ages)

**10980 Heckscher Drive, Fort George, Jacksonville; (904) 251-3335. Open 8:00 a.m. to 8:00 p.m. in summer and 8:00 a.m. to 6:00 p.m. in winter. Admission is 50 cents per person 6 years of age and older.**

Situated at the mouth of the St. Johns River, this claw of sand is popular with swimmers, surfers, anglers, and campers.

## Where to Eat

Small fish camps and their restaurants are about all you find along this remote strip, with the exception of the restaurant listed here.

**Sandollar Restaurant.** 9716 Heckscher Drive, Fort George, Jacksonville; (904) 251-2449. Perched at the mouth of the St. Johns near the ferry landing, with great views, seafood, and sandwiches. Lunch and dinner daily. $$–$$$

# Mayport

Here the route splits in two directions. You can continue along Route A1A's coastal drive, or head into Jacksonville and take the town route back to the beaches.

### Mayport Ferry, St. Johns River Ferry Service (all ages)

**Route A1A; (904) 241-9969. Ferry departs weekdays at 6:00, 6:20, and 7:00 a.m., and on the half hour and hour throughout the day until 10:00 p.m.; and on Saturday and Sunday at 6:20 and 7:00 a.m., and on the half hour and hour throughout the day until 10:00 p.m. The ride costs $2.50 for motorcycles, $5.00 for cars, and $1.00 per bicycle and pedestrian.**

The scenic quality of Route A1A reaches a nostalgic peak as it winds down to the mouth of the St. Johns River, which one must cross by car ferry. The ride takes only five minutes.

# Smart **Travel**

- Many of the best, most educational kids' toys are found in attraction gift shops, such as the one at Cummer Museum of Art and Gardens and the Museum of Science and History, where I bought Aaron Amber InsectNside—a slab of orange-yellow hard candy encasing a real (and edible!) cricket, asparagus fern, and larva. (Gross! Cool!) Steer them toward purchases that will entertain them in the car or on the plane.

- If you're traveling much of the state of Florida by road, try this to keep the kids involved. Create a map of the state marked with the outline of roads you'll be traveling and cities you'll be visiting. Have them color the stretch of road covered each time you reach a city along it.

- When traveling the interstate, detour the "are we almost there" chant by trying this: Tell your children the exit number where you'll be stopping next for an attraction, meal, or the night. They can then clock your progress by watching exit sign numbers. Involve a little math and ask them how many more exits you have to go.

- Another trick for keeping them occupied in the car: Keep a bag or box of car-only toys, games, puzzle books, picture books, coloring books, crayons, etc. Put it away between trips. That way it will be fresh and new each time you bring it out. Add a surprise for each trip.

- A picnic lunch at a rest stop or town park gives kids—and you—a chance to stretch.

## Kathryn Abbey Hanna Park (all ages)

**500 Wonderwood Drive, Jacksonville; off Route A1A; (904) 249-4700. Admission is $1 per person 8:00 to 10:00 a.m., then $3 per car from 10:00 a.m. to close.**

A litany of beaches continues from Mayport southward. One of the local favorites, Hanna Park encompasses 450 acres devoted to wide, ocean-swept beach, heavily wooded nature trails (favored by mountain bikers), picnic areas, volleyball, kayak and other water-sports rentals, and freshwater fishing. Campsites are available. Lifeguards supervise in summer. It's a terrific place for an all-day family picnic in the park.

## Where to Eat and Stay

See the Jacksonville Beach area listings for dining and lodging options.

# Weekend Jaunt: Jacksonville

If you opt to take the route through town for some metropolitan input before continuing down the beaches, follow Route A1A from Fort George along the north bank of the St. Johns, where it turns into Heckscher Drive/Route 105, a scenic riverside drive marred by smokestacks.

Jacksonville is a big city (the fifteenth largest in the United States) and one of Florida's most industrial metropolitan areas. The smell of paper mills can be offensive, especially to children, when the wind's in the wrong direction. Still, it offers plenty of family entertainment and fun within its boundaries and along its beaches (see Jacksonville Beach listings). Downtown has undergone a renaissance along the St. Johns River, resulting in lively shopping, museums, and entertainment districts. The city is a bit difficult to navigate, especially confusing to a first-timer. For best results buy a city map and make a point to visit the old historic neighborhoods of San Marco and Riverside Avondale to get in touch with Jacksonville's soul.

## Jacksonville Zoo and Gardens (all ages)

**370 Zoo Parkway; (904) 757-4462; www.jaxzoo.org. Open 9:00 a.m. to 5:00 p.m. daily (extended hours on weekends through Labor Day). Admission is $11.00 for adults, $9.50 for seniors, $7.50 for children ages 3 to 12; children under 3, free. The train runs from 10:00 a.m. to 4:30 p.m. Monday through Friday, 9:00 a.m. to 6:00 p.m. Saturday and Sunday. Train admission is $4 for adults, $2 for children ages 3 to 12; under 3 free. Wildlife Carousel $2.**

On Jacksonville's north side, the zoo enchants with a train ride, walk-through aviary, baby animal nursery, petting zoo, Chimpanorama, and African beasts roaming freely. Demonstrations and shows about alligators, other reptiles, and birds hold children's attention. New exhibits include Range of the Jaguar, Savanna bloom garden, Giraffe Overlook, and a play park with a splash pool.

## Jacksonville Landing

**2 Independent Drive; off Highway 1; (904) 353-1188; www.jacksonvillelanding.com. Open 10:00 a.m. to 8:00 p.m. Monday through Thursday, 10:00 a.m. to 9:00 p.m. Friday and Saturday, noon to 5:30 p.m. Sunday.**

Downtown Jacksonville is on the move. On the northern riverfront, Jacksonville Landing makes for a lively shopping, dining, and entertainment experience. Toy Factory (904-353-4874) is a really fun shop.

# On a **Budget**

- **Kingsley Plantation Historic Site,** Fort George, free admission
- **Huguenot Memorial Park,** Fort George, admission 50 cents per person six years or older
- **Kathryn Abbey Hanna Park,** Mayport, admission $1 from 8:00 to 10:00 a.m.
- **Jacksonville Historical Center,** Jacksonville, free admission
- **Jacksonville Maritime Museum,** Jacksonville, free admission
- **Fort Caroline National Memorial,** Jacksonville, free admission
- **Castillo de San Marcos National Monument,** St. Augustine, admission is free for guests ages fifteen and younger

## Kids Kampus (ages 2 to 6)
**Next to Metropolitan Park on the Northbank.**

This city park is incredible fun. Among the interactive gizmos and equipment, kids will find a toddler splash pool with geysers and sculptures, a sand area with mechanical diggers, a replicated Timucuan village, a wind machine, and kid-size streetscapes.

## Southbank Riverwalk
**Off Highway 1.**

Facing Jacksonville Landing from across the river, this jaunty 1.2-mile boardwalk offers more excitement and cultural activity, including the Friendship Fountain and three museums listed below. Water taxis cross between the two areas (admission: $3 adults, $2 children one-way; kids under age 3 ride free). Public restrooms are provided at the marina.

## The Museum of Science & History (all ages)
**1025 Museum Circle, Southbank; (904) 396-6674; fax (904) 396-5799; www.themosh .org. Open 10:00 a.m. to 5:00 p.m. Monday through Friday, 10:00 a.m. to 6:00 p.m. Saturday, and 1:00 to 6:00 p.m. Sunday. Admission (which includes the planetarium) is $9.00 for adults, $7.50 for seniors and military, $7.00 for children ages 3 to 12; under 3 free.**

Here's a painless way to introduce learning into a vacation. Toddlers will have fun in the two-story, play-and-learn tree house in Kidspace. (How nice! They provide rubber aprons and a hand dryer for playing in the waterworks.) Everyone will be fascinated by the Atlantic Tails exhibit, where the kids can see the skeletons, listen to the voices, and track the migration patterns of whales, dolphins, and manatees. The Florida Naturalist Center showcases fish, turtles, baby alligators, and other live creatures. Tonga, a twenty-five-pound alligator snapping turtle lives in the courtyard. Hands-on stations demonstrate principles of vision, sound, electricity, and motion. History exhibits upstairs scan the early settlement of the St. Johns River and northern Florida's Civil War days. The museum also hosts special programs, planetarium shows, and live animal demonstrations.

### Jacksonville Historical Center (ages 5 to 13)

**Southbank Riverwalk; tour address: 317 A. Phillip Randolph Boulevard, Jacksonville; (904) 665-0064. Open 1:30 to 3:30 p.m. Thursday. Admission is free.**

The center takes a less high-tech stroll through Jacksonville bygone days at the James E. Merrill house, depicting family life in 1903.

### Jacksonville Maritime Museum (ages 7 to 13)

**Southbank Riverwalk; 1015 Museum Circle; (904) 398-9011. Open 10:30 a.m. to 3:30 p.m. Monday through Friday, 1:00 to 5:00 p.m. Saturday and Sunday. Admission is free or by donation.**

Local seafaring history spills from model, art, and photographic displays. Part of the museum is devoted to a 16-foot model of the aircraft carrier *Saratoga* and to Jacksonville-built World War II ships.

### Cummer Museum of Art and Gardens (ages 3 to 13)

**829 Riverside Avenue; (904) 356-6857. Open 10:00 a.m. to 9:00 p.m. Tuesday and Thursday; 10:00 a.m. to 5:00 p.m. Wednesday, Friday, and Saturday; and noon to 5:00 p.m. Sunday; closed Monday. Admission is $8 for adults; $5 for seniors, military, and students; children 6 and under are free.**

If you think art museums are too highbrow for small fry, try this one. In Art Connections they will enjoy getting involved in art by mingling with characters in a re-created masterpiece, painting by computer, or touching replicated elements from pieces in the collection. Besides its excellent hands-on section, Cummer has an impressive traditional gallery and beautiful riverside gardens where children can run.

## What's in **a Name?**

Well, Jacksonville by the original name Cowford probably didn't smell as sweet. It was first named for the narrow throat in the St. Johns River, where cattlemen could cross their herds. In 1822 the name was changed to honor Andrew Jackson.

# Port of **Import**

During the 1991 Gulf War, Jacksonville was the busiest military port in the country, moving more supplies and personnel than any other port in the United States.

### Jacksonville Jaguars (ages 5 to 13)
**Alltel Stadium; 1 Stadium Place, on the east end of downtown; (904) 633-2000. Ticket prices start at $38.**

The NFL team plays home games here September through December and is the source of extreme city pride.

### Fort Caroline National Memorial (ages 5 to 13)
**12713 Fort Caroline Road; (904) 641-7155; www.nps.gov/timu. Call ahead for directions. Open 9:00 a.m. to 5:00 p.m. daily. Admission is free.**

French Huguenots originally settled this area in 1564, creating the first Protestant colony in North America. Northeast of town, a 680-acre park remembers their brave new world with a fort exhibit, a hammock nature trail, ranger-led walks, and a museum of nicely presented ecology and French and Timucuan exhibits, including a 6-foot owl totem that is the largest wood effigy recovered in North or South America. The site is headquarters for the 46,000-acre Timucuan Ecological and Historic Preserve, which also contains the nearby Ribault Monument and wilderness trails in its Theodore Roosevelt Area.

### Tree Hill—Jacksonville's Nature Center (all ages)
**7152 Lone Star Road; off Arlington Road; (904) 724-4646; www.treehill.org. Open 8:00 a.m. to 4:30 p.m. Monday through Saturday; tours Saturday at 10:00 a.m. Admission is $2.00 for adults ages 18 and older, $1 for children.**

It interprets the environment of a hardwood forest via nature trails throughout forty acres and indoor local wildlife and rain forest exhibits. You can also explore butterfly, herb, and organic vegetable gardens and Turtle Town. Special family programs and guided tours take place monthly.

## Where to Eat

**Dave & Buster's.** 7025 Salisbury Road; (904) 296-1525. A restaurant within a mega-arcade—what could make kids happier? There are games and pastimes for everyone, and the food is much better than you'd expect from a video arcade—pizza, salads, pasta, steak, seafood (the grilled mahimahi is superb), sandwiches, plus kids' selections. Open daily for lunch and dinner. $$–$$$

**River City Brewing Co.** 835 Museum Circle; (904) 398-2299. Delicious eclectic, Asian, and tropically inclined food; kids' menu; dining indoors or outdoors along the river. Lunch and dinner Monday through Saturday; brunch, Sunday. Near Southbank attractions. $$–$$$

## Where to Stay

Jacksonville hotels are designed primarily for business travelers. Most vacationers head to the beaches. Accommodations downtown are less expensive than on the beach. Best rates are on weekends.

**Hilton Jacksonville Riverfront.** 1201 Riverplace Boulevard; (904) 398-8800 or (800) HILTONS; www.hilton.com. The Hilton rises above the rest on the St. Johns River, near all the riverfront action, and provides a grand black-marble lobby, 291 tastefully decorated rooms and suites, a swimming pool, and a restaurant. $–$$

## For More Information

**Jacksonville and the Beaches Convention and Visitors Bureau.** 550 Water Street, Suite 1000, Jacksonville 32202; (904) 798-9111 or (800) 733-2668; www.jaxcvb.com.

# Jacksonville Beach

Follow Route A1A south from Mayport. From Jacksonville, go east on the Arlington Expressway and take Route 10 (Atlantic Boulevard) or continue along Highway 90 (Beach Boulevard). The beaches lie about 30 miles east of downtown and I-95. First Street South, 2 blocks off A1A, is the main oceanfront drag.

Jacksonville Beach sands are generally well populated, and teens will find a lot of the action they crave. Some parts are undesirable, with girlie shows and a run-down look. The beach community begins at Atlantic Beach and Neptune Beach to the north. Atlantic Beach is least rowdy and tacky.

### Adventure Landing (all ages)

1944 Beach Boulevard; (904) 246-4386; www.adventurelanding.com. The water park portion is open seasonally. Other attractions are open 10:00 a.m. to 11.00 p.m. Monday through Thursday and Sunday, 10.00 a.m. to midnight Friday and Saturday. Admission to the water park is $25.99 for adults, $21.99 for children under 42 inches, and $15.99 for "Nite Splash." Free for children 3 and younger, and 10 percent discount to senior citizens and military people with identification. Tax is extra. Other rides and attractions are individually priced.

You could easily spend a day here, and it's a good place to do so when the weather's hot. The water park has a shipwreck-themed play area, the Hydro-Pipe, and a water coaster that actually goes uphill—well, for a short distance anyway. Not as intimidating as some water parks, its rides are tame to mildly wild, with lots for toddlers. It has a surf pool like many others do, but this one provides inner tubes, which makes it more fun. On the river inner-tube ride, you can ride with your young one on a double inner tube, another plus. Batting cages, go-karts, bumper boats, and two miniature golf courses provide dry outdoor activity. Inside the huge, air-conditioned arcade, kids of all ages find food and games—including laser tag—from which you'll have trouble tearing them away.

### Atlantic Beach Town Center (ages 5 to 12)
**Atlantic Boulevard, Atlantic Beach.**

Here's a fun place to stroll through one-of-a-kind shops and along the beach, and have lunch or dinner. Stop at the Book Mark (299 Atlantic Boulevard, Atlantic Beach; 904-241-9026), which has a children's room in addition to a great selection of Florida-related books.

## Where to Eat

**First Street Grille.** 807 North First Street; (904) 246-6555. Casual but upscale dining on the beach, indoors or out. Seafood, burgers, and light bites. Lunch and dinner daily. $$–$$$

**Sundog Diner.** 207 Atlantic Boulevard, Atlantic Beach; (904) 241-8221. This neighborhood kind of place has a diner façade outside and a retro look inside, complete with Dave Clark Five and Monkees tunes. The kids' menu is extensive, as is the regular menu—from meat loaf sandwich to seafood and sausage étouffée. Open daily for lunch and dinner. $–$$

## Where to Stay

The beaches hold a steady stream of chain hotels and other accommodations.

**Sea Turtle Inn.** 1 Ocean Boulevard, Atlantic Beach; (904) 249-7402 or (800) 874-6000; www.seaturtle.com. More stylish than most beach accommodations. Small pool and dining on-site. $–$$$

## For More Information

**Jacksonville and the Beaches Convention and Visitors Bureau.** 550 Water Street, Suite 1000, Jacksonville 32202; (904) 798-9111 or (800) 733-2668; www.jaxcvb.com.

# St. Augustine

Follow Route A1A south out of Jacksonville Beach. Continue on it or split off onto coastal Route 203, which takes you along Ponte Vedra Beach's privileged resorts and homes, then reconnects with Route A1A. The trip from Jacksonville Beach to St. Augustine takes about a half hour.

Anyone who believes Florida has no history hasn't been to St. Augustine. Nor have they traveled its 144 blocks of sites listed on the National Register of Historic Places. St. Augustine's reputation as North America's oldest city plays a dominant theme in its realm of tourism, which tends toward the overdone. Despite its commercialism, the town's historic district provides a great way for kids to experience Florida's deep historical context and everyday life in the colonial era.

## Guana Tolomato Matanzas National Estuarine Research Reserve
(ages 4 to 13) 🦈

**North of St. Augustine at 2690 South Ponte Vedra Boulevard, Ponte Vedra Beach; (904) 825-5071. Visitor center open 9:00 a.m. to 4:00 p.m. daily. Closed on state holidays. Admission is $2 for adults 17 and up, $1 for children ages 10 to 17; under 10 free. Driving tour of nature trails is $3 per car extra.**

Historians generally concur that Spanish explorer Juan Ponce de León probably made his first landing near the spot today preserved at Guana. Route A1A shoots through the middle of the park, which is lined with low shrubs and saw palmettos (*guana* is Spanish for "palm") for a visually soothing drive. Accesses allow you to park and enjoy the beach and other facilities. From the park's beach you can swim, surf, and fish. Other activities include nature study, fishing, and boating on the Guana and Tolomato Rivers, and hiking or biking on 9 miles of old service road.

## Fountain of Youth National Archaeological Park (ages 5 to 13) 🏛

**11 Magnolia Avenue; (904) 829-3168 or (800) 356-8222. Open 9:00 a.m. to 5:00 p.m. daily. Admission is $7 for adults, $6 for seniors, $4 for children ages 6 to 12; under 6 free.**

The first historic attraction you'll reach in this city of historic attractions, it too claims Ponce de León's point of arrival in 1513 and St. Augustine's first colony. Stroll through excavations of the original colony, a planetarium, and life-size exhibits. You can even take a sip from Ponce de León's fountain and see how young it makes you feel.

# Doorway **Defense**

Door frames in St. Augustine's colonial homes were built to accommodate the tallest family member, at 5 feet or less. When the tall Timucua Indians attacked, the diminutive doorways slowed them down, either by causing them to duck or by knocking them out.

### Ripley's Believe It or Not! (ages 6 to 13)

19 San Marco Avenue; (904) 824-1606; www.gtmnerr.org. Open 9:00 a.m. to 7:00 p.m. Sunday through Thursday, 9:00 a.m. to 8:00 p.m. Saturday. Admission is $14.99 for adults, $11.99 for seniors, $7.99 for children 5 to 12; under 5 **free.**

Always fascinating for wide-eyed young ones, this first Ripley's is housed in a Moorish 1887 structure with exhibits that stretch the imagination to the limit. See the London Bridge re-created from 264,345 matchsticks, the Lord's Prayer carved into a grain of rice, a soda-can manatee, and a stuffed two-headed calf. Be careful when you make faces in the mirror; you never know who may be looking! Some of the stuff is a bit macabre for the very young and impressionable.

### Visitor Information Center (ages 4 to 13)

10 Castillo Drive; across the street from Ripley's; (904) 825-1000. Center admission and movie are **free.**

Stop in for a **free** introduction to St. Augustine via diorama displays and video. Pick up your printed information with discount coupons here. The center shows a forty-five-minute dramatic movie presentation of St. Augustine's founding, titled *Struggle to Survive*. In the vicinity you'll find the Huguenot Cemetery (tours available; ask at the information center), the Gates to old St. Augustine, and Davenport Park, with a playground and restored old carousel, which you can ride for $1. Packages for the movie and other museums are available.

### Castillo de San Marcos National Monument (all ages)

1 South Castillo Drive; (904) 829-6506; www.nps.gov/Casa. Open 8:45 a.m. to 4:45 p.m. daily. Admission is $7 for adults; children 15 and younger, **free.**

The colonial fort dominates the entrance to St. Augustine's celebrated historic district. In early times it was the entrance, and its walls completely encircled the town. Construction on the fort began in 1672 to replace previous wooden fortresses. Made of coquina rock, the massive fort kept enemies of Spanish, British, and American settlers at bay for 235 years. Like most forts, its strategic waterside location offers great views and picture-taking opportunities. Kids love the firing of the old cannons by period-uniformed soldiers.

# Fort **Facts**

- Historians estimate that if Castillo de San Marcos were built today, using the same coquina rock and taking the same twenty-three years to complete, it would cost $79 million.
- The fort's soft, coquina rock walls stood strong because they could absorb cannon shot. One historian describes the outer wall as looking like a chocolate chip cookie.

### St. Augustine's Restoration Area (ages 5 to 13) 🏛
**Along St. George Street between South Street and Orange Street.**

In St. Augustine's historic waterfront district, small, specialized museums and living-history rituals reveal the town's historic importance, while crafts shops, galleries, restaurants, and other stores sell goods and victuals of all manner behind vintage storefronts. Pedestrian-only St. George Street is the center of activity in the restoration area, which holds buildings dating back to 1566.

### Oldest Wooden Schoolhouse (ages 5 to 9) 🏛
**14 St. George Street; (904) 824-0192 or (888) 653-7245. Open 9:00 a.m. to 5:00 p.m. daily, with extended summer hours. Admission is $3.00 for adults, $2.50 for seniors and military, $2.00 for children ages 6 to 12; children under 6 free.**

Students can appreciate how colonial kids learned their lessons and can receive a diploma of their own. An audio-animated schoolmaster and dunce explain elementary procedures in colonial days, pointing out the dungeon under the staircase, to which unruly students were sentenced. Explore the lovely gardens outdoors and ring the old school bell. The gift shop carries school-related items.

### Colonial Spanish Quarter Museum (ages 5 to 13)
**53 St. George Street; (904) 825-6830; www.historicstaugustine.com. Open from 9:00 a.m. to 5:30 p.m. daily. Admission is $6.89 for adults, $5.83 for seniors and military, $4.24 for students ages 6 to 18, or $13.78 for families.**

Costumed artisans, craftspeople, and street musicians keep alive the skills, arts, and crafts—blacksmithing, thread spinning, thatched roofing, hearth cooking, and more—of colonial days. Children can participate in some of the crafts or simply listen to costumed guides explain the history of the museum's ten homes and workshops. Learn about the lifestyles of eighteenth-century Spanish officers commissioned to this strange new land so far from home.

### Dow Museum of Historic Houses (ages 8 to 13)

149 Cordova Street; (904) 823-9722; www.old-staug-village.com. Open 10:00 a.m. to 4:30 p.m. Monday through Saturday and 11:00 a.m. to 4:30 p.m. Sunday. Admission is $7 adults, $6 seniors, $5 students.

This new-old attraction contains ten historic buildings dating from 1790 to 1910 and archaeological sites dating from the sixteenth century. The oldest structure was once occupied by Napoleon Bonaparte's nephew, Prince Murat. Reenactors bring history alive.

### Government House Museum (ages 8 to 13)

48 King Street; (904) 825-5033. Open 10:00 a.m. to 4:00 p.m. Tuesday through Saturday. Admission is $2 (plus tax) for adults and seniors, $1 for children ages 6 to 18.

Browse exhibits detailing the city's cultural and architectural development.

### Museum of Weapons and Early American History
(ages 6 to 13)

81-C King Street; (904) 829-3727. Open 9:30 a.m. to 5:00 p.m. daily. Admission is $4 for adults, $1 for children ages 6 to 12; under 6 **free.**

It houses armaments from the Civil War and before.

# Road **Markers**

Follow this tour from its beginning at northernmost Amelia Island and down the coast along Route A1A's meanderings. The road travels for a long stretch through pristine parklands. At Mayport, you can either continue along A1A or take a city detour into Jacksonville via Heckscher Drive, a panoramic riverside route. Routes 10 (Atlantic Boulevard), 202 (J. Turner Butler Boulevard), and Highway 90 (Beach Boulevard) return you to the beaches. Avoid all in rush-hour traffic. Highway 1 and I-95, incidentally, run parallel to Route A1A and more directly north-south. If you have the time, you should stick to the coastal road with its delightful quirks—including an old-fashioned car ferry across the mouth of the St. Johns.

Within Jacksonville, Highways 1 or 17 and I-95 get you downtown efficiently, when it isn't rush hour, that is. Interstate 295 skirts the downtown. Interstate 10 intersects with both and heads west. Highway 301, at the western edge of town, goes south to Starke and Gainesville through rural heartland territory. North of Jacksonville, Route A1A connects to I-95.

## Lightner Museum

**75 King Street; (904) 824-2874; www.lightnermuseum.org. Open 9:00 a.m. to 5:00 p.m. daily. Admission is $8 for adults, $2 for children 12 to 18, free for children under age 12 when accompanied by an adult.**

The museum is located at Flagler's old Hotel Alcazar, one of his magnificent creations. The museum's three floors concentrate on America's Gilded Age of industrial prosperity with a "Brilliant Period" cut-glass display, antique furnishings, mechanical musical instruments, and Tiffany stained glass.

## The Oldest (Gonzalez-Alvarez) House (ages 6 to 13)

**14 St. Francis Street; (904) 824-2872. Open 9:00 a.m. to 5:00 p.m. daily. Admission is $8 for adults, $7 for seniors, and $4 for children ages 6 to 18. Tickets also good for admission to the Museum of Florida's Army, the museum gardens, a research library, and a historical museum.**

The kids can experience how families lived in old St. Augustine. A home for more than 250 years, the house displays Spanish colonial, British Victorian, and American Territorial styles.

## Nights of Lights Festival (ages 4 to 13)

**(904) 829-1711 or (800) OLD-CITY; www.getaway4florida.com.**

St. Augustine's history most dramatically comes to life during period reenactments in the Old City from the third week of November through January 31. At Christmastime, the pageantry of night-guard detail lights the streets during Grand Illumination and Night Watch. Torch processions and fife-and-drum bands recall eighteenth-century tradition early in the season. Historic and holiday events continue throughout the month of December and into January.

## St. Augustine Sightseeing Train (all ages)

**170 San Marco Avenue; (904) 829-6545 or (800) 226-6545; www.redtrains.com. Tours run from 8:30 a.m. to 5:00 p.m. Admission is $18.99 for an adult three-day pass, $5.99 for children ages 6 to 12; under 6 free. Attraction admission packages range from $30 to $84 each.**

Save your feet and car brakes by hooking up with this tour. (And stop circling the historic district endlessly in search of a parking spot.) You can board from several locations. Tours are narrated, and the train lets you on and off at will. It's a good way to get an overview of the town's layout and history. With a good narrator, you can learn in great detail about St. Augustine's fabulous architecture, divided between the colonial era and the Flagler era—from the 1880s through the turn of the twentieth century, during which time the great railroad king Henry Flagler came to town to build hotels that looked like castles, magnificent churches, and a cache of other historical treasures.

# Top Family **Resorts**

1. **Amelia Island Plantation,** Amelia Island

2. **Ritz-Carlton,** Amelia Island

3. **Marriott at Sawgrass Resort,** Ponte Vedra Beach

## Tour St. Augustine (ages 6 to 13)

**(904) 641-1009 or (800) 797-3778. Open 9:00 a.m. to 8:00 p.m. Monday through Thursday, 9:00 a.m. to 9:30 p.m. Friday and Saturday. Walking tour at 8:00 p.m. every night. Admission for walking tour $12 for those 6 and older.**

Kids into goose-bump tales? Take them on A Ghostly Experience. The haunted tour of St. Augustine provides ninety minutes of terror-tinged yarns and lore of the town's scariest places, including the dungeons of Castillo and the oldest (Huguenot) cemetery. The Historic Villages of St. Augustine is an interactive walk where kids can build a Timucuan canoe, grind corn into flour, and witness a blacksmith at work. Other theme tours are also available.

## *Victory III* **Scenic Cruise** (all ages)

**Municipal Marina; (904) 824-1806 or (800) 542-8316; www.scenic-cruise.com. Departs daily. Call for current seasonal schedule. Tickets cost $15.00 for adults, $16.75 for seniors, $9 for children ages 13 to 18, and $7.00 for children 4 to 12.**

For seabound adventure, take a scenic seventy-five-minute tour narrated by a local Minorcan- descended family. Snacks, beverages, beer, and wine are available on board.

## **Anastasia State Park** (all ages)

**1340-A Route A1A South; (904) 461-2033; www.dep.state.fl.us/parks/District_3/ Anastasia/index.html. Open 8:00 a.m. to sunset daily. Park entrance is $5 per vehicle of eight persons or fewer, $1 per extra passenger, cyclist, or pedestrian.**

At the historic district, Route A1A crosses the Bridge of Lions to the home of the beautiful hard-packed beaches that gave birth to the sport of beach paddle tennis. The best access is at the state recreation area, which encompasses 4 miles of sandy beach, offering volleyball, ocean swimming, surfing, sailboarding, fishing, and coastal camping. Go for a sunset drive on the beach, when you'll find it at its emptiest and loveliest—bathed in twilight, edged in dunes, and distanced from city life. During the day you can rent sailboards and take lessons from Anastasia Watersports (904-460-9111) or rent surf and boogieboards from Surf Station (904-471-WIND), or kick back and watch the shorebirds. There are oak-shaded picnic facilities near the beach.

### St. Augustine Alligator Farm and Zoological Park (all ages)

Southeast of the historic district on Route A1A; 999 Anastasia Boulevard; (904) 824-3337. Open 9:00 a.m. to 5:00 p.m. daily, to 6:00 p.m. in summer. Admission is $19.95 for adults, $10.95 for children ages 5 to 11; under 5 **free.**

One of St. Augustine's most popular kid attractions concentrates on reptiles rather than reenactments. Like many places in St. Augustine, it is designated the oldest of its kind in America (opened 1893). It is as much about crocodiles as it is about gators. If you don't know the difference now, you will after your visit. The farm represents the world's only complete collection of crocodilians (which include alligators, crocodiles, caimans, and gavials—twenty-three species in all) from around the world. Monkeys, birds, and snakes also share the park. Entertaining wildlife shows educate your family about crocodilians and other reptiles—no gator wrestling here.

### St. Augustine Lighthouse and Museum (ages 7 to 13)

Old Beach Road off Route A1A; 81 Lighthouse Avenue; (904) 829-0745; www.staugustine lighthouse.com. Open 9:00 a.m. to 6:00 p.m. daily (extended to 7:00 p.m. in summer). Admission to the museum and grounds is $6 for adults, $5 for seniors, and $4 for children ages 6 to 11; **free** for children ages 5 and younger. Admission to the museum and tower is $8 for adults, $7 for seniors, and $6 for ages 6 to 11, **free** for children ages 5 and younger. Children must be 44 inches tall to climb the tower.

Climb a 165-foot, 219-step lighthouse built in the late 1800s. Notice the cracks in its circular wall, a legacy of the earthquake that shook Charleston, South Carolina, in 1886. The visitor center holds maritime archaeological exhibits and flashes back to the history of the black-and-white-striped tower, which is the town's oldest brick structure.

### Lighthouse Park

Across the street from the lighthouse.

A good place for a picnic after you've climbed the lighthouse. You'll find a boat ramp, fishing pier, and restaurant.

## Top Family **Beaches and Parks**

1. **Fort Clinch State Park,** Fernandina Beach

2. **Anastasia State Park,** St. Augustine

3. **Kathryn Abbey Hanna Park,** Mayport

4. **Washington Oaks State Gardens,** Palm Coast

# Day **Trip**

From Route A1A, south of St. Augustine, take Routes 206, 207, and 100 southwest to Palatka, about a half hour away, to see some of Florida's astounding interior natural sights.

### Ravine Gardens State Park (ages 6 to 13)

1600 Twigg Street, Palatka; (386) 329-3721. Open 8:00 a.m. to sunset daily. Park entrance is $4 per vehicle of eight persons or fewer, $1 per extra passenger, cyclist, or pedestrian. The prime attraction in this river town is an unusual park. Its striking namesake feature becomes particularly picturesque in spring, when the azaleas and camellias bloom.

### Mike Roess Gold Head Branch State Park (ages 5 to 13)

West of Palatka at 6239 Route 21, Keystone Heights; a side trip off Route 100 on Route 21; (352) 473-4701. Open 8:00 a.m. to sunset daily. Park entrance is $4 per vehicle of eight persons or fewer, $1 per extra passenger, cyclist, or pedestrian. Rolling sand hills, marshes, springs, lakes, mill ruins, and a deep ravine are contained within almost 2,400-acre confines. Take a cool dip in Lake Johnson, or toss in a line and try for some bass or speckled perch. Nature trails penetrate into the habitat of fox squirrels, gray foxes, scrub jays, and black bears. Lakefront cabins and a primitive campground accommodate overnighters.

## Fiesta Falls (ages 4 to 13)

818 A1A Beach Boulevard; (904) 461-5571. Open 10:00 a.m. to 9:30 p.m. Monday through Friday and 9:00 a.m. to 10:00 p.m. Saturday and Sunday. Admission is $7.95 for adults, $6.95 for children ages 3 to 12 and for seniors.

Themed around old town's Spanish colonial motif, this eighteen-hole miniature golf course holds a Spanish galleon, waterfalls, and multileveled holes.

## Marineland (all ages)

About 18 miles south of St. Augustine on Route A1A; 9600 Ocean Shore Boulevard, St. Augustine; (904) 460-1275 or (888) 817-3283; www.marineland.net. Open 8:30 a.m. to 4:30 p.m. daily. General admission is $5.00 for ages 13 and up, $2.50 for children. Dolphin encounter prices vary from $65 to $400.

Diving, snorkeling, and dolphin encounters are the more unusual offerings at Marineland, which is Florida's—the world's!—first marine animal attraction (opened in 1938). Then there are the typical dolphin and seal shows, plus tropical fish aquariums.

## Washington Oaks State Gardens (all ages) 🏕️

**2 miles south of Marineland; 6400 North Ocean Shore Boulevard, Palm Coast; (386) 446-6780. Open 8:00 a.m. to sunset daily. Park entrance is $4 per vehicle of eight persons or fewer, $1 per extra passenger, cyclist, or pedestrian.**

This park takes you away into a land of mixed, crazy-quilt environments. Huge coquina boulders decorate the park's ocean beach, and peaceful ornamental gardens line its riverfront. It's a great place to sun, picnic, and explore along the nature trail. On weekends at 1:30 p.m. you can join in on interpretive walks of the gardens, trail, or beach.

## Where to Eat

**A1A Ale Works.** 1 King Street; (904) 829-2977. A minibrewery, but fine and fun for kids as well as adults. Menu has a Cuban-Caribbean flair. Lunch and dinner daily. $$–$$$

**Santa Maria Restaurant.** 135 Avenida Menendez; on the dock at the marina; (904) 829-6578. You'll love the view. The kids will love the little trapdoors at many of the tables, handy for feeding the birds outside and the catfish below. The food is typical fried fish-house fare, and you're probably better off going for lunch. Just be sure to ask for a trapdoor table. Lunch and dinner. Closed Wednesday during lunchtime. $$

## Where to Stay

Aside from the accommodations below, St. Augustine offers everything from chain hotels and family-run motels to historic B&Bs, which, though charming, are not ideal for families.

**Days Inn Historic.** 1300 North Ponce de Leon Boulevard; (904) 824-3383 or (800) DAYS INN. Handily located near Old City attractions, with pool, restaurant, and 124 rooms. $$

**Ponte Vedra Inn & Club.** 200 Ponte Vedra Boulevard, Ponte Vedra Beach; (904) 285-1111 or (800) 234-7842. Upscale lodging, a renowned spa, golfing, and kid-friendly amenities (swimming pools—including a wading pool—the beach, a playground, and a nursery) make this a top choice for family vacations. $$$–$$$$

**Sawgrass Marriott Resort and Beach Club.** 1000 PGA Tour Boulevard, Ponte Vedra Beach; (904) 285-7777 or (800) 457-4653. Massive 508-room resort known for its world-class golfing (ninety-nine holes and home of the Players Championship at Sawgrass tournament) and kids' program. $$$–$$$$ (Ask about summer family packages.)

## For More Information

**St. Augustine, Ponte Vedra, and the Beaches Visitors and Convention Bureau.** 88 Riberia Street, Suite 400, St. Augustine 32084; (904) 829-1711 or (800) OLD-CITY; www.visitoldcity.com.

# More Things to See and Do in
# Northeast Florida

- **G. Howard Bryan Museum of Southern History,** Jacksonville; (904) 388-3574
- **Jacksonville Museum of Modern Art,** Jacksonville; (904) 366-6911
- **Peterbrooke Chocolatier,** Jacksonville; (904) 398-4812; www.peter brooke.com
- **Spanish Military Hospital,** St. Augustine; (904) 827-0807
- **Old Jail and Florida Heritage Museum,** St. Augustine; (904) 829-3800; www.historictours.com
- **Mission of Nombre de Dios,** St. Augustine; (904) 824-2809; www .missionandshrine.org
- **Fort Matanzas National Monument,** St. Augustine; (904) 471-0116
- **World Golf Hall of Fame,** St. Augustine; (904) 940-4123; www.world golfhalloffame.org

## Annual Events

**Jacksonville Jazz Festival.** Jacksonville; (904) 630-3686. Eight days of concerts and activities. Held in April. **Free.**

**Beaches Festival Weekend.** Jacksonville Beach; (904) 247-6236. The beaches "open" with a parade, sand-castle-building contest, and food vendors the last full weekend of April. **Free.**

**Isle of Eight Flags Shrimp Festival.** Fernandina Beach; (904) 261-3248 or (904) 261-0203. Seafood feasting in May with a pirate theme. **Free.**

**Drake's Raid.** St. Augustine; (800) OLD-CITY. A reenactment of Sir Francis Drake's sixteenth-century attack on the Spanish colony, early in June. **Free.**

**Halloween Nights: Old Haunts in the Old City.** St. Augustine; (800) OLD-CITY. October brings family activities, haunted tours, and festivities through the Historic District.

**Nights of Lights.** St. Augustine; (904) 829-1711 or (800) OLD-CITY. November through January, holiday festivities feature colonial reenactments. **Free.**

**Victorian Seaside Christmas.** Fernandina Beach; (904) 261-3248. Beginning Thanksgiving weekend, it lights up downtown and provides a variety of activities, including sleigh rides on the beach.

# East Central
# Florida

M uch of east central Florida was built with an eye toward travel—whether by train, race car, motorcycle, or spaceship. Still, the area balances space-age technology with untamed wilderness to present attractions and temperaments that are intriguingly diverse, from bald eagles to launch shuttles, citrus groves to drive-on beaches, surfboards to sea turtle nests.

This chapter covers the area from Flagler Beach and Daytona Beach to Stuart and Hobe Sound, with short detours inland.

## TopPicks for Family Fun in East Central Florida

1. Living the dream at John F. Kennedy Space Center

2. Shuttling into simulated space at Astronaut Hall of Fame/U.S. Space Camp Florida, Titusville

3. Feeling the thunder at Daytona International Speedway/Daytona USA, Daytona Beach

4. Staring at giant sloth bones and scary African masks at Museum of Arts and Sciences, Daytona Beach

5. Feeling like an ancient explorer at the pristine and quiet Merritt Island National Wildlife Refuge, Titusville

6. Shredding the waves at Sebastian Inlet

7. Cruising on the St. Johns River, Sanford

8. Manatee spotting at Blue Spring State Park, Orange City

9. Playing surrogate parent to a nest of sea turtle hatchlings at Hobe Sound National Wildlife Refuge, Hobe Sound

# EAST CENTRAL FLORIDA

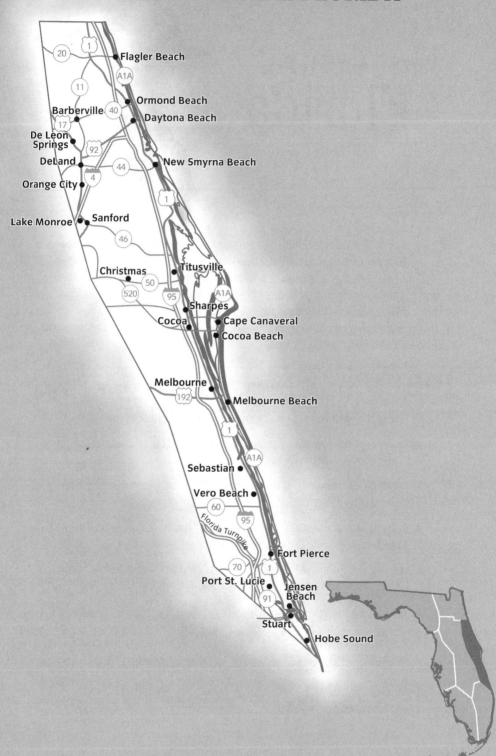

# Ormond Beach and Environs

Located about a half hour south of St. Augustine Beach–Marineland along Route A1A or Highway 1.

First stop: Flagler Beach, named for Henry Flagler, Florida's choo-choo Sugar Daddy. Although Flagler was one of the earliest settlers of Ormond Beach, to the south, the town and its big brother, Daytona Beach, are more well known today for the automobile and its race-car pioneers.

To the south of the Flagler Beach area, the Halifax River widens the split between mainland and barrier island. Route A1A continues to take the coastal route into Ormond Beach.

### Gamble Rogers Memorial State Recreation Area (all ages)
**3100 South A1A, Flagler Beach; (386) 517-2086. Open 8:00 a.m. to sunset daily. Main park entrance is $4 per vehicle of eight persons or fewer, $1 per extra passenger, cyclist, or pedestrian; entrance for beach only is $4 per car.**

Cradled between the Atlantic and the Intracoastal Waterway, it pleases nature observers with two waterfronts and 144 acres. Camp, picnic, swim, fish, and watch the shorebirds come to feed at low tide.

### Bulow Plantation Ruins State Historic Site (ages 5 to 13)
**Follow signs west off Route A1A to Route 100 and turn south on Route 2001 (Old King's Road; mailing address: P.O. Box 655, Bunnell 32010); (386) 517-2084. Open 9:00 a.m. to 5:00 p.m. daily. Admission is $3 per vehicle. Canoe rentals are available at $10 per hour or $40 per day.**

This state site oddly juxtaposes elements of times past. On one hand, you'll explore ruins of a sugar mill and other plantation structures dating back to the early 1800s. It feels something like an Indiana Jones adventure. In an open-air interpretive center, you get a taste of Seminole Indian heritage and culture through artifact displays. While there, you can have a picnic and paddle a canoe along a 13-mile trail on Bulow Creek, through reclaimed oak and magnolia forest where sugarcane once fluttered.

### The Casements (ages 7 to 13)
**25 Riverside Drive and Granada Boulevard (Route 40), Ormond Beach; (386) 676-3216. Open 8:30 a.m. to 5:00 p.m. Monday through Friday and 8:30 a.m. to noon Saturday. Guided tours 10:00 to 11:30 a.m. Saturday. Donations are requested.**

The town's premier attraction, it was once the winter home of multimillionaire John D. Rockefeller. The circa-1912 palace today serves as a cultural center and museum that showcases historic Boy Scout memorabilia, Hungarian folklore, and Rockefeller artifacts.

# Smart **Travel**

- Pack plenty of books for the trip. Suggested topics: space travel, sea turtles, Navy frogmen, and citrus. During summer vacation, a few school workbooks keep the brain from lapsing.

- Sea lice are the bane of swimmers along the East Coast. Actually the larvae of thimble jellyfish, they get caught in swimsuits and emit an itchy venom that can drive you crazy. Watch for posted signs at beaches that warn of sea lice. Immediately after exiting the water, remove swimsuits and shower.

- Tar balls, remnants of old oil spills, are another common problem in these waters. Pack a tar solvent.

- Among the top injuries reported at Canaveral National Seashore are splinters from boardwalks. Be sure to keep the little ones shod to and from the beach, and remind them not to run their hands along the railing.

- When swimming around fishing piers, stay well clear to avoid being accidentally hooked.

## Ormond Beach Performing Arts Center (ages 4 to 13) 🎵
**399 North Highway 1, Ormond Beach; (386) 676-3375. Tickets are reasonably priced.**

Across the Intracoastal Waterway formed by the river, via Route 40, you'll find cultural and natural reasons to leave the alluring shoreline. Besides community theater and touring concert arts and drama productions, this center presents children's theater workshops and productions.

## Tomoka State Park (ages 5 to 13) 🏛️ 🏕️ 🖼️
**2099 North Beach Street, Ormond Beach; (386) 676-4050. The park is open 8:00 a.m. to sunset daily; the museum, 9:30 a.m. to 4:30 p.m. Park entrance is $4 per vehicle of eight persons or fewer, $1.00 per extra passenger, cyclist, or pedestrian. Admission to the museum is free.**

Before there was Tomoka State Park, a Timucuan Indian village and later a plantation, circa 1766, occupied these 1,900 acres. Set between the lovely Tomoka and Halifax Rivers, it offers great canoeing and fishing, as well as camping, hiking, picnicking, and the Fred Dana Marsh Museum, where the works of an Ormond Beach sculptor and architect are gathered.

## For More Information

**Daytona Beach Area Convention and Visitors Bureau.** 126 East Orange Avenue, Daytona Beach 32114; (386) 255-0415 or (800) 545-0415; www.daytona beach.com.

**Ormond Beach Chamber of Commerce.** 165 West Granada Boulevard, Ormond Beach 32174; (386) 677-3454; www.ormondchamber.com.

See Daytona Beach listings for nearby restaurants and hotels.

# Weekend Jaunt: DeLand and Vicinity

From Ormond Beach, head for the contrasting beauty and culture of Florida's inlands along Route 40 to Barberville. Follow Highway 17 south to De Leon Springs, DeLand, and Orange City. South of Orange City, you can hop on Interstate 4 west to reach Sanford and Lake Marion, then return to Daytona Beach via I-4 east.

### Barberville's Pioneer Settlement for the Creative Arts

(ages 5 to 13)

West of Ormond Beach about 20 miles on Highway 40, located 2 blocks west of the intersection of Highway 17 and Route 40; 1776 Lightfoot Lane, Barberville; (386) 749-2959. Open 9:00 a.m. to 4:00 p.m. Monday through Friday and 9:00 a.m. to 2:00 p.m. Saturday. Admission with guided tours is $4 for adults, $3 for children ages 5 to 12.

The ten-acre wooded complex is dedicated to preserving traditional folk arts such as pottery, woodwork, and blacksmithing. The kids get a vision of life in early Florida and can visit a vintage railroad depot. In November, the attraction hosts a two-day Fall Country Jamboree, with artisans, crafters, music, and a corn boil.

## Top Family **Beaches and Parks**

1. **Golden Sands County Park,** Vero Beach

2. **Fort Pierce Inlet State Park,** Fort Pierce

3. **Stuart Beach,** Stuart

4. **Playalinda Beach,** Canaveral National Seashore

5. **Daytona Beach,** Daytona Beach

## Top Family **Resorts**

1. **Club Med Sandpiper,** Port St. Lucie

2. **Hutchinson Island Marriott,** Stuart

3. **Driftwood Resort,** Vero Beach

### De Leon Springs State Park (ages 5 to 13)

**Ponce de Leon Boulevard and Burt Parks Road off Highway 17; 601 Ponce de Leon Boulevard, De Leon Springs; (386) 985-4212. Open 8:00 a.m. to sunset daily. Park entrance is $5 per vehicle of eight persons or fewer, $1 per extra passenger, cyclist, or pedestrian.**

South of Barberville, the site of an erstwhile sugar plantation later became a health resort and today is protected as a state park. Much of its modern-day reputation is stacked on the popularity of an on-site pancake house (see below). Work off a hearty meal there with a hike, a swim in the old spring-fed resort pool, or a canoe trip in the springs. One day in August, the park's A Day in Florida History features living-history presentations staged at camps for Timucuans, Spanish soldiers, Seminole Indians, and Civil War soldiers.

### Old Spanish Sugar Mill & Griddle House

**De Leon Springs State Park, De Leon Springs; (386) 985-5644.**

Make your own flapjacks on the griddle built into your table. Servers bring you pitchers of stone-ground, five-grain, and unbleached flour pancake batter, along with apples, bananas, chocolate chips, or any other condiments you request. The griddles raise the ambient temperature, so it's best to try this in cool weather. The restaurant, inside the gates at De Leon Springs State Park, opens daily for breakfast and lunch (when you can grill your own sandwiches). $

### Lake Woodruff National Wildlife Refuge

(ages 6 to 13)

**2045 Mud Lake Road, De Leon Springs; off Highway 17; (386) 985-4673; www.lakewoodruff.fws.gov/. Open dawn to dusk daily. Admission is free.**

Devoted naturalists head here to explore by foot or bike the nature trails, which penetrate pine and hardwood forest and ring dikes built around bird-feeding ponds.

### Hontoon Island State Park (ages 4 to 13)

**2309 River Ridge Road, DeLand; off Route 44 west of town; (386) 736-5309. Open 8:00 a.m. to sunset daily. Park entrance is free.**

Surrounded by the St. Johns and Huntoon Dead Rivers, the park can be reached by private boat or a free passenger shuttle that operates from 8:00 a.m. until one hour before sunset. This is a nice place to spend a lazy day with a fishing pole in hand as the little ones swing on the playground. Six miles of trails accommodate bikers and hikers. Six rustic cabins and twelve campsites are available.

### Blue Spring State Park (all ages)

**2100 West French Avenue, Orange City; (386) 775-3663. Open 8:00 a.m. to sunset daily. Park entrance is $5 per vehicle with up to eight passengers, $1 for extra passengers, bicyclists, and pedestrians.**

Manatees are the star attraction. They winter here, drawn by balmy 72-degree waters. So are families, who also enjoy the park's many recreational opportunities: fifty-one campsites, picnicking, swimming, scuba diving, and canoeing. Manatee educational programs are scheduled mid-November through mid-March.

The last weekend in January, the park cohosts the Blue Spring Manatee Festival. Besides entertainment and other festivities, the event offers the opportunity to see endangered-species exhibits. You can take a shuttle bus to the park to observe manatees when weather permits, attend an educational program, and tour the park's historic Thursby House, which is open to the public Wednesday through Sunday.

### St. Johns River Cruises (ages 5 to 13)

**At Blue Springs State Park (mailing address: P.O. Box 521673, Longwood 32752-1673); (407) 330-1612; www.sjrivercruises.com. Cost for two hours is $18 for adults, $16 for seniors, $12 for children 3 to 12; under 3 free. Ecotours depart 10:00 a.m. and 1:00 p.m. daily. Seasonal tours available 3:30 p.m. January through April.**

It concentrates on the natural sights along local waterways during its two-hour and full-day cruises. Spot manatees, alligators, deer, wild hogs, bald eagles, and other rare birds along the scenic route.

### Rivership *Romance* (ages 4 to 13)

**Monroe Harbour Marina; 433 North Palmetto Avenue, Sanford; (407) 321-5091 or (800) 423-7401. Admission for a three-hour tour is $38 for adults, $28 for children ages 3 to 12.**

Perched on the edge of a bulge in the St. Johns River known as Lake Monroe, Sanford is the perfect place from which to embark on a narrated tour of the historic, wilderness-fraught waterway. (The town is also known as the Celery Capital of the World, but don't tell your kids that or they'll never want to go.) One of the most popular tours is aboard this replica of a 1940s steamer for lunch or dinner and dancing.

## Central Florida Zoological Park (all ages)

On the western shore of Lake Monroe, right off I-4's exit 52; 3755 Highway 17/92 (P.O. Box 470309, Lake Monroe 32747); (407) 323-4450; www.centralfloridazoo.org. Open 9:00 a.m. to 5:00 p.m. daily; closed Thanksgiving and Christmas Day. Admission is $9.95 for adults, $7.95 for seniors, $5.95 for children ages 3 to 12.

It conducts a variety of seasonal programs designed to enlighten children about animal behaviors and endangerment. They range from Children's Storytime at the Zoo to Nature Niche, a weeklong study for six- to twelve-year-olds. Many of the zoo's animals are endangered species from around the world, including the red-ruffed lemur, clouded leopard, Aruba island rattlesnake, and Bali mynah bird.

## Where to Stay

**DeLand Country Inn Bed & Breakfast.** 228 West Howry Avenue, DeLand; (386) 736-4244; www.bnbfinder.com. Charming 1900 home with five bedrooms done in lace and fancy wallpaper sits right downtown, so you can porch sit and watch the world go by, or stroll through little DeLand, checking out antiques shops, parks, and the campus at Stetson University. It's kid- and pet-friendly; go for a swim in the screened pool, or play board games or basketball. Great breakfast, too. $–$$

**Hontoon Landing Resort & Marina.** 2317 River Ridge Road, DeLand; (386) 735-2474 or (800) 248-2474. Rooms, suites, and cottages overlooking the St. Johns River. Houseboat and pontoon rentals. $–$$

## For More Information

**DeLand Area Chamber of Commerce.** 336 North Woodland Boulevard, DeLand 32720; (386) 734-4331; www.deland chamber.org.

# On a **Budget**

- **The Casements,** Ormond Beach, by donation
- **Lake Woodruff National Wildlife Refuge,** De Leon Springs, free admission
- **Sugar Mill Botanical Gardens,** Port Orange, free admission
- **New Smyrna Beach Sugar Mill Ruins,** New Smyrna Beach, free admission
- **Merritt Island National Wildlife Refuge,** Titusville, free admission
- **Fort Christmas,** Christmas, free admission
- **Jack Island Preserve,** Fort Pierce, free admission

# Daytona Beach

Anyone who has heard of Florida beaches has heard of Daytona Beach, for one reason or another. Its name sounds most often from the lips of college spring breakers and race-car fans.

Motor sports in Daytona Beach got its start on the hard-packed beaches, so it's not surprising that it is one of the few places in Florida that still allows cars to drive on most of its 23-mile-long beach. (Enter at marked beach ramps off Route A1A for $5 a day, 8:00 a.m. to 7:00 p.m., February through November—free the rest of the year.) This contributes to its reputation as a party town, but it's just as much a family attraction. Along the beach, which stays well trafficked all day, you can rent all kinds of cool beach toys, including golf carts, four-wheelers, reclining bicycles, and boogieboards. Sun Splash Park, at 611 South Atlantic Avenue, provides interactive fountains and other cool-down features.

To get to Daytona's other claims to fame, cross the Intracoastal Waterway at Highway 92. Find historic attractions in the downtown area by heading to the south of Highway 92 (International Speedway Boulevard) on Beach Street. Stroll lovely City Island Park or browse downtown stores, many of which occupy historic buildings. To get to the high-test attractions, head out on the highway, 92 that is.

### Boardwalk Amusement Area and Main Street Pier (all ages)
**Ocean Avenue (off Route A1A); (386) 253-1212 for pier information. The pier is open 6:00 a.m. to 11:00 p.m. daily (hours extended in summer); its restaurant, 11:00 a.m. to 10:00 p.m. Admission to the fishing end of the pier, past the restaurant, is $5.00 for adults ($12.50 with pole rental), $3.50 for children ages 12 and under, $1.00 for spectators. Admission to Sky Lift is $6.00.**

By day (at night it turns into a rowdier scene), take the kids to the Boardwalk, with its tents full of video games, rides, a castle-motif band shell, and, on the 1,000-foot-long pier, a gondola Sky Lift. It's like a fairgrounds on the beach! The beach around the pier has been declared pedestrian-only and is closed to vehicular traffic. From the pier, you can also charter fishing boats.

### Pirate's Island Adventure Golf (ages 4 to 13)
**3420 South Atlantic Avenue, Daytona Beach Shores; (386) 767-9397. Open 10:00 a.m. to 10:00 p.m. September through February and 9:00 a.m. to 11:00 p.m. March through August. Admission is $9.49 for adults, $7.49 for children ages 5 to 12.**

Not far off the beach you'll find more miniature golf and small amusement parks than even the most ambitious parents could exhaust in a week's stay. This eighteen-hole course is a nice one.

### Ponce de Leon Inlet Lighthouse (ages 6 to 13)

**4931 South Peninsula Drive, Ponce Inlet; (386) 761-1821; www.ponceinlet.org. Open 10:00 a.m. to 5:00 p.m. daily, with extended summer hours. Admission is $5.00 for adults, $1.50 for children ages 11 and under.**

Don't be fooled by all the amusement park and speed-demon attractions: There's history in Daytona Beach, too. The area's most popular vintage structure stands watch at the beach's south end. The lighthouse was built more than a hundred years ago. You can still climb its 203 spiraling steps to the top of a 175-foot red tower (the second tallest in the United States) and sigh at the sweeping panorama. A small colony with historic buildings surrounds the tower; one houses an antique French-cut lighthouse lens that kids like for its prism effect. After you've climbed the lighthouse, you can buy a certificate attesting to your accomplishment in the gift shop.

### Lighthouse Point County Park (all ages)

**5000 South Atlantic Avenue, Ponce Inlet; (386) 756-7488. Admission is $3.50 per car of eight passengers or fewer, $1.00 per extra passenger.**

For a quieter beach scene, without the anxiety beach traffic can cause parents with toddlers, spend your sun time here. This end of the island is much quieter, and the fifty-five-acre beach is more natural, edged in small dunes. A jetty keeps waters calm.

### Halifax Historical Museum (ages 6 to 13)

**252 South Beach Street; (386) 255-6976; www.halifaxhistorical.org. Open 10:00 a.m. to 4:00 p.m. Tuesday through Saturday. Admission is $4 for adults, $1 for children under age 12. Thursday after noon by donation.**

The museum resides in an old bank building and holds memorabilia from prehistoric Indian eras to the early days of beach car racing. You can see a wood-carved model of what the boardwalk area looked like in 1933.

### Angell & Phelps Chocolate Factory (ages 4 to 10)

**154 South Beach Street; (386) 252-6531; www.angellandphelps.com. Open 9:30 a.m. to 5:30 p.m. Monday through Friday. Admission is free.**

What kid, at whatever age, wouldn't love a trip to a chocolate factory? Take a free thirty-minute guided tour of this one and see how more than a hundred kinds of candies are made. The Angell & Phelps Restaurant and Wine Bar serves casual gourmet dishes such as soups and sandwiches, chili, and wraps.

### A Tiny Cruise Line (ages 5 to 13)

**Halifax Harbor Marina, 425 South Beach Street; (386) 226-2343. Ticket prices for a one-hour excursion are $12.44 for adults, $7.51 for children ages 4 to 12; $18.54 and $11.03 for two hours. Tax is extra.**

Boat tours on the Halifax River are themed variously for estate-gawking, wildlife-sighting, downtown history, and sunset and city lights.

## Museum of Arts and Sciences (ages 7 to 13)

1040 Museum Boulevard; (386) 255-0285; www.moas.org. Open 9:00 a.m. to 5:00 p.m. Monday through Saturday and 11:00 a.m. to 5:00 p.m. Sunday. Admission is $12.95 for adults, $10.95 for seniors, and $6.95 for children 6 to 17; under 6 free. The museum fee includes the planetarium show, but planetarium tickets may be purchased separately at $4 for adults and $3 for children 6 to 17. Planetarium shows are scheduled at 3:00 p.m. Tuesday through Friday and 2:00 and 4:00 p.m. Saturday and Sunday.

This attraction will surprise you with its many layers of enrichment possibilities. Centered on the ninety-acre Tuscawilla Preserve, its approach to discovery is holistic. For the wee ones, there's a 13-foot-tall skeleton of a 130,000-year-old giant ground sloth and the skeleton of a huge armadillo ancestor, plus the museum's drawers and showcases full of other fossils. Older children will enjoy the free world's largest Cuban art collection, Indian artifacts, and exhibits from thirty different African cultures. Other components range from changing displays of fine art to hikes through coastal hammock environment and shows in the planetarium.

## Daytona International Speedway and Daytona USA
(ages 6 to 13)

1801 West International Speedway Boulevard; (386) 255-2700 (speedway) or (386) 947-6800 (Daytona USA); www.daytonausa.com. Track tours are conducted 9:30 a.m. to 5:00 p.m. daily when there's no racing. Daytona USA open 9:00 a.m. to 7:00 p.m. daily (hours extended during racing events). Admission is $24 for adults, $19 for seniors and for children ages 6 to 12; under 6 free.

Each March, thousands flock here for the energy and excitement of Daytona 500 NASCAR stock-car racing. Other major Speedweek events include the Pepsi 400 NASCAR race in July, the Rolex 24 sports-car race in February, and the Daytona 200 for motorcycles in March. Year-round, you can travel backward by race car via a video wall showing early racing films, then take the thirty-minute narrated Speedway tour by tram. A highlight is a stop on the rim road behind turn four for a heightened overview of the grounds.

Opened in July 1996, Daytona USA further traces the history and hysteria of motor sports with interactive displays that allow visitors to assist at a pit stop, broadcast a race, design and test a stock car, and talk to their favorite drivers through video. Famous race cars, such as actor Paul Newman's Ford Mustang Cobra and each year's Daytona 500 winner, are on display. From a 55-foot theater screen, a film about the Daytona 500 race brings you as close to being there as you can get without fighting traffic. Buy your race-car souvenirs at the gift shop or at any one of several motor sports shops in the area.

### Shenandoah Stables (ages 7 to 13)

**1759 Tomoka Farms Road; (386) 257-1444. Rides cost $25 per hour. Children under age 7 can ride with an adult for $5 extra.**

It takes reservations for family rides along country trails and offers lessons on horses and ponies. Ask about the kids' summer riding program.

## Where to Eat

**Lighthouse Landing.** 4940 South Peninsula Drive, Ponce Inlet; (386) 761-9271. The oldest restaurant on Florida's east coast. Waterside place, picnic tables, fish, and sandwiches indoors or out. Lunch and dinner daily. $–$$$

**Ocean Deck.** 127 South Ocean Avenue; (386) 253-5224; www.oceandeck.com. The upper deck offers fine dining. Down below at beach level, things are more casual and family appropriate. Open daily for lunch and dinner, it serves a wide variety of sandwiches, seafood, salads, and appetizers. $$

## Where to Stay

**Plaza Resort.** 600 North Atlantic Avenue; (386) 255-4471 or (800) 225-0329; www .plazaresortandspa.com. Formerly the Holiday Inn, this recent remake has upgraded the hotel and added a spa, but it's still affordable, with a beach location, swimming pool, and snack bar that families like. $$–$$$

**Shores Resort and Spa.** 2637 South Atlantic Avenue, Daytona Beach Shores; (386) 767-7350 or (800) 525-7350. One of Daytona's most luxurious accommodations; 214 guest rooms, pools, exercise facility, restaurant and bar, tennis courts, and room service. $$–$$$$

## For More Information

**Daytona Beach Area Convention and Visitors Bureau.** 126 East Orange Avenue, Daytona Beach 32114; (386) 255-0415 or (800) 544-0415; www.daytona beach-tourism.com.

# Port Orange and New Smyrna Beach

Along Highway 1 just south of Daytona Beach.

### Sugar Mill Botanical Gardens (ages 4 to 13)

**Take Herbert Street west off Highway 1 and follow the signs; 950 Old Sugar Mill Road, Port Orange; (386) 767-1735. Open 8:00 a.m. to 6:00 p.m. daily. Admission is free. To arrange a free guided tour, call (386) 767-0996.**

Remnants of Florida's sugar days persist despite the ravages of war and the elements. Twelve acres of peaceful gardens enshrine two distinctly different eras of

Florida history. The site originally processed sugar, and several ruins remember the era. Forty years ago, it was turned into Bongoland, a theme park now extinct, although dinosaur statues remain. Throw in botanical gardens, and you have an off-beat attraction with enough variety for everyone in the family.

### Go-Kart City (all ages)

**4114 South Nova Road, Port Orange; (386) 761-2882. Open daily; hours vary according to demand. Admission for go-karts is $6.50 per ride (four laps), with multiride rates; "bullet" karts (faster) are $7.50 per ride. Golfing is $5 for adults, $4 for seniors and children 6 to 10, $2 for children 4 or 5.**

Let 'em live their race-car fantasies on a ¼-mile track. Tots can buddy-ride **free** with parents. Nonracers can play games in the video arcade, or play eighteen holes on the minigolf course.

### Public Beach

**Take the causeway at Route 44, turn left onto Peninsula Drive, and then right onto Flagler Avenue. Open sunrise to sunset daily. Admission is $5 per car.**

The town of New Smyrna Beach has three marvelous beach accesses. The public beach is a small-town version of Daytona, where you can drive your car onto the 9-mile stretch of sand, while avoiding all the crowds and college boogie. Surfers and other boardsters like it here, especially at the north-end jetty, which also appeals to anglers.

### Canaveral National Seashore at Apollo Beach

**Follow Route A1A across the south causeway and continue south about 6 miles; visitor center at 7611 South Atlantic Avenue, New Smyrna Beach; (386) 428-3384. Park open 6:00 a.m. to 6:00 p.m. in winter, 6:00 a.m. to 8:00 p.m. in summer; visitor center open 9:00 a.m. to 5:00 p.m. Admission is $3 per person.**

This is minimally developed with parking lots, nature trails, and restrooms. South of there, entrance is by foot only, and eventually you'll reach Klondike Beach. (More about Canaveral National Seashore appears under Titusville.)

### New Smyrna Beach Sugar Mill Ruins (ages 6 to 13)

**West of Highway 1 and south of Route 44 on Mission Drive. Admission is free.**

Sugar-coated history lessons continue. The county park makes low impact on the haunting, primitive beauty of undisturbed ruins and nature. This is a great place for a hike on the hammock trail, then a picnic away from it all.

## For More Information

**Southeast Volusia Chamber of Commerce.** 115 Canal Street, New Smyrna Beach 32168; (386) 428-2449 or (877) 460-8410; www.sevchamber.com.

# Titusville

About a half hour south of New Smyrna Beach on Highway 1.

The whole town, small as it is, revolves around the space theme, thanks to its role in hosting NASA. Still, Titusville remains natural and uncommercialized because it shares its shores with the pristine realms of two vast, nationally protected areas. Only for the few days surrounding a launch does the town fill with tourists and do hotel rates rise. Otherwise, most of the trade is day-trippers, who come from the Orlando area just to tour the Space Center.

### Merritt Island National Wildlife Refuge (ages 5 to 13)

**3.5 miles east of Titusville on Route 402 (P.O. Box 6504, Titusville 32782); (321) 861-0667. The refuge is open daily during daylight hours; the visitor center is open 8:00 a.m. to 4:30 p.m. Monday through Friday and 9:00 a.m. to 5:00 p.m. Saturday and Sunday. April through October, the center closes on Sunday. Admission is free.**

Cross the Intracoastal Waterway—here the Indian River—to find a solitary world of wildlife that coexists with, and survives in spite of, the space-age neighbor that shares its realm. The refuge's 140,000 acres, together with bordering Canaveral National Seashore, provide habitat for 1,045 plant species, 310 bird species, and 21 threatened or endangered animal species, including the bald eagle, wood stork, manatee, and loggerhead turtle. Stop at the visitor center on Route 402 to get your bearings and background, then explore by car, foot, or bike along the trails.

### Canaveral National Seashore (ages 5 to 13)

**Route 402; visitor center at 7611 South Atlantic Avenue, New Smyrna Beach; (386) 428-3384. Open 6:00 a.m. to 6:00 p.m. in winter, 6:00 a.m. to 8:00 p.m. in summer. Admission is $3 per person.**

Behold this wonderfully undiscovered beach world! Its 25-mile-long stretch has three sections. Easiest to reach and most family friendly is Playalinda Beach, still minimally developed with only pit toilets and beach walkovers. Thirteen parking lots line the 4-mile stretch. Secluded at its north end, it was once popular with nudists. Although the county has banned nudism, it still occurs on this most secluded of Florida beaches. Two other beaches, Apollo and Klondike, are most easily accessed from New Smyrna Beach (see New Smyrna listings).

Natural and gorgeous, Playalinda is the kind of beach you never want to leave. Sea turtles like it, too. Though they lay their eggs along the entire length of the East Coast and on the West Coast, too, this area begins a stretch of the state's heaviest concentration of turtle nests. With all this nature, it feels strange to look down the way and see a launch pad. The contrast is dramatic, but the duality seems to work. The beach does close around rocket launches, so call ahead.

# Ninja **Turtles**

May through September brings loggerhead, leatherback, and green turtles ashore. Mammoth, 300-pound mother turtles drag themselves above the shoreline in the stealth of night, leaving tractorlike tracks to mark their visit. Into their sandpit nests, they drop about a hundred eggs and are on their way, maternal duties complete. In summer you'll see their nests staked or wired off. Sixty days later, the eggs hatch, the baby turtles dig their way out of the sand, and then, like little ninjas, they scurry toward the moonlight reflected on the water.

### North Brevard Historical Museum (ages 7 to 13)
301 South Washington Avenue (Highway 1 North); (321) 269-3658. Open 10:00 a.m. to 3:00 p.m. Tuesday through Saturday. Admission is free or by donation.

Get a quick bite of history at this museum in the thick of downtown's historic renovation. It exhibits photographs, furniture, clothing, and other items that depict early local lifestyles. And since everything in the area must have a space spin, it displays the handprints of the original Mercury astronauts.

### American Police Hall of Fame and Museum (all ages)
6350 Horizon Drive; (321) 264-0911; www.aphf.org. Open 10:00 a.m. to 6:00 p.m. daily. Admission is $12 for adults, $8 for seniors and children ages 4 to 12, and free for kids ages 3 and under. Law enforcement officers are also admitted free.

Do your kids have a fascination with cops and robbers? If so, take them to see a real jail cell, electric chair, police cars, and weapons.

### Titusville Playhouse (ages 4 to 13)
301 Julia Street off Highway 1 South; (321) 268-1125. Tickets cost $10 to $16, less for students and seniors.

Also downtown, you'll find the playhouse lodged in the Emma Parrish Theatre, a restored silent movie house from the turn of the twentieth century. It hosts the Rising Stars Children's Theatre.

# Road **Markers**

Continuing down Route A1A, the resort towns reel off with their special brand of wide, firm beaches and attractions both classic and contemporary. This straight shot down the coast begins in the environs of Daytona Beach, just south of which it swings inland along Routes 40 and 17 to examine some hidden natural treasures around the town of DeLand. Then it's easy cruising down Highway 1 or parallel Route A1A along the so-called Space Coast and Treasure Coast, which are among the least discovered sections of Florida's eastern shores. A1A is the more scenic, but at times congested, route, especially around Melbourne Beach. Highway 1 is more utilitarian. Between Fort Pierce and Stuart, try Route 707 (Indian River Drive) for a scenic crusade. Interstate 95 skirts the region inland from the shore, for a zippier trip.

### Valiant Air Command Warbird Museum (ages 7 to 13)

**6600 Tico Road; off Route 405; (321) 268-1941. Open 9:00 a.m. to 5:00 p.m. daily. Admission is $12 for adults, $10 for seniors and active military personnel, $5 for children ages 4 to 12; children under 4 free.**

Although spaceships are more commonly associated with the area, you can get your fill of aviation history here. Displays preserve memories of aviation battle from World War I to the Vietnam War, including aircraft, uniforms, flying gear, and artwork.

### Kennedy Space Center (ages 3 to 13)

**Kennedy Space Center (follow signs off Highway 1 and head east on Route 405 to Route 3); (321) 449-4444; www.KennedySpaceCenter.com. Open 9:00 a.m. to 6:00 p.m. daily, except certain launch days and Christmas. Standard admission to the visitor complex is $29 plus tax for adults and $19 plus tax for children ages 3 to 11, and does not include the Astronaut Hall of Fame. The Space Center offers a two-day Maximum Access Admission ticket good for both the visitor complex (which includes Astronaut Encounter, IMAX space films, and the KSC Tour, plus deals on food and merchandise), and Astronaut Hall of Fame exhibits and simulators. It costs $38 plus tax for adults, and $28 plus tax for children ages 3 to 11.**

This is why folks come to Titusville, and it's a great reason, especially for kids. It is, after all, the only space shuttle launch site in the world. For devoted space buffs, it's the ultimate, especially since the completion of its five-year, $130 million makeover. It takes several hours to fully tour the array of exhibits dealing with space exploration. Toddlers love the space-age playground. Older children are intrigued by flashy, multimedia presentations in the humorous Robot Scouts exhibit and by the futuristic look

# Space **Camp**

The Space Center has a weeklong day camp for kids eight to fourteen, dubbed Camp Kennedy Space Center. It features an exciting array of fun activities and robust, hands-on learning, plus free twelve-month passes to the visitor complex for each camper and four free tickets for family members to the Astronaut Hall of Fame. Campers ride a 3D-360° simulator, G-Force Simulator, and ⅙ Gravity Trainer; climb a Zero-G Wall; operate a simulated Mars rover; meet an astronaut; and even design space exploration vehicles. Specially trained teachers lead the program, which is based at the Astronaut Hall of Fame, with occasional excursions to the nearby main campus at Kennedy Space Center visitor complex. Registration costs $295, plus tax, per camper, and includes all activities and transportation, hot lunches, afternoon snacks, and an official space center T-shirt. One spring session is available, and there are weekly sessions during summer, from June to August. Reservations are required; call (321) 449-4400 or write Camp Kennedy Space Center, Delaware North, Park Services, DNPS, Kennedy Space Center 32899.

at humans on Mars in "Exploration in the New Millennium." Kids will love climbing aboard a replica of the space shuttle *Explorer* and meeting an astronaut in person.

With a Maximum Access pass, visitors get access into the two IMAX theaters with screens more than five stories high. *The Dream is Alive* chronicles the history and drama of space travel. Guided bus tours take you past gates barring the general public, into NASA's inner workings and to three attractions. LC39 Observation Gantry is a multilevel deck looking out on Kennedy's two launch pads. At the Apollo/Saturn V Center, interactive displays and multimedia shows illustrate NASA's moon missions. See a real *Saturn V* orbiter and touch a moon rock. Gift shops and a wide variety of eateries throughout the Space Center provide souvenirs and sustenance.

For a special treat, sign up for the "Dine With an Astronaut" program. You get to lunch with a real space hero, ask questions, and take pictures with those who have "the right stuff." As part of another program called ATX Astronaut Training Experience, visitors ages fourteen and older can take a whirlwind route through hands-on training, space flight preparation, and space shuttle simulators, and they even leave with cool ATX gear.

In the 1980s the six surviving *Mercury 7* astronauts conceived of a place where space travelers could be remembered—much like baseball players and other sports figures. Their dream was realized in 1990 as the U.S. Astronaut Hall of Fame, in

Titusville, adjacent to the Space Center. It has become an official part of the Kennedy Space Center Visitor Complex, which spent $700,000 on improvements and celebrated a formal grand opening in 2003. The Hall of Fame tells the personal side of human space exploration history through artifacts once owned by astronauts, interactive exhibits, and astronaut training simulators. It also houses the world's largest collection of astronaut memorabilia, exhibits, and tributes to the heroes of *Mercury, Gemini,* and *Apollo,* plus a fine collection of spacecraft, such as a *Mercury Sigma 7* capsule, *Gemini* training capsule, and an *Apollo 14* command module. Astronaut training simulators allow guests to feel the pressure of four times the force of gravity, ride a rover across Mars, and land a space shuttle.

## Where to Eat

**Kloiber's Cobbler Eatery.** 337 South Washington Avenue; (321) 383-0689. In a historic department store setting, this family-run cafe sells the freshest in bakery goods, salads, soups, and deli sandwiches. Try the meat loaf sandwich on black bean–jalapeño cheese bread and some homemade ice cream or cobbler. Open for breakfast and lunch Monday through Saturday and dinner Tuesday through Saturday. $

## For More Information

**Titusville Area Chamber of Commerce.** 200 South Washington Avenue, Titusville 32780; (321) 267-3036; www.titusville.org.

# Detour: Christmas, Florida

Continue west on Route 50 to reach the town of Christmas, most famous for its postmark, which many seek for their holiday greetings.

**Fort Christmas** (ages 4 to 13)
1300 Fort Christmas Road; (407) 568-4149. Park is open 8:00 a.m. to 8:00 p.m. in summer, 8:00 a.m. to 6:00 p.m. in winter. Museum is open 10:00 a.m. to 5:00 p.m. Tuesday through Saturday, 1:00 to 5:00 p.m. Sunday. Admission is **free.**

The town's existence is based on the fort, which was constructed beginning on Christmas Day 1837, for the Second Seminole War, and later replicated. Visit the museum and enjoy a picnic in the play area.

**Midway Airboat Tours** (ages 8 to 13)
28501 East Route 50; (407) 568-6790. Open 9:00 a.m. to 6:00 p.m. daily. Cost for forty-five-minute rides is $35 for adults and $25 for children 4 to 11; under 4 **free.**

Airboat rides are a loud but distinctively Floridian way to explore the state's inland waters. Excursions explore the rampant wildlife on the St. Johns River and connecting lakes.

# Cocoa

About twenty minutes south of Titusville on Highway 1. Historic Cocoa Village lies along Brevard Avenue, just south of King Street (Route 520).

### Horseback Trail Rides (ages 8 to 13)

1020 Camp Road, Sharpes; 6 miles south of Route 405 off Highway 1; (321) 632-7085. Four scheduled rides depart between 9:00 a.m. and 5:30 p.m. daily. Rates are $30 per ninety-minute ride. No one under age 6 or over 225 pounds is permitted. For children under 6 there is a 30-minute walkaround for $10.

A horseback ride slows down the space-age pace to a clip-clop trip through primal woodlands. Call ahead for reservations and directions.

### Brevard Museum of History and Science (ages 5 to 11)

2201 Michigan Avenue (off Highway 1); (321) 632-1830. Open 10:00 a.m. to 4:00 p.m. Monday through Saturday and noon to 4:00 p.m. Sunday. Admission is $6.00 for adults, $5.50 for seniors, $4.50 for children ages 5 to 16; 4 and under free.

It occupies twenty-two acres of interpreted environment. Trails lead through marsh, sand hills, and hammock. Indoors, kids can get their hands on science experiments in the Discovery Room; see displays from the Ice Age, pioneer days, and Space Age; and visit changing exhibits.

### Brevard Community College Planetarium and Observatory
(ages 5 to 13)

1519 Clearlake Road; (321) 433-7373; www.brevardcc.edu/planet. Schedule changes monthly. Planetarium admission is $7 for adults, $6 for seniors, $4 for children ages 4 to 12; under 4 free. Observatory and exhibits are free.

It offers planetarium programs, high-tech stargazing, and intergalactic movies three stories high.

## For More Information

**Cocoa Beach Area Chamber of Commerce.** 400 Fortenberry Road, Merritt Island 32952; (321) 459-2200.

# Cape Canaveral and Cocoa Beach

Head back north on Highway 1 and take Route 528, also known as Bennett Memorial Causeway, to cross Merritt Island to Cape Canaveral. Cocoa Beach lies south of Cape Canaveral on Route A1A.

### Jetty Park (ages 4 to 13)

**400 East Jetty Road, north of Route 528, Cape Canaveral; (321) 783-7111; www.jetty park.org. The park is open until 9:00 p.m. for fishing. Day parking costs $5 per car, $7 per recreational vehicle.**

One of the best locations for launch watching, this is also a great spot for beaching, camping, picnicking, pier fishing, and cruise ship gazing. It has a general store, a playground, a bake shop, and concessions.

### TRAXX at Jungle Village Family Fun Center (all ages)

**South of Route 528 on Route A1A; 8801 Astronaut Boulevard, Cape Canaveral; (321) 783-0595. Open 10:00 a.m. to midnight Sunday through Thursday, 10:00 a.m. to 1:00 a.m. Friday and Saturday. Fees are charged per attraction.**

Life-size jungle animal sculptures herald your approach. The center assembles all the makings of a half-day's entertainment, with three varieties of race track, thirty-six-hole miniature golf course, laser tag, game arcade, and snack bar. Look for the elephant wearing sunglasses.

### Cocoa Beach Pier (ages 8 to 13)

**401 Meade Avenue, Cocoa Beach; (321) 783-7549. Cost for parking Friday through Sunday is $7. Admission to fishing end of pier is $1.00 for spectators, $3.50 for fishing adults, and $3.00 for seniors and children under age 12.**

A local landmark, it measures 800 feet in length. Besides fishing, you'll find equipment rentals, restaurants, bars, shops, and live entertainment. It's also the site of festivals—such as the Labor Day Pro-Am Surfing Festival—launch watches, and informal gatherings.

### Ron Jon Surf Shop (ages 5 to 13)

**Routes A1A and 520; 4151 North Atlantic Avenue, Cocoa Beach; (321) 799-8820; www .ronjons.com. Open twenty-four hours daily.**

Surf's up—about as up as it gets in Florida—at Cocoa Beach and vicinity. Much of the area's surfing reputation is based on the looming, visually loud presence of Ron Jon; it's the cathedral of water sports. The park around it displays ten sand sculptures of beach sports.

## Where to Eat

**Marlins Bar & Grill.** Cocoa Beach Pier, 401 Meade Avenue, Cocoa Beach; (321) 783-7549. Watch surfers while you chow down on wings, burgers, mahimahi, and seafood. Inside and outside seating; kids' menu. Open daily for lunch and dinner. $–$$

## Where to Stay

**Hampton Inn.** 3425 North Atlantic Avenue, Cocoa Beach; (321) 799-4099 or (877) 49-BEACH. With beach access and an above-the-rest view of the cruise ship port and two waterfronts, this is one of Cocoa Beach's finest offerings. Pool and complimentary continental breakfast. $$–$$$

# Melbourne and Melbourne Beach

Route A1A continues its crawl through resort town after resort town. Cocoa Beach blends into Melbourne Beach.

By the time you reach Route 518, the Eau Gallie Causeway, you may want to take a retreat to something more mentally satisfying in the charming, historic district of Eau Gallie.

### Brevard Museum of Art and Science Center (ages 5 to 13)

1463 Highland Avenue, Melbourne; (321) 242–0737. Open 10:00 a.m. to 5:00 p.m. Tuesday through Saturday and 1:00 to 5:00 p.m. Sunday. Admission is $5 for adults, $3 for seniors, $2 for students and children older than 2.

Sensory stimuli include feeling a dinosaur egg and tasting freeze-dried space food. The center also offers changing exhibits, field trips, films, and workshops.

### Brevard Zoo (all ages)

8225 North Wickham Road, Melbourne; off I-95's exit 73; (321) 254-9453; www.brevard zoo.org. Open 9:30 a.m. to 5:00 p.m. daily (gate closes at 4:15 p.m.). Admission is $10.50 for adults, $9.50 for seniors, $7.50 for children ages 2 to 12. Train fare is $3.00 for ages 2 and up. Kayak trips cost $5.00 per person.

Animals indigenous to Florida and Australia are at home here. See black jaguars, 600-pound tapirs, a giant anteater, kangaroos, dingoes, and two-toed sloths. At "Paws

On" kids can try to outrun an alligator or outjump a frog. "Animal Encounters" petting zoo, a mini-train, and otter feedings give the place a personal, interactive touch. The Wetlands Outpost provides the opportunity to kayak.

## For More Information

**Melbourne/Palm Bay Area Chamber of Commerce.** 1005 East Strawbridge Avenue, Melbourne 32901; (321) 724-5400 or (800) 771-9922; www.melpb-chamber .org.

# Sebastian

### Sebastian Inlet State Park (ages 5 to 13)

970 South Route A1A, Melbourne; (321) 984-4852 or (561) 589-9659 for camping. Open twenty-four hours daily. Park entrance is $5 per vehicle of eight persons or fewer; $1 per extra passenger, cyclist, or pedestrian, $3 for a single-occupancy vehicle or motorcycle.

The coast's fame for surfing and turtle nesting continues. The surfing reputation crests at Sebastian Inlet, which slices through the middle of this park. The north side of the 587-acre park attracts beachers, surfers, and picnickers. Surfing contests are hosted year-round. A rock-barricaded "pool" in the inlet provides safe swimming for tots. The park accommodates anglers and boaters with its jetties, bridge catwalks, a bait shop, and a marina with a boat ramp, boat tour of the Indian River, and canoe and kayak rentals. South of the inlet, a small campground draws mostly fishing types, while a day-use area beach (no admission fee) is great for snorkeling and diving. Snorkeling gear is for rent in the park. In summer rangers lead nighttime turtle walks to observe loggerheads and other sea turtles nesting on the beach.

### McLarty Treasure Museum (ages 7 to 13)

Sebastian Inlet State Park; 13180 Route A1A, Vero Beach; (772) 589-2147. Open 10:00 a.m. to 4:30 p.m. daily (last showing of the museum's film begins at 3:15 p.m.). Admission is $1 for persons ages 6 and older.

Part of the state park, the museum reveals the reason why this slice of coastline, from Sebastian Inlet south to Fort Pierce Inlet, is labeled the Treasure Coast. In 1715 a hurricane thrashed and dashed into the rocks a treasure-laden Spanish fleet returning from Mexico. Erected on the site of a Spanish salvage camp, the museum relates the story of the wreck and salvaging efforts and the Ais Indians who met the fleet's 1,500 survivors. It displays recovered treasure, from forks to pieces of eight. An observation deck lets you watch ongoing salvaging, most active in calm summer weather, or, if you're really lucky, migrating whales.

## For More Information

**Sebastian River Area Chamber of Commerce.** 700 Main Street, Sebastian 32958; (772) 589-5969; www.sebastian chamber.com.

# Vero Beach

About ten minutes south of Sebastian Inlet via Route A1A.

The true value of the Treasure Coast becomes apparent as you follow one of the most scenic portions of Route A1A south of Sebastian Inlet through Vero Beach to Fort Pierce Inlet.

North of Vero Beach along Indian River Shores, the beach parks are perfect for families: small, well maintained, and varied. Treasure Shores Park and Golden Sands County Park have playgrounds, lifeguards, picnic shelters, and barbecue grills. The wave action ranges from gentle to awesome. Admission and parking are **free.**

Vero Beach is a pretty, artsy town on its beach side, with lots of fun shops to explore. The beaches in the village are more crowded and narrow than those to the north. Jaycee Park, off Ocean Drive (Route A1A) at Mango Road, makes a nice picnic spot, with tables, grills, lots of trees, lifeguards on the beach, and a playground.

The town of Vero Beach spills onto the mainland, where museums and other cultural attractions await.

## Central Florida Surf School (ages 7 to 13)

**1085 Morningside Drive; (321) 727-8464; www.surfschoolcamp.com. Most lessons are held at Fort Pierce Inlet State Park. Private lessons start at $100 per hour, two-hour minimum. Group lessons are $130 for a five-hour day (9:30 a.m. to 2:30 p.m.).**

For one-on-one surfing lessons in the Vero Beach–Sebastian Inlet area, contact Lou Maresca at the Surf School. He also sells and rents equipment and rooms. Ask about summer and monthly camps.

## Dodgertown (ages 6 to 13)

**4401 Twenty-sixth Street; (772) 569-4900. Spring training tickets for the Dodgers are $18 to $20. Tickets for the Vero Beach Devil Rays (minor league) are $6 for adults, $5 for seniors and children ages 6 to 12; under 6 free. There is a summer sports camp for kids 14 and under ($110 for three days) and a one-week "fantasy" camp for adults (approximately $3,000; includes hotel and food).**

Mainland side, the star attraction is baseball, specifically Los Angeles Dodgers spring training baseball. In fact, the town derives much of its identity from the team, which has long had its headquarters here.

### Indian River Citrus Museum (ages 7 to 13)

**2140 Fourteenth Avenue, off Route 60 (Beachland Boulevard); (772) 770-2263. Open 10:00 a.m. to 4:00 p.m. Tuesday through Friday. Admission is by donation.**

In Indian River County, the other buzzword is *citrus*. Indian River produces some of the world's largest and juiciest oranges and grapefruit. How it won its reputation is the subject of photographs, antiques, farm tools, and memorabilia tracking the area's history from the early 1800s. You get a video viewing of modern-day techniques.

### Indian River County Historical Society Exhibit Center (ages 4 to 13) 

**2336 Fourteenth Avenue; (772) 778-3435. Open 10:00 a.m. to 4:00 p.m. Monday through Friday. Admission is free or by donation.**

If you're one who gets all steamed up over train memorabilia, you'll be happy here. It's set up in a historic railroad ticket office. You'll see a miniature railroad and other exhibits dealing with local history.

## Where to Eat

**Ocean Grill.** 1050 Sexton Plaza; (772) 231-5409. Overhanging the beach, a combination of nautical and medieval decor. Excellent lunches and seafood and steak dinners. Open for lunch Monday through Friday, dinner daily. Ask for a kids' menu. $$$–$$$$

## Where to Stay

**Disney's Vero Beach Resort.** 9250 Island Grove Terrace; (800) 359-8000; www.dvcresorts.com. Part of the Disney Vacation Club network; 115-room inn with minigolf course, slide pool, restaurants, tennis, basketball, play area, river cruises. $$$–$$$$

**Driftwood Resort.** 3150 Ocean Drive; (772) 231-0550. Funky place that began in the early 1900s as a way to put washed-up beach debris to use (thus, its name). Standard rooms, efficiencies, two-bedroom apartments—each with its own personality. Swimming pools and restaurant. $$–$$$$

## For More Information

**Vero Beach–Indian River County Chamber of Commerce.** 1216 Twenty-first Street, Vero Beach 32960; (772) 567-3491; www.IndianRiverChamber.com.

# Fort Pierce

As you follow Route A1A, Fort Pierce begins on the south end of North Hutchinson Island, continues across the bridge (known as the North Bridge) onto the mainland (where A1A briefly merges with Highway 1), and spreads to still another island, the north end of Hutchinson Island, back on Route A1A. The bridge that crosses to Hutchinson is known as the South Bridge.

The Fort Pierce portion of Hutchinson Island (which also holds the beach adjuncts of Jensen Beach and Stuart) is the most developed, freckled with small resorts, surf shops, restaurants, and other tourism-related places. It has its share of beaches, with extensive boardwalks and picnic and fishing facilities.

### Pepper Park (all ages)
**3300 North Route A1A, North Hutchinson Island. Open dawn to dusk daily.**

A top choice for family recreation, it takes up both sides of the road, spreading from ocean to bayfront. The ocean part is older, with a nice beach and timeworn facilities, including tennis and basketball courts and picnic pavilions. Lifeguards supervise on the beach. The other side of the road crosses into a world tailor-made for fishing, hiking, canoeing, boating, and picnicking. Two boat docks, one of them for canoes, and six fishing piers reach into Wildcat Cove.

### UDT-SEAL Museum (ages 7 to 13)
**3300 North A1A; (772) 595-5845. Open 10:00 a.m. to 4:00 p.m. Tuesday through Saturday (also Monday, January through April) and noon to 4:00 p.m. Sunday. Admission is $6 for adults, $3 for children ages 6 to 12.**

Within Pepper Park you can visit a museum that deals with a most unusual aspect of local history—the training of Navy frogmen in 1943 for the D-Day invasion. It tells the story of Underwater Demolition Teams and the Navy's SEAL (Sea Air and Land) program. Outside, a collection of specialized naval watercraft, a helicopter, and other large specimens begin this foray into special naval tactics.

### Jack Island Preserve (ages 10 to 13)
**Off Route A1A (watch carefully for the entrance signs). Open 8:00 a.m. to sunset daily. Admission is free.**

Part of Fort Pierce Inlet State Park (see page 96), it juts into the Indian River. You can hike the peninsula's diked perimeter or trek into its center via a mile-long mangrove wetlands trail.

## Fort Pierce Inlet State Park (ages 4 to 13) 🅰

Southernmost end of North Hutchinson Island; 905 Shore Winds Drive; (772) 468-3985. Open 8:00 a.m. to sunset daily. Park entrance is $5 per vehicle of eight persons or fewer; $1 per extra passenger, cyclist, or pedestrian; $3 per single occupancy vehicle.

This is the place to go for beach recreation off the main road. You and the kids can sun yourselves on a choice of two beaches, fish, surf, have a picnic, hike into a coastal hammock, or play on the playground. Inlet Beach fronts the pass between North Hutchinson and Hutchinson Islands. Swift waters mean unsafe swimming conditions. On the ocean side, Jetty Park (aka North Beach) is protected from waves by its fishing jetty, making it safer for children. Lifeguards are on duty for added protection.

## Harbor Branch Oceanographic Institution (ages 10 and up)

5600 Highway 1 North; about fifteen minutes north of the North Bridge Causeway on the mainland; (772) 465-2400; www.hboi.edu. Open 10:00 a.m. to 5:00 p.m. Monday through Friday. Admission is **free.**

Harbor Branch is one of the leading centers for exploration of the world's oceans. Learn about the vital role our oceans play in almost every aspect of our lives, even if we call Nebraska or North Dakota home. Displays, interactive exhibits, and videos inform and entertain. At the new Ocean Discovery Center you can become a "Marine Biologist in Training."

## St. Lucie County Historical Museum (ages 4 to 13) 🅒

414 Seaway Drive; off Route A1A alongside the South Bridge; (772) 462-1795. Open 10:00 a.m. to 4:00 p.m. Tuesday through Saturday and noon to 4:00 p.m. Sunday. Admission is $4.00 for adults, $1.50 for children ages 6 to 17; under 6 **free.**

At the north end of Hutchinson Island, take another peek at citrus and its local importance. Nicely framed vignettes show other aspects of local history, too, including one devoted to the sixteenth-century shipwreck of a Spanish treasure fleet and another of a Seminole Indian camp. Kids will love the 1919 fire engine and charming little pioneer home. The museum is located next to a waterfront park where you can picnic and fish.

## Florida **Trivia**

**Cocoons of the Deep** Harbor Branch Oceanographic Institution is known for its underwater research using manned submersibles, like the one used to explore the *Titanic* wreck. Its displays show the Link Trainer, a submersible simulator that is predecessor to today's amusement park motion simulator rides.

### Beach Horseback Riding (ages 10 and up)
Frederick Douglass Memorial Park, 3500 South A1A; (772) 468-0101. Rides available 10:00 and 11:30 a.m. and 1:00, 2:30, and 3:30 p.m. on the first, second, and fourth Sunday of each month. Cost is $35 per person. Reservations required.

Hoof it down a stretch of pristine beach.

## Where to Eat

**Mangrove Mattie's.** 1640 Seaway Drive (Hutchinson Island); (772) 466-1044. Seafood and pasta, and a picture-window view of Fort Pierce Inlet, beachers, and boat traffic. Lunch and dinner daily. $$–$$$

## For More Information

**St. Lucie County Tourist Bureau.** 2300 Virginia Avenue, Fort Pierce 34982; (772) 462-1535 or (800) 345-TGIF; www.visitst luciefla.com.

# Jensen Beach

Take Route A1A ten minutes south of Fort Pierce on Hutchinson Island. To get to the mainland, cross the Intracoastal Waterway at Route 732.

Things get much quieter as you head south down Hutchinson Island. You'll see signs for beach accesses every few miles. Many have limited or no facilities and are favored by surfers and solitude-seekers.

### Sea Turtle Beach (all ages)
Jensen Beach Causeway at Route A1A. Open 8:00 a.m. to 8:00 p.m. daily.

This is the best beach for families who appreciate lots of activities. The vast stretch, 1,500 feet long, has lifeguards, extensive food concessions, volleyball, and picnic tables. The park manages to remain in a nicely maintained natural state despite its popularity.

### Rosemeyer's Boat Rental (all ages)
Across the Jensen Beach Causeway at Jensen Beach Boulevard and Northeast Indian River Drive; 3321 Northeast Indian River Drive; (772) 334-1000. Open 8:00 a.m. to 5:00 p.m. daily.

On-the-water opportunities are abundant on this part of the coast. Diving, surfing, windsurfing, and fishing—both deep-sea and back-bay—provide endless adventure of the $H_2O$ variety. Create your own adventures with a boat rental from Rosemeyer's.

# The Day My Son **Joined the Circus**

Aaron had just turned eight, but a shy and awfully cautious eight. That's why it came as such a surprise when he grabbed the Club Med "Dolphins" (ages eight to twelve) Mini-Club activity sheet from my hand and proclaimed he would do the waterskiing, scuba diving, water polo, and circus.

Although parents aren't allowed, I snuck in to watch the daily circus practice under the guise of a travel writer. Run by circus professionals from around the world, it was no wimpy pretend circus. Kids were hanging from trapeze swings, others were doing flips off the trampoline, all practicing for the big show Thursday night. The next time we visited Club Med, Aaron had aged a year and the resort had added excitement in the form of a half-pipe (artificial competition ramp). He had the extra thrill of meeting and watching a performance by Tony Hawk, a member of Club Med's champion extreme and professional sports team. With its skating ramp, Club Med offers lessons for older kids with a yen to go pro.

*—C.K.W.*

## Club Med Sandpiper ⊖

**Northwest of Jensen Beach at 3500 S.E. Morningside Boulevard, Port St. Lucie; (772) 398-5100 or (800) 258-2633; www.clubmed.com.**

It is one of the few Florida resorts with a kids' program that includes infants, ages four to twenty-three months. Kids as young as four years old can get their fins wet on the Scuba Experience. The resort also caters to older children and adults, with circus courses in juggling, trapeze, and clowning. Each Thursday night the kids put on a circus under the real Big Top. Like all Club Meds, the emphasis is on activity, and there is plenty to do at this riverside property with its golf, river beach, swimming pools, trampoline, fitness center, sailing and waterskiing lessons, tennis courts, in-line skating and half-pipe ramp, pitch-and-putt course, basketball, volleyball, and beach shuttle. It has a French flair, and kids get exposed to people from many cultures. Ask about special family plans. $$$$ (Rates are per adult and include all meals and activities.)

## Where to Eat

**Conchy Joe's.** 3945 Northeast Indian River Drive; just across and north of the Jensen Beach Causeway; (772) 334-1130. Seafood and ribs. Bahamian style with view of the Indian River. Kids' menu. Lunch and dinner daily. $$–$$$

## For More Information

**Jensen Beach Chamber of Commerce.** 1910 Northeast Jensen Beach Boulevard, Jensen Beach 34957; (772) 334-3444; www.jensenchamber.com.

# Stuart

Just south of Jensen Beach along Route A1A. Downtown centers around Osceola Avenue, north of and parallel to Route A1A.

Downtown Stuart has a rejuvenated appeal to shoppers and historians, but getting there from Hutchinson Island can be confusing. There's even an intersection called Confusion Corner. Most visitors, however, head to the beach, which occupies the southernmost portion of Hutchinson Island.

### Stuart Beach (all ages)

**Route A1A. Open sunrise to sunset. Admission is free.**

Families love Stuart Beach, and why not? It has everything you could ever hope to find on a Florida beach: lifeguards, an outdoor cafe, a playground, a nature interpretation station, picnic shelters with grills, a volleyball net, basketball courts, and a concession where you can rent boogieboards, volleyballs, and basketballs.

### Elliott Museum (ages 7 to 13)

**825 Northeast Ocean Boulevard; (772) 225-1961; www.elliottmuseum.goodnature.org. Open 10:00 a.m. to 4:00 p.m. Monday through Saturday and 1:00 to 4:00 p.m. Sunday. Admission is $6 for adults, $2 for children ages 6 to 13.**

On park grounds at Stuart Beach, this museum presents a curious assortment of inventions by Sterling Elliott, including the stamp machine, automatic knot-tyer, and four-wheel bicycle. There's also an impressive, eclectic collection of classic automobiles and Indian artifacts, and a vintage general store.

### Florida Oceanographic Coastal Center (ages 4 to 13)

**890 Northeast Ocean Boulevard (Route A1A); (772) 225-0505; www.fosusa.org. Open 10:00 a.m. to 5:00 p.m. Monday through Saturday and noon to 4:00 p.m. Sunday. Admission is $8 for adults, $4 for children ages 3 to 12.**

Touch tanks, aquariums, a mounted fish collection, interactive puzzles and activities, and guided nature walks acquaint youngsters with local sea and land habitat and inhabitants.

# East Central **Climes**

Temperatures average between 62 to 88 degrees along this spell of coastline and are generally more temperate than inland since air and water temperatures are moderated by the Gulf Stream. The average yearly humidity is 76 percent. Summer, of course, is hottest, most humid, and rainiest, but showers are usually brief. Winters may require long sleeves and pants legs, especially in the evening, but usually allow a just share of swimsuit time. Statistics show that the region enjoys an average of 230 days of sunshine per year.

### Hutchinson Island Marriott
**555 Northeast Ocean Boulevard; (772) 225-3700 or (800) 775-5936.**

Among Florida's top family destination resorts, 200 acres large, the Marriott is well respected for its golfing and kids' programs. There's a marina, four restaurants, bars, swimming pools, thirteen tennis courts, and any number of rental options, many of which front the beach. $$$–$$$$

### *Island Princess* (ages 5 to 13)
**Hutchinson Island Marriott, 555 Northeast Ocean Boulevard; (772) 225-2100. Cost of nature tour is $18.95 for adults, $14.50 for children under age 10.**

This yacht departs from the marina for several excursions. Recommended for children is Wednesday's two-hour nature cruise. You need not be a resort guest to enjoy it.

### Gilbert's Bar House of Refuge (ages 7 to 13)
**301 Southeast McArthur Boulevard; off Route A1A; (772) 225-1875. Open 10:00 a.m. to 4:00 p.m. Monday through Saturday and 1:00 to 4:00 p.m. Sunday. Admission is $4 for adults, $2 for children ages 6 to 13.**

Another unusual museum, this one dwells in a structure that once harbored nineteenth-century shipwreck survivors along these often cruel shores. The only remaining such structure where once stood ten, it today harbors turn-of-the-twentieth-century period furnishings from the time the Bessie family manned the lifesaving facility.

### Bathtub Reef Beach (all ages)
**Southeast McArthur Boulevard.**

A favorite of families with small kids, it lives up to its name: A rare marine-worm reef creates a calm pond of Atlantic waters. However, facilities are a bit shabbier than at other local beaches. Lifeguards are around at peak activity periods. Posted notices warn of possible swimming dangers and surf conditions.

## Where to Eat

**Prawnbroker Grill.** Harbour Bay Plaza, 3754 Southeast Ocean Boulevard; (772) 288-1222. Specializing in fresh seafood and steaks, with creative nightly specials and kids' menu. Dinner daily. $$$

## For More Information

**Stuart/Martin County Chamber of Commerce.** 1650 South Kanner Highway, Stuart 34994; (772) 287-1088 or (800) 524-9704; www.goodnature.org.

# Hobe Sound

Head south on Route A1A, also known as Dixie Highway, about fifteen minutes from Hutchinson Island.

The teeny town of Hobe Sound makes a pleasant stop for antiques and crafts shoppers. Outside of town, the community is known for its natural treasures. Route 707 takes you through Jupiter Island with its mansions and its preserved beaches.

### Blowing Rocks Preserve (ages 7 and up)

On Jupiter Island, 574 South Beach Road, Hobe Sound; (561) 744-6668. Open 9:00 a.m. to 4:30 p.m. daily. Beach access fee $2 per person; **free** for children 12 and under. Guided nature walks on Sunday at 11:00 a.m.

Blowing Rocks is named for the 50-foot plumes forced up after storms or during high tides. The preserve has beach dunes, mangrove wetlands, and tropical and upland trees. There is a butterfly garden with native plants.

### Hobe Sound National Wildlife Refuge (ages 7 to 13)

Visitor center at 13640 Southeast Federal Highway; (772) 546-2067. The center is open 9:00 a.m. to 3:00 p.m. Monday through Friday. Admission is **free.** The island portion of the refuge is open sunrise to sunset daily. Admission to the refuge's beach portion, which lies on the north end of Jupiter Island (take Route 707/Bridge Road, east from Route A1A), is $5 per car.

It hosts environmental education programs, summer kids' camps, nature hikes, exhibits, and sea-turtle walks. Its beach is a prime nesting site for sea turtles. The tiny but packed full interpretative center on the mainland contains a big, old, soft vinyl manatee toy and glass boxes filled with a baby alligator, a baby crocodile, and snakes. Easy nature trails take you around the placid waterfront.

## Jonathan Dickinson State Park (ages 5 to 13)

16450 Southeast Federal Highway (Highway 1); (772) 546-2771. Open 8:00 a.m. to sunset daily. Park entrance is $4 per vehicle of eight persons or fewer, $1 per extra passenger, cyclist, or pedestrian.

Many people overlook Jonathan Dickinson because it lacks beaches. Its treasures are estuarine instead. Take the family there to camp, rent a cabin, hike, canoe, or enjoy pontoon tours into its 11,600 acres of forest—host to wildlife such as deer and Florida scrub jays.

## Loxahatchee River Adventures (ages 6 to 13)

Jonathan Dickinson State Park; 16450 Southeast Federal Highway; (561) 746-1466. Tours depart at 9:00 and 11:00 a.m. and 1:00 and 3:00 p.m. daily. Cost is $14.50 for adults, $9.50 for children ages 6 to 12, plus the car entrance fee to the park. Canoe rentals available beginning at $14 for two hours and $5 for each additional hour.

Guided pontoon rides from the park on the wild and scenic Loxahatchee River are provided four times daily.

# More Things to See and Do **in East Central Florida**

- **Ormond Memorial Art Museum and Gardens,** Ormond Beach; (386) 676-3347
- **Pirate's Cove Adventure Golf,** Ormond Beach; (386) 676-9326
- **Safari River Tours,** Debary; (386) 668-1002
- **Atlantic Race Park,** Daytona Beach Shores; (386) 226-8777
- **Speed Park Motorsports,** Daytona Beach; (386) 253-FAST
- **New Smyrna Speedway,** New Smyrna; (386) 427-4129
- **Andretti Thrill Park,** Melbourne; (321) 956-6706
- **Brevard Museum of Art and Science,** Melbourne; (321) 242-0737
- **Mel Fisher's Treasure Museum,** Sebastian; (772) 589-9875
- **Manatee Observation and Education Center,** Fort Pierce; (772) 466-1600, ext. 3071
- **New York Mets Spring Training,** Port St. Lucie; (772) 871-2115
- **Maritime and Yachting Museum,** Jensen Beach; (772) 692-1234
- **Stuart Heritage Museum,** Stuart; (772) 220-4600

## For More Information

**Hobe Sound Chamber of Commerce.** 8994 Southeast Bridge Road (P.O. Box 1507), Hobe Sound 33475; (772) 546-4724; www.hobesound.org.

## Annual Events

**Blue Spring Manatee Festival.** Orange City; (386) 775-3663. In January the park cohosts the Blue Spring Manatee Festival with entertainment, endangered species exhibits, and tours.

**Seafest.** Port Canaveral; (321) 459-2200. Seafood, arts, crafts, and entertainment three days in late March.

**Daytona 500 NASCAR Stock Car Races.** Daytona Beach; (386) 253-7223. The biggest motor sports event in Florida, held in April.

**Ron Jon's/Robert August Easter Surfing Festival.** Cocoa Beach; (321) 452-4145. Spring contests, entertainment, fun.

# Central
# Florida

Tourism in central Florida is dominated by the world of Disney and the kids' fantasy land of amusement parks that have sprung up on its shirttails. The Orlando-Kissimmee hub can provide enough for a month's worth of family vacation, if you and your wallet could take it.

You don't have to travel far from Walt Disney World and the Orlando area to find the real Florida, minus the animatronics. In the region's farthest reaches, you can discover snatches of the old Cracker days, when cowboys and orange growers scratched a living out of the swamps and prairies. Here, along the shores of year-round warm springs, Florida tourism was born.

# TopPicks for Family Fun in Central Florida

1. Cavorting with Mickey Mouse at the Magic Kingdom, Walt Disney World

2. Riding the movies at Universal Studios Orlando

3. Entering the funny-paper world of Islands of Adventure, Orlando

4. Seeing 3-D at Disney–MGM Studios, Walt Disney World

5. Looking into the future at EPCOT, Walt Disney World

6. Exploring underwater secrets at SeaWorld Adventure Park, Orlando

7. Kissing a dolphin at Discovery Cove, Orlando

8. Being a "science guy" (or gal) at Orlando Science Center, Orlando

9. Peeking into Florida's past at the Florida Museum of Natural History, Gainesville

# CENTRAL FLORIDA

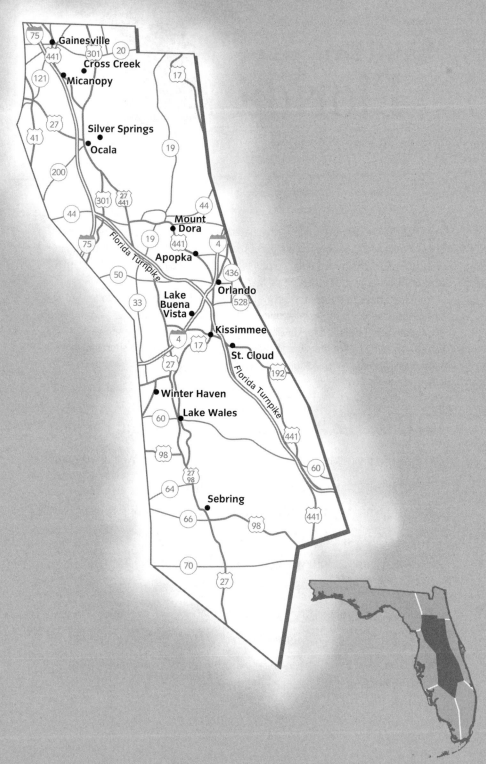

This tour of central Florida takes you to both extremes—the time-frozen temperament and the futuristic facade.

# Gainesville and Environs

East of Interstate 75 at Highway 441.

Gainesville, once ranked the nation's best place to live by *Money* magazine, is first and foremost a college town, home of the University of Florida Gators—and birthplace of Gatorade! This keeps it youthful, spirited, and cultured. Natural attractions in its northern and southern environs keep it bonded to the environment.

### Devil's Millhopper State Geological Park (ages 5 to 13)
4732 Millhopper Road (Route 232); (352) 955-2008; administrative office: 12720 Northwest 109th Lane; (386) 462-7905. Open 9:00 a.m. to 5:00 p.m. Wednesday through Sunday; closed Monday and Tuesday. Make reservations for a free ranger-guided tour on Saturday at 10:00 a.m. by calling (386) 462-7905. Admission to the site is $2 per vehicle or $1 per pedestrian or bicyclist.

Here is a special place where waterfalls and lush fern growth make you feel as though you've stumbled into the Garden of Eden. The unusual landscaping is due to a five-acre, 120-foot-deep sinkhole—232 steps to the bottom!

### San Felasco Hammock State Preserve (ages 5 to 13)
Route 232, 4 miles northwest of town; 12720 Northwest 109th Lane, Alachua; (386) 462-7905. Open 8:00 a.m. to sunset daily. Park entrance is $2 per vehicle of eight persons or fewer, $1 per extra passenger, cyclist, or pedestrian.

This park presents still another unusual face of natural Florida, where springs play hide-and-seek amid the honeycombed limestone foundation and more than 150 species of trees occupy the forest along a nature trail. Wild turkeys, white-tailed deer, and bobcats also dwell here.

### Florida Museum of Natural History (ages 4 to 13)
University of Florida, UF Cultural Plaza, Hull Road and Southwest Thirty-fourth Street, Gainesville; (352) 846-2000; www.flmnh.ufl.edu. Open 10:00 a.m. to 5:00 p.m. Monday through Saturday and noon to 5:00 p.m. Sunday and holidays. Closed Thanksgiving and Christmas Day. Admission is free, but there may be fees for special exhibits.

This newly rebuilt museum teaches young learners about northern Florida limestone-based geology and the region's incredible dunes. Special exhibits rotate through the year. It's a not-to-be-missed attraction in Gainesville, with permanent exhibits showing ancient civilizations and fossils, a walk-through cave, and an Indian village. Among the new additions is a butterfly rain forest.

# Road **Markers**

This excursion roughly follows Highway 441 from the Gainesville area south to Orlando, then along Interstate 4 through Kissimmee, and south on Highway 27 into the state's quirky midsection.

I-4 between Orlando and Tampa, often under construction (especially at the west end), can be a nightmare to drive, particularly in winter season. The construction is widening the road, so hopefully more lanes will disperse the traffic before the traffic catches up with the upgrade. In the meantime, it's best to avoid that route and take Highway 27 south, even if it does wind through towns and stoplights.

### Morningside Nature Center (ages 5 to 13)
3540 East University Avenue, Gainesville; (352) 334-2170; www.natureoperations.org. Open 9:00 a.m. to 5:00 p.m. daily. Admission to park and farm is **free.** Reenactments held Saturday, except in summer.

Costumed actors re-create the lifestyles of a nineteenth-century farmer in its ten-acre Living History Farm, with an 1840 cabin and other vintage structures. Also in the 278-acre park, 5 miles of trails travel through cypress and pine forests, where more than 130 species of birds live. Spy some from the wildlife observation blind.

### Santa Fe Community College Teaching Zoo (ages 4 to 13)
3000 Northwest Eighty-third Street, Gainesville (near I-75); (352) 395-5611. Open 9:00 a.m. to 2:00 p.m. Saturday and Sunday, Monday through Friday by appointment. Admission is **free.**

You can see endangered and other animals from around the world.

### Paynes Prairie Preserve State Park (ages 5 to 13)
South of town on Highway 441; 100 Savannah Boulevard, Micanopy; (352) 466-3397. The visitor center is open 9:00 a.m. to 4:00 p.m. daily. The park is open daily from 8:00 a.m. to sunset. Park entrance is $4 per vehicle of eight persons or fewer, $1 per extra passenger, cyclist, or pedestrian.

It introduces visitors to northern Florida's social and natural history with inside exhibits and outdoor nature trails, living history, biking, canoeing, and camping. Sandhill cranes and alligators are common to its 22,000 acres of predominantly marshy terrain, plus the kids can try spotting American bison and Spanish horses. A visitor center with museum traces the region's Amerindian roots.

## Gainesville to Hawthorne Rail Trail (ages 8 to 13)

**Parking at 3400 Southeast Fifteenth Street. Parking and access to the trailhead is open 8:00 a.m. to sunset daily.**

The 17-mile trail begins at Boulware Springs City Park and takes you through the Paynes Prairie wilderness to the town of Hawthorne. There are restrooms at mile 1 and mile 6.6.

## Marjorie Kinnan Rawlings State Historic Park (ages 10 to 13)

**Route 325, 21 miles southeast of Gainesville at Cross Creek; (352) 466-3672. The grounds are open 9:00 a.m. to 5:00 p.m. daily. You can enter the home by tour only, conducted every hour on the hour (except noon) from 10:00 a.m. to 4:00 p.m. Thursday through Sunday (except August and September). Admission to the park is $2 per person; tours of the home are $3 for adults, $2 for children 6 to 12, and free for children under 6.**

Prepare the kids with readings from *The Yearling*, then proceed to the home where the author once lived the spartan life. She's the region's local hero, and guides at the site dress in period costume to relate her life of farming oranges, hunting gators, and cooking cooter (turtle). Arrive early in the day because tours are limited in number, which means a long wait as the day rolls on.

## Micanopy

As you make your way south on Highway 411, stop in Micanopy, where tourism first hit Florida. Today the town, which strings along Cholokka Boulevard parallel to the highway, has turned into a restored enclave for artisans and antiques vendors. Some of the shops sell vintage toys.

## Where to Eat

**Emiliano's Cafe and Bakery.** 7 Southeast First Avenue, Gainesville; (352) 375-7381. Redbrick walls, a bakery, and sidewalk seating. Specialties have a Cuban-Caribbean flair. Lunch and dinner Tuesday through Saturday. $–$$

**Harry's.** 110 Southeast First Street, Gainesville; (352) 372-1555. Cajun-style po'boys, soups, and other dishes in a New Orleans setting with sidewalk seating. Lunch and dinner daily. $–$$

## Where to Stay

Lodging is typically inexpensive in Gainesville.

**Bambi Motel Budget Host.** 2119 Southwest Thirteenth Street, Gainesville; (352) 376-2622 or (800) 34-BAMBI. Playground, pool, and thirty-four rooms. $

## For More Information

**Alachua County Visitors and Convention Bureau.** 30 East University Avenue, Gainesville 32601; (352) 374-5231 or (866) 778-5002; www.visitGainesville.net.

# Ocala

About 35 miles south of Gainesville on Highway 441 or I-75.

One of the nicest ways to spend time in Ocala is looking at the scenery, whether from a car, a bike, or horseback.

### Horse Farms (all ages)

Horses are a recurring theme around town. The area's 400-plus horse farms raise 10 percent of North America's thoroughbred race horses and provide some of the hill-heaving countryside's prettiest sights. Highways 441 and 301, and Routes 220, 225, 225A, and 475A are among the most scenic. Some of the farms allow visitors to tour. To tour the countryside by horse and buggy, call Ocala Carriage & Tours; (352) 867-8717; www.ocalacarriage.com. The company offers an hour carriage ride in the country for four, priced at $95. Reservations only.

### Young's Paso Fino Ranch (ages 6 to 13)

**8075 Northwest Route 326; (352) 867-5305. Seventy-five-minute trail rides start at 9:00 and 11:00 a.m. and 1:00 p.m. Monday through Saturday. Cost is $38 per rider, and riders must be age 6 or up. Tours of the horse barns are $7.50 per person, 10:00 a.m. and 2:00 p.m. Monday through Saturday.**

To actually ride a horse in these parts, stop here. You can take a tour of the barn, follow a wooded trail astride a gentle Paso Fino horse, or sit in on a horse show with dancing and live music. Children ages four or above are welcome, but they must be six or older to ride. Go in the spring when the foals are born, or in the summer for special kids' programs.

### Don Garlits Museum of Drag Racing (ages 5 to 13)

**13700 Southwest Sixteenth Avenue; (352) 245-8661. Open 9:00 a.m. to 5:00 p.m. daily. Admission is $15 for adults, $13 for seniors and students, $6 for children 5 to 12; under 5 free.**

Race fans of a different stripe will want to look at the retired dragsters and the antique automobile displays here.

### Discovery Science Center (all ages)

**1211 Southeast Twenty-second Road; (352) 401-3900. Open 9:00 a.m. to 4:00 p.m. Tuesday through Friday; closed Saturday, Sunday, and Monday. Admission is $2.**

Dress up like a firefighter—hose and all—or run your own veterinary "office." There's also a hands-on "weather station" connected to various interactive computer exhibits children will like. Put on your own puppet show at the museum's stage area, or enjoy the outside exhibits, including a former limestone quarry with a partial boardwalk that will help your kids blow off steam.

# Movie **Star**

Silver Springs has starred in more movies and television shows than Harrison Ford. Six Tarzan movies, *Creature from the Black Lagoon*, *The Yearling*, *Never Say Never Again*, and *Smokey and the Bandit* are among major films shot on location at the park. It also starred in the *Sea Hunt* television series, episodes of *I Spy*, *One Life to Live*, National Geographic specials, and other movies, TV shows, and commercials dating back to the silent movie *The Seven Swans* in 1916.

## Silver Springs (all ages)

1 mile east of Ocala on Route 40; 5656 East Silver Springs Boulevard, Silver Springs; (352) 236-2121; www.silversprings.com. Open 10:00 a.m. to 5:00 p.m. daily. General admission is $33.99 for adults, $30.99 for seniors, $24.99 for children ages 3 to 10; under 3 **free.** Includes boat rides and entrance into the museums and other attractions. Parking is $7.

One of the original glass-bottom boat rides took early visitors through the jungles and over the clear spring waters of Silver Springs. Florida's first tourist attraction continually grows and has kept up with the times by adding a petting zoo, a Jeep safari, World of Bears, and Panther Prowl. The squeamish will want to sidestep the "Creature Feature" show, starring scorpions, bats, and giant Madagascar hissing cockroaches. Don't miss the white alligator exhibit. Big Gator Lagoon is home to more than twenty gators and crocodiles. Once the site of *Tarzan* filming, the park hosts a healthy population of free-roaming monkeys in addition to its contained animals. The tiny tots will like the playland. You can dine at one of seven food outlets; no food or drink is allowed to be brought into the park (except bottled water). Call for a schedule of special entertainment events.

## Wild Waters Water Park (ages 4 to 13)

At Silver Springs; (352) 236-2121; www.wildwaterspark.com. Open in warm months, generally sometime in March to sometime in September, 10:00 a.m. to 6:00 p.m. Admission is $23.99 plus tax for adults, $20.99 for children shorter than 48 inches. **Free** to those 2 and younger. Parking costs $7.

Have a wet blast on the water slides and flumes—Thunderbolt, Hurricane, Silver Bullet, Osceola's Revenge, or Twin Twister—or in the wave pool with tubes. Tots can slide down a frog's tongue or play in the Cool Kids Cove. The Caribbean Sprayground squirts 'em down with misters and fountains.

### Juniper Springs (all ages)

**Route 40 east of Ocala; 3199 Northeast County Road 315, Silver Springs; (352) 625-3147 or (352) 236-0288. The park and its visitor information center are open daily 8:00 A.M. to 8:00 P.M. Park entrance fee is $4 per person over age 5.**

The Ocala area has it up on all other parts of central Florida as far as natural attractions go. The continental United States' southernmost national forest, Ocala National Forest, is a 400,000-acre refuge for wildlife and sportsfolk alike. A gurgling land of warm (72-degree) springs and sand pines, it offers camping, swimming, hiking trails, wildlife sighting, canoeing, and diving in several recreational areas. Most popular and scenic is Juniper Springs, where an ancient waterwheel-powered mill edges see-through waters. A 7-mile canoe run takes you past alligators, limpkins, turtles, and other wildlife.

## Where to Eat

**Harry's.** 24 Southeast First Avenue; (352) 840-0900. Jambalaya, red beans and rice, seafood gumbo, po'boys, and other Cajun specialties. Lunch and dinner daily. $–$$

## For More Information

**Ocala–Marion County Chamber of Commerce.** 110 East Silver Springs Boulevard, Ocala 34470; (352) 629-8051; fax (352) 629-7651; www.ocalacc.com.

## Where to Stay

**Holiday Inn–Silver Springs.** 5751 East Silver Springs Boulevard, Silver Springs; (352) 236-2575 or (800) HOLIDAY. One hundred and three rooms, pool, and restaurant. $

# Mount Dora

Take Highway 441 south of Ocala 45 miles.

A picture-pretty town that refuses to join the twenty-first century, Mount Dora provides a restful contrast to the flurry of activity that awaits to the south. Downtown is a baker's window full of Victorian wedding-cake homes and browsable antiques shops. The chamber of commerce hands out historic tour maps.

### *Miss Dora* (ages 5 to 13)

**Gator Inlet Marina; 1505 Highway 441, Tavares; (352) 343-0200. Departs at 11:00 a.m. and 2:00 p.m. Monday to Saturday, 1:00 and 3:00 p.m. Sunday. Fare is $15 for adults, $10 for children ages 3 to 10; under 3 free.**

To see Mount Dora's wild side, take this sixteen-person pontoon boat canal tour between two lakes—Eustis and Dora—decorated with cypress trees and birds.

## Where to Eat

**The Gables Restaurant.** 322 Alexander Street; (352) 383-8993. Salads, burgers, sandwiches, and entrees. Seating indoors and outdoors in the garden. Lunch and dinner daily. $–$$

## Where to Stay

**Lakeside Inn.** 100 North Alexander Street; (352) 383-4101. Pretty historic property on the lake with pool, restaurant, lounge, tennis courts, nearby shopping, and a boardwalk to a natural island on the lake. $–$$$

## For More Information

**Mount Dora Area Chamber of Commerce.** 341 Alexander Street (P.O. Box 196), Mount Dora 32757; (352) 383-2165; fax (352) 383-1668; www.mountdora.com.

# Orlando

Located at the crossroads of I-4 and the Florida Turnpike. From Mount Dora, continue along Highway 441 for about a half hour to reach I-4.

Vacationland of the world, Orlando and its attractions come in two parts. Downtown you'll find culture, museums, and the showtime atmosphere of Church Street Station and environs.

Orlando's most publicized attractions and resorts lie south of downtown on the west side of town, along I-4 and International Drive. Although Disney World is not actually contained within Orlando, it affects it deeply, and most people associate it with Orlando. The city itself was a quiet little town that went bonkers in 1971, when Disney moved in. The whole south end of town rides like an amusement park where sky beams, neon lights, larger-than-life sneakers and teddy bears, and sinking and upside-down buildings fight for your attention. It's a stream of fun, but be prepared to pay and stand in line for it.

## Central Florida **Climes**

The average temperature ranges from 50 to 90 degrees. Humidity ranges from 55 to 88 percent. Winter months average daytime highs of 70 with low humidity. Thunderstorms cool hot, humid summer days. Be sure to take shelter at the first sound of an approaching thunderstorm, as central Florida is the nation's lightning capital.

## Kelly Park (all ages)

**North of Orlando in Apopka; 400 Kelly Park Road, Apopka; (407) 889-4179. Admission is $1. Free for children ages 5 and under.**

Cool off in an inner tube or just a swimsuit. Picnic tables, grills, nature trails, volleyball courts, and horseshoes make for an old-fashioned family fun day. You can even camp overnight.

## Wekiwa Springs State Park (all ages)

**Wekiwa Springs Road between Apopka and I-4; 1800 Wekiwa Circle, Apopka; (407) 884-2009. Open 8:00 a.m. to sunset daily. Park entrance is $5 per vehicle of eight persons or fewer, $1 per extra passenger, cyclist, or pedestrian.**

Another cool place for a summer swim, it provides a playground, canoeing, hiking, picnicking, and camping within its 6,900 acres.

## Mennello Museum of American Folk Art (ages 5 to 13)

**900 East Princeton Street; (407) 246-4278; www.mennellomuseum.com. Open 10:30 a.m. to 4:30 p.m. Tuesday through Saturday, noon to 4:30 P.M. Sunday. Admission is $4 for adults, $3 for seniors; under 12 free.**

For a day of culture, head to the Loch Haven neighborhood with its science museum, galleries, and other attractions. This small museum offers a dose in child-bright colors and an outdoor sculpture garden on the lake, featuring the work of Earl Cunningham and changing exhibits.

## Amway Arena (ages 6 to 13)

**8600 West Amelia Street; 1 block off I-4; (407) 89-MAGIC or (800) 338-0005; www .orlandomagic.com. Off-season (single game) ticket prices from $10 to $95.**

Basketball fans travel far (without penalty) to watch the Orlando Magic at Amway, formerly the T. D. Waterhouse Centre. The NBA team plays October through April.

# Top Family **Resorts**

1. **Holiday Inn Family Suites,** Lake Buena Vista

2. **Portofino Bay Hotel,** Universal Orlando

3. **Holiday Inn Sunspree,** Lake Buena Vista

4. **Hyatt Regency Grand Cypress,** Lake Buena Vista

5. **Grand Floridian,** Walt Disney World

6. **Polynesian Resort,** Walt Disney World

## Orlando Science Center (ages 4 to 13)

777 East Princeton Street; (407) 514-2000 or (888) 672-4386; www.osc.org. Open 10:00 a.m. to 6:00 p.m. Sunday through Thursday and 10:00 a.m. to 9:00 p.m. Friday and Saturday. Admission is $14.95 for adults, $13.95 for seniors, $9.95 for children 3 to 11; 2 and under free. On Friday and Saturday admission is lower after 6:00 p.m.

With all the flash and spark of Orlando, it winds you around four floors of touch, poke, and play exhibits. Lift a Volkswagen Beetle, walk into a giant mouth, spin a cloud, stick your head into a tornado, and stand inside a kaleidoscope. There's a special Kid's Town, where no one over 48 inches tall is allowed to enter. NatureWorks takes a walk on the wild side. Other exhibits include 1-2-3 Math, Physics Park, Body-Zone, and Light Power. CineDome theater projects in-the-round films on a screen eight stories high, and live shows take place in the Adventure Theater. Some of the exhibits and the observatory present special programs, and traveling exhibits visit. Exhibits and programs were designed to meet school curriculum requirements. There's a lot to see here—it outlasts the attention spans of children under age ten.

## Orlando Museum of Art (ages 5 to 13)

2416 North Mills Avenue; near Orlando Science Center; (407) 896-4231; www.omart .org. Open 10:00 a.m. to 4:00 p.m. Tuesday through Friday, noon to 4:00 p.m. Saturday and Sunday. Admission is $8 for adults, $7 for seniors and students, $5 for children ages 6 to 18. Locals admitted free from 1:00 to 5:00 p.m. on Thursday.

The kids can learn about art the fun way in the interactive Children's Gallery. The museum's permanent collection includes works by Georgia O'Keeffe, Andy Warhol, Roy Lichtenstein, and Childe Hassam, along with ancient art.

## Orange County Regional History Center (ages 6 to 12)

65 East Central Boulevard; (407) 836-8500 or (800) 965-2030; www.thehistorycenter .org. Open 10:00 a.m. to 5:00 p.m. Monday through Saturday, noon to 5:00 p.m. Sunday. Admission is $7.00 for adults, $6.50 for seniors, $3.50 for children ages 3 to 12.

Moved downtown to the historic old city hall building, it has expanded to include more hands-on scenes of old Orlando, from 12,000 years past and ancient natives to Seminoles, pioneers, and Cinderella's Castle. Begin your sashay through time in the Orientation Theater, set on an Old Florida back porch.

## Lake Eola Park (all ages)

Rosalind Avenue and Robinson Street; (407) 246-2827. Paddleboat rentals are $10 for thirty minutes.

Much overlooked, but a great place for a picnic, this downtown refuge offers sculpture, lighted fountains, concerts, a pagoda, mossy oaks, a scenic walk, and graceful swan paddleboats.

## Universal Studios and Islands of Adventure Orlando
(ages 3 to 13) 🚂

1000 Universal Studios Plaza; (407) 363-8000 or (888) U-ESCAPE; www.universalorlando
.com. Parks open at 9:00 a.m.; closing times vary. One-day admission to each park is
$71.36 for adults, $59.64 for children ages 3 to 9 (tax included). Multiple-day, multipark passes save money, as do purchase of Internet-only specials from the parks'
Web site. Multiday, multipark flex tickets are available for visits to Universal Studios,
Islands of Adventure, SeaWorld, Wet 'n' Wild, and Busch Gardens Tampa Bay. Florida
residents can score special deals at certain times of the year. Admission to CityWalk
is free. Parking fees are $8 for cars, $9 for large vehicles. Generally, no parking fees
after 6:00 p.m.

With brashly entertaining parks, Universal Studios Orlando nears the top of the list of
must-do attractions in Orlando. The original park, Universal Studios, features rides
based on beloved blockbusters, such as *E.T., Earthquake, Jaws, Twister,* and *Men in
Black*. However, the newest generation of technologically sophisticated attractions is
even more fantastic, such as the psychological thrill ride Revenge of the Mummy or
Shrek, namesake of the Oscar-winning film. It features a stunning four-dimensional
film, which is amazing enough without the extra special effects that help guests realistically see, hear, and feel the action from their seats. Through the magic of "Ogrevi-
sion," the characters Princess Fiona, Donkey, and all the others come to life. Jimmy
Neutron's Nicktoon Blast, a similarly high-tech attraction that takes you on a rocket
trip to fight the evil Oublar from the planet Yokian, is a favorite, too. Preschoolers love
the Funtastic World of Hanna-Barbera, Barney's Backyard, Fievel's Playland, and Curious George Goes to Town. Woody Woodpecker's Nuthouse Coaster is tame enough
for the first-time thrill rider. Shows and tours take you to back lots or Nickelodeon
Studios, where visitors can tour a set. A new addition is the Blue Man Group, the
poker-faced, blue-painted mimes who put on an eclectic all-ages show. It can be
messy, and front rows get free ponchos.

Islands of Adventure appeals more evenly to all ages. Tots take a trip through the
pages of *Cat in the Hat* at Seuss Landing. At Toon Lagoon, they are awed by the color
and humor of their favorite funny-pages characters. Older adventurers love the monstrous roller coaster called the Incredible Hulk, which blasts them out of a dark tunnel
from 0 to 40 mph in two seconds, only to drop them into thin air and then shoot
them through water a couple of stories below. The park also boasts the world's first
dual racing roller coasters, called Dueling Dragons, at the Lost Continent. The park
also holds lots of interactive areas, including the Jurassic Park Discovery Center, and
offers a fun assortment of shows.

The Universal Express system makes it possible for one-day ticket-holders in
either park to reserve a time on most attractions, saving time in line; they can hold
only one reservation at a time. Resort guests enjoy "no-wait" privileges all day.

CityWalk is a lively complex of restaurants, movie theaters, and clubs. Two resorts
complete the Universal scene, all accessible by water taxi, bus, or foot.

## Wet 'n' Wild (ages 4 to 13)

**6200 International Drive; (407) 351-WILD; www.wetnwild.com. Open daily; hours vary. Admission is $36.95 for persons ages 10 and older, $30.95 for children ages 3 to 9; online discounted tickets for Florida residents. Tube rental $4. Parking costs $8 per car, $9 per recreational vehicle.**

One of the most popular and spectacular of the region's many water parks, it boasts multipassenger rides, a miniature park for kiddies, high-speed slides, a surf pool, and cable-pulled knee-boarding. Hydra Fighter lets riders create their own momentum by shooting water guns, but the line to get on moves painfully slow. Pools are heated in cold weather.

## Skull Kingdom (ages 8 to 13)

**5933 American Way (off International Drive); (407) 354-1564. Open 10:00 a.m. to midnight daily. Admission to the Horror Show is $8.99 from 10:00 a.m. to 5:00 p.m. (partial show) and $14.04 from 5:00 p.m. to midnight (full show). Admission to the Magic Show is $15.97 to $24.45, including food (pizza and drinks, so there is no set eating time); there are various combinations of this with the Horror Show.**

Skull Kingdom occupies a castle that you enter through the mouth of a skull. A white-knuckled march takes you through dark, narrow hallways and monster-airbrushed doors. Plus there's a Ghoulish Face Painting Gallery and arcade games.

## Pirate's Dinner Adventure (ages 5 to 13)

**6400 Carrier Drive; off International Drive; (407) 248-0590 or (800) 866-AHOY; www.piratesdinneradventure.com. The box office and preshow room opens at 6:30 p.m. daily. Admission for dinner and show is $55.95 plus tax for adults and $35.95 plus tax for children ages 3 to 11.**

The newest in the genre of dining experience pits swashbuckling buccaneers against one another in competition and mutiny (with feigned acts of hand-to-hand violence). The audience participates in the fun; children from the audience are used in many scenes. The stage is a floating pirate's brig. Entertainment is musical and dramatic with feats of circuslike skill. Dinner is a multicourse affair, with special kids' meals available and freely poured beverages (beer, wine, and cola—you can request something without caffeine for the kids). Before and after the show, you are treated to entertainment and partying with the pirates.

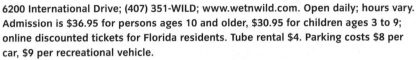

# Top Family **Beaches and Parks**

1. **Juniper Springs,** Ocala National Forest

2. **Wekiwa Springs State Park,** Apopka

3. **Lake Kissimmee State Park,** Lake Wales

# Smart **Travel**

- Admission prices are sky-high in the Orlando area, but you rarely have to pay full fare. Look for coupons in locally distributed brochures and materials, from hotel guest services, in restaurants, at other attractions, on the Internet, practically everywhere you look. Florida residents are often eligible for discounts. The Orlando Magicard offers discounts at seventy-six local establishments and is available through the Orlando/ Orange County Convention and Visitors Bureau; (800) 551-0181. The Orlando FlexTicket packages admission to Universal Studios, Sea- World, and Wet 'n' Wild theme parks and is available through individual park Web sites or by calling any of the participating parks.

- If you're including Disney or Universal Studios Escape in your Florida vacation, make it the grand finale. If you do Disney first, other attrac- tions and activities pale. "Save the best for last."

- Don't be in a great hurry to get your toddler to Disney World. Although the Magic Kingdom does have its Mickey's Starland for teeny ones, it's generally most attractive to children ages seven and older. Young chil- dren have a hard time distinguishing fantasy from reality and can be scared even by the most seemingly benign attractions, such as Snow White. They also have a difficult time waiting in lines for an hour or more at a time. Universal's Islands of Adventure is the best major theme park for starters.

- When theme park–bound, bring backpacks and wear comfortable shoes and hats for the long haul. Suggested items: water spray bottle for hot days, sweaters for cool evenings, portable umbrellas or rain ponchos, apples and healthful snacks, frozen containers of drinking water and juice, sunscreen, bags of money. The wet rides at Universal's Islands of Adventure may require a change of clothes and locker rental.

- To save money, stamina, and sanity, consider taking an afternoon break from your theme park day. We usually leave about 2:00 P.M., go have lunch somewhere reasonably priced, go to the hotel to nap or chill out, then return when the weather has cooled and crowds have somewhat thinned.

- Many of the large theme park attractions don't serve kid-size portions in their restaurants and food stands, oddly enough (well, not so odd in a place where squeezing the last cent from your wallet seems to be the goal). Bring extra plastic cups so that you can split soft drink portions among little ones. Split meals and snacks. One cheeseburger at Disney's Animal Kingdom easily fed two second-graders.

- When visiting large attractions, have a plan in case a child gets separated and lost. Instruct small children to stay put at the spot where he or she last saw the adults in the party. With older children, you can agree upon a spot to meet in case someone gets lost, or keep in touch with cell phones. Tuck notes into the pockets of small children with name of parents and home, cell phone, or hotel phone number.

- Disney T-shirts and other merchandise are sold at bargain prices at discount stores outside Disney World.

- To prevent scorching feet between rides at water parks, wear beach slippers.

## Wonderworks (ages 5 to 12)

**Pointe Orlando, 9067 International Drive; (407) 351-8800; www.wonderworksonline .com. Open daily 9:00 a.m. to midnight. Admission is $19.95 for adults ($22.95 with laser tag), $14.95 for seniors and children ages 4 to 12 ($17.95 with laser tag). Laser tag alone costs $4.95 per person.**

The fun begins outside this tossed-upside-down building that creaks as if to topple when you walk by. With its disaster orientation, it may have stolen some of Orlando Science Center's thunder—but at a much higher price and less of a learning focus. Interactive games let you experience an earthquake, hang gliding, and aging. Dance on a keyboard and morph your voice to alien qualities. This place is lots of fun.

## SeaWorld Adventure Park (all ages)

**7007 SeaWorld Drive (exit 29B westbound or 30A eastbound off I-4); (407) 351-3600 or (800) 4ADVENTURE; www.seaworld.com. Open 9:00 a.m. daily, with varying closing hours. Admission is $64.95 for adults, $53.95 for children ages 3 to 9 (tax not included). Parking is an additional $10 for cars, $12 for recreational vehicles.**

Killer whales, dolphins, sharks, and sea lions were the original stars at SeaWorld. The ever-evolving attraction has since added a sure-to-wow-'em Wild Arctic theme park with a simulated flight over the northlands and face-to-face encounters with polar bears (separated by Plexiglass). Key West has moved to central Florida—sandy boardwalks, tropical blossoms, Bahamian cuisine, street entertainers, mangroves, and all. Journey to Atlantis is a thrilling flume ride and mythical sensory encounter all in one. The looping Kraken roller coaster, which is floorless and one of the tallest, fastest, and largest in Orlando, will thrill your teens. And older kids will love some of the parks' special programs, like Shark Deep Dive, where they descend into the shark tank with scuba or snorkel gear to see the massive creatures up close, or "sea trainer for a day," a day with the staff to see how marine animals are cared for and trained. The Waterfront, a five-acre entertainment, shopping, and restaurant complex designed to resemble a Mediterranean seaport, features street performers, musicians, and fun shows, like Kat 'n Kaboodle, with sixteen exotic species of trained cats doing amazing feats. You can also watch chefs flip pizza, cook on a Mongolian wok, and sample the cuisine of faraway places.

## Discovery Cove (ages 6 to 13)

**6000 Discovery Cove Way; (877) 4-DISCOVERY; www.discoverycove.com. Open daily 9:00 a.m. to 5:30 p.m. All-inclusive admission with dolphin encounter is $259 to $279 per person, depending on the season, plus tax. Without dolphin encounter, admission runs $159 to $179 per person, depending on the season, plus tax.**

Across the street from SeaWorld, its parent park, Discovery Cove expands the dolphin interaction program begun there into an all-inclusive (well, almost, anyway) resort experience. For the full price you get a dolphin encounter, which includes about forty-five minutes of instruction and forty minutes in the water with a dolphin, a trainer, and about eight other people. The package includes a cafeteria-style lunch, one free photograph taken as you enter the park, use of snorkel equipment (you keep the snorkel), and access to the park's freshwater river pool, saltwater ray and coral reef pools, aviary island, beach, lockers, showers, towels, and a seven-day pass to SeaWorld. The kids will love feeding the birds and petting the rays. Snacks, beverages, and dolphin interaction photos cost extra (at typical theme park prices). Admission is limited to 1,000 people per day, and reservations are required. Children must be age six or older to swim with the dolphins.

## Gatorland

**14501 South Orange Blossom Trail; (407) 855-5496 or (800) 393-JAWS; www.gatorland .com. Open 9:00 a.m. to dusk daily. Admission is $19.95 for adults, $12.95 for children ages 3 to 12, plus tax.**

Not far from the hubbub, yet a world away, Gatorland holds on to Orlando's Cracker roots with gator-wrestling shows and native snake demonstrations. You'll see alligators from a foot long to 3 feet wide. There are also a wet and dry playground, after-dark events, and a crocodile land. If you dare, snack on some gator ribs or gator nuggets at Pearl's Smokehouse. It serves more normal fare as well and provides a smokehouse jungle gym for the kids.

# My Son, **the Gator Rassler**

One photo on my son's kindergarten "All About Me" poster pictures him sitting astride a fierce, 8-foot alligator, prying open its jaws. The caption underneath it, written in five-year-old scratch, reads "My Pet."

I can't say his teacher enjoyed the humor as much as we did. You can hardly tell that the gape-mouthed gator is made of molded plaster, merely a lifelike facsimile of the real thing. I snapped the shot at Gatorland in Orlando, where the rest of the 4,000 alligators are alive and writhing—from darling little hatchlings you wish you could hold to some so wide you'd never get your arms across them (were you ever so inclined and able to make it past that nasty overbite in the first place). Bring your camera in case your child finds a "pet" he or she wishes to safely capture. Snap from a distance, lest it snap first. —*C.K.W.*

## Where to Eat

**Cafe Tu Tu Tango.** 8625 International Drive; (407) 248-2222; www.cafetutu tango.com. Something for Mom, Dad, and the kids. An all-appetizer menu with an artist's theme. Lunch and dinner daily. $$–$$$

**Flipper's Pizzeria.** 7480 Universal Boulevard; (407) 351-5643. With four other locations. Yummy, handmade pizza, excellent salads with homemade dressings for Mom, even good desserts, and the prices are reasonable. Flipper's even delivers to your hotel room if you're too tired to go out after a big day at the theme parks. $

**One of the Largest McDonald's in All the World.** 6875 Sand Lake Road (exit 74A off I-4); (407) 351-2185. Only in Orlando! McDonald's restaurant, pizzeria, and Mickey D's ice cream parlor, plus a magnificent playland and two stories of video games. $

**Tchoup Chop (pronounced chop-chop).** Royal Pacific Resort, 6300 Hollywood Way, (407) 503-2467. The Polynesian-Asian menu, conceived by celebrity chef Emeril Lagasse, is a treat for adults, featuring such items as blue crab claws, Kahlua pork, and a pineapple upside-down cake that tastes like homemade. It's not really suitable for young children, but well-behaved teens and accompanying adults can treat themselves to its luxurious calm and gourmet fare after a hectic day at the theme parks. $$$

**Wild Jack's Orlando Grill & Co.** 7364 International Drive; (407) 352-4407. Kids love the wild west decor and cowboy boot–shaped glasses. Prime steaks, fiery Southwestern specialties, ribs, and wonderful homemade soups and desserts. Open daily for dinner. Reservations recommended. $$–$$$

## Where to Stay

**Hyatt Regency Grand Cypress.** 1 Grand Cypress Boulevard (off Route 535 at I-4 exit 27); (407) 239-1234 or (800) 233-1234; www. hyatt.com. Near Disney, 1,500 acres and 750 guest accommodations in a luxury atrium hotel, restaurants, golf, cave and waterfall wrap pool with water slides, tennis, horseback riding, pitch and putt-putt golf, playground, and Camp Hyatt and Family Camp programs. $$$$

**Royal Pacific Resort.** 6300 Hollywood Way; (407) 503-3000 or (888) 273-1311; www.universalorlando.com. Opened in June 2002 on a fifty-three-acre site directly across the street from Universal's Islands of Adventure park, it is a luxurious tropical retreat with one of the city's largest swimming pools, a 12,000-square-foot monster designed to resemble a South Seas lagoon, complete with extensive landscaping, water cannons, fake beach, and water polo equipment. Its proximity to Universal is its best feature, but another great perk for guests is that your room key provides no-wait access to Universal parks and rides, and other benefits such as free use of the water taxi line. The hotel's restaurant, Tchoup Chop, is an elegant eatery that makes a nice reward for adults who have endured a whole day in a noisy theme park. Hard Rock Hotel opened in January 2001 with the same park privileges. $$$–$$$$

## For More Information

**Orlando/Orange County Convention and Visitors Bureau, Official Visitor Center.** 8723 International Drive, Suite 101, Orlando 32819; (407) 363-5872 or (800) 551-0181; www.orlandoinfo.com.

# Walt Disney World

Exit 67 off I-4 takes you to the bull's-eye of the Orlando area family target.

Here awaits a vacationland unto itself, 7,100 developed acres complete with umpteen resorts, several major theme and water parks, stores, restaurants, nightlife complexes, sports arenas—you name it. If you plan to spend several days at Walt Disney World, look into its various pass options. They begin in price and scope with a Four-Day Park-Hopper Pass (good for Magic Kingdom, EPCOT, Disney–MGM Studios, and Disney's Animal Kingdom), which costs $225.78 for guests ages 10 and older, $189.57 for children ages 3 to 9. Florida residents can take advantage of discounted rates. One-day, one-park tickets to the Magic Kingdom, EPCOT, Animal Kingdom, or Disney–MGM cost $71 for guests ages 10 and older, $60 for children ages 3 to 9; under 3 free. Other park admissions are listed separately. All ticket prices are subject to tax and change. Parking at the attractions is $11. For general information on any Walt Disney World attraction, call (407) W-DISNEY or visit www.disneyworld.com. Times vary according to season. Call or search "park hours" on the Web site for up-to-date information.

## The Magic Kingdom (ages 6 to 13)

**Normally open daily at 9:30 a.m. Closing times vary. Call ahead for exact times and a schedule of which attractions may be closed for repairs.**

The park has to be on the wish list of every kid who has ever seen a Disney film or tape. It's the first place most families take their youngsters, but beware: Don't take them here at too early an age. The realistic effects of such classic attractions as Pirates of the Caribbean, the Haunted Mansion, and even Snow White's Scary Adventures can frighten preschoolers. If you do have tots, Mickey's Toon Town Fair is the best place for them, while you send the older kids off to survive Space and Splash Mountains. They'll also enjoy three new attractions featuring popular Disney characters. Goofy's crop duster takes off from a barn in Barnstormer at Goofy's Wiseacre Farm, while riders on Buzz Lightyear's Space Ranger Spin must save the toy universe from sinister Emperor Zurg. Sights, sounds, and sometimes yucky smells plague the new security recruit in Stitch's Great Escape while looking for the six-limbed alien. There is also the Spectro Magic Parade at night, dazzling with fiber optics and half a million lights.The Magic Carpets of Aladdin, in the Adventureland area of the park, has sixteen, four-passenger carpets circling around a giant Genie's bottle with funny-looking camels spitting refreshing squirts of water at airborne riders for extra fun. Check out the open-air marketplace called the Agrabah Bazaar where you can buy frosty fruit treats that are nutritious and delish.

## Disney's Animal Kingdom (ages 5 to 13)

**Open 7:00 a.m. to 8:00 p.m.**

Disney finally decided to follow the ecotourism trend, but of course in a big, big way. This largest of Disney theme parks concentrates on animals—real, imaginary, and extinct. Quite frankly, it doesn't measure up to Magic Kingdom or EPCOT, which charge the same entrance fee. The headliner attractions are DINOSAUR, Kali River Rapids, Kilimanjaro Safaris, and Expedition Everest. The first, the centerpiece of Dinoland, U.S.A., is a rollicking ride into the past with animatronic dinosaurs, a mild roller coaster, and typical Disney effects. The young ones especially will like playing in the nearby Boneyard play area, where they can slide, climb, and dig for bones. Africa's safari ride takes you to a wildlife preserve where real live animals—gazelles, elephants, Nile crocodiles, kudus, and giraffes—await around every corner and thin drama adds the Disney dimension. The new Expedition Everest thrills kids with hairpin turns on a high-speed train ride around Forbidden Mountain, which is guarded by a snarling Yeti. The best attraction is tucked into the roots of the impressive (though not alive) Tree of Life. It's Tough to Be a Bug is cute and fun 3-D entertainment. (And the lines are much shorter!) Camp Minnie-Mickey is tot friendly, with character greeting areas and theme shows from *Lion King* and *Pocahontas*. Naturally, you'll find plenty of shops and food stands throughout the park.

# Vacationland **Fun Facts**

- It takes more than a million yards of fabric to costume the cast at Walt Disney World.
- Shamu's swimming pool at SeaWorld holds 1.7 million gallons of water.
- Universal Studios' King Kong, the largest animated figure ever built, is covered with 7,000 pounds of fur.

## EPCOT (ages 8 to 13)
**Future World is open 9:00 a.m. to 7:00 p.m.; World Showcase, 11:00 a.m. to 9:00 p.m.**

At EPCOT (Experimental Prototype Community of Tomorrow) younger children enjoy front-of-the-park Future World attractions. Honey, I Shrunk the Audience is especially popular. New for little ones is the Seas with Nemo and Friends, where a cruise in a clamobile ends with a Turtle Talk with Crush. Older kids will go for the new Mission: SPACE, which launches guests on a simulated space adventure. During this one-of-a-kind astronaut-like adventure in Future World, guests experience everything from a pulse-racing liftoff to "weightlessness" among the infinite reaches of outer space. World Showcase is more suited to parents and older kids. There you can tour eleven countries in one day, taste their culinary specialties, and buy their wares.

## Disney–MGM Studios (ages 6 to 13)
**The park generally opens daily at 9:00 a.m.; closing hours vary throughout the year.**

Thrill seekers line up first for the Twilight Zone Tower of Terror, whose thirteen-story elevator plunge makes their hair stand straight up. The little ones will love meeting Aladdin's genie, Belle of *Beauty and the Beast* fame, and other characters off the Disney screen. Even the older ones will get a kick out of the Muppet-Vision 3-D attraction. The Voyage of the Little Mermaid is sure to enchant, while Star Tours is a rollicking adventure through outer space with an absent-minded droid in the cockpit. Lights, Motors, Action Extreme Stunt Show is a new attraction straight from Paris Disneyland. A live spectacle with specially designed cars, motorcycles, and Jet Skis sparked with pyrotechnics shows how action stunts are created for the movies. The nighttime Fantasmic! show stars Mickey Mouse. Don't miss one of the park's best coasters, Aerosmith's Rock 'n' Roller Coaster, which spins its riders through loops in the dark to the tunes of Aerosmith.

### Disneyquest Indoor Interactive Theme Park (ages 5 to 13)

**Downtown Disney West Side; (407) 824-2222; www.disneyquest.com. Open daily 10:30 a.m. to midnight. Admission is $36 plus tax for guests age 10 and older, $33 plus tax for children ages 3 to 9.**

Five stories of indoor interactive entertainment challenge visitors of all ages. The latest additions include a 3-D experience titled Pirates of the Caribbean: Battle for Buccaneer Gold and SongMaker, where up to four people can cut their own musical CD by mixing singers, lyrics, and a variety of musical styles. Kids will love taking home their personalized and self-designed CD in jewel case.

### Disney's Wide World of Sports (ages 5 to 13)

**Admission for the Sports Experience, a multisport playground where kids can test their agility, and most sports events are $11.25 for guests ages 10 and older, $8.50 for children ages 3 to 9.**

Two hundred acres devoted to sports, it hosts the Atlanta Braves in spring training season (March through early April), Harlem Globetrotters training, and world-class tennis, soccer, karate, and other tournaments. The Sports Experience, formerly an attraction at Super Bowl host cities, has its permanent home here, allowing wannabe football players a chance to test their skills. Tiny future quarterbacks can play in the Kid's Zone with authentic NFL equipment.

### Walt Disney World Water Parks (ages 6 to 13)

Each of these water parks has its own theme. For an extra $20 at Typhoon Lagoon you can do a half hour of snorkeling-assisted scuba. Must be age 7 or older.

- Typhoon Lagoon. Admission is $39 for adults, $33 for children ages 3 to 9, plus tax; under 3 **free.** Speed down Mount Mayday in an enclosed slide.
- Blizzard Beach. Admission is $39 for adults, $33 for children ages 3 to 9, plus tax; under 3 **free.** Drop straight down at 55 mph.

## Disney Sports **Trivia**

- Wide World of Sports fields are always playable, thanks to drainage systems that remove 5 to 7 inches of rainfall per hour.
- Two of the largest air-conditioning units in all of Disney World cool the complex's fieldhouse.

# Where to Eat

Disney World dining spans the realm of hot pretzel stands and gimmickry to fine dining and cutting-edge cuisine. Each park and each resort has its own selections, demonstrating a wide range of ethnic styles. Most are fit for families.

**California Grill.** Disney's Contemporary Resort, 4600 North World Drive, Lake Buena Vista; (407) 824-1576. Bright, sky-high setting, new California-style cuisine. Lunch and dinner daily. $$$

**Character meals.** For priority seating call (407) WDW-DINE. For a special treat, take the kids to a Disney character breakfast, lunch, or dinner to eat with Captain Hook, Cinderella, and other celluloid stars. These meals come at a premium, so to save money, look for the characters at the theme parks instead. Character meals are hosted by Magic Kingdom, EPCOT, Disney's Animal Kingdom, Downtown Disney Marketplace, Disney's Beach Club Resort, Contemporary Resort, Grand Floridian Resort, Polynesian Resort, Old Key West Resort, and Wilderness Lodge Resort. $$-$$$

**Cinderella's Royal Table.** Cinderella's Castle in Magic Kingdom. Buffet-style dining with Cinderella and friends. Breakfast. $$ (plus park admission)

**Coral Reef Restaurant.** EPCOT; (407) WDW-DINE. Kids will love dining "under the sea," with an eye-to-eye aquarium view. Seafood, naturally, is the specialty. Lunch and dinner daily. $$$

**Disney–MGM Studios.** Sandwiches, burgers, seafood, and pasta. $–$$

**ESPN Club.** Disney's Boardwalk; (407) WDW-DINE. Welcome, sports fans, to the ultimate sports cafe, with seventy-five monitors, chili, burgers, barbecue pork sandwiches, salads, entrees, and desserts. Breakfast, lunch, and dinner daily. $$$

**Rainforest Cafe.** Downtown Disney, Walt Disney World, also at Disney's Animal Kingdom; (407) 827-8500; www.rainforest cafe.com. Tropical theme—complete with active volcano—and cuisine with live and animated wildlife. Lunch and dinner daily. $$-$$$

# Where to Stay

Resort accommodations at Disney World cover all the bases, from the woodsy campground of Fort Wilderness to ones themed for sports, music, and luxury. One advantage to staying at a Disney resort, besides close proximity and **free** transportation to the parks, is early admission privileges on certain days and park ticket sales at hotel guest desks. Another is character meals and appearances. Children under age eighteen stay **free** in rooms with parents. For reservations for most Disney resorts, call (407) W-DISNEY or visit www.disneyworld.com.

**Animal Kingdom Lodge.** Feel like you're staying on an African wildlife reserve, with a view of grasslands, birds, and other animals outside your window. African architecture, hand-carved furnishings, restaurants, and pools. $$$$

**Disney's All-Star Sports Resort.** 1701 West Buena Vista Drive, Lake Buena Vista; (407) 939-5000. One of Disney's most affordable hotels, where oversized football, baseball, basketball, surfing, and tennis paraphernalia bedeck the property. There are 1,920 rooms. $–$$

**Disney's Caribbean Beach Resort.** 900 Cayman Way, Lake Buena Vista; (407) 934-3400. On a lake with seven beaches and a marina. There are 1,700 rooms, most with water views. Restaurant, bars, playground, whirlpool, and game room. $$$-$$$$

**Grand Floridian.** The ultimate in Disney grandeur, it evokes Florida's old wooden hotels of the railroad era. Kid activities and evening club, My First Facial in the spa for ages 10 to 14, beach, water activities, game room, character breakfast, teatime, and dinner, plus other dining options. $$$$

**The Polynesian Resort.** 1600 Seven Seas Drive, Lake Buena Vista; (407) 824-2000. Great for small kids because of its Minnie Mouse character breakfast and Neverland evening child-care facility. To enter, kids crawl through Wendy's (of Peter Pan fame) window. $$$$

# Kissimmee and Lake Buena Vista

East of I-4 along Highway 192 (Irlo-Bronson Memorial Highway). Lighted mile markers help locate attractions along this busy strip.

A quiet cow town that burgeoned into Tourist Town, U.S.A., with the arrival of a certain mouse, Kissimmee has attractions that reflect its split personality. Highway 192, aka Irlo-Bronson Memorial Highway or Vine Street, is the town's main thoroughfare.

## Holiday Inn SunSpree Resort

**13351 Route 535 (exit 27 off I-4), Lake Buena Vista; (407) 239-4500 or (800) 366-6299; www.kidsuites.com.**

In 1995 the resort came up with an entirely new concept for family accommodations. Its KidSuites are based on the belief that parents and children need their separate space—and beds—while on vacation. Bunk beds and media centers are part of cubby rooms separated by walls—decorated as forts, circuses, racetracks, and such—from the rest of the room. When considered with the hotel's excellent and wonderfully flexible kids' programs, they mount up to a near-perfect family vacation situation. Kids eat **free** with parents or in their separate kids-only restaurant. Swimming pools, a state-of-the-art video arcade with computer island, plus all sorts of special kid-oriented bonuses are also located on the property. Other accommodations are roomy suites with some kitchen facilities. $–$$$

### Old Town (ages 3 to 13)

**5770 West Irlo-Bronson Memorial Highway, Kissimmee; (407) 396-4888 or (800) 843-4202; www.old-town.com. Open 10:00 a.m. to 11:00 p.m. daily. Admission to the haunted house is $7 for adults, $5 for children, plus tax. Separate admission for other rides.**

Mom can shop, Dad can eat, and the kids can ride go-karts, a Ferris wheel, a roller coaster, or an antique merry-go-round. Everyone hold hands while visiting the haunted house. A two-hour babysitting service is available in the children's play zone, Yellow Submarine. Where else can you still get Pepsi for a quarter?

### Medieval Times Dinner and Tournament (ages 5 to 13)

**4510 West Irlo-Bronson Memorial Highway, Kissimmee; (407) 396-2900 or (888) WE-JOUST; www.medievaltimes.com. Showtimes vary. Admission to medieval village and dinner show is $54.95 for adults, $34.95 for children ages 3 to 12. Birthday celebrants are admitted free with two paying adults. Seniors get a 10 percent discount. Tax and gratuity are extra on all admissions.**

Learn what it was like to live in the Middle Ages from authentically costumed village artisans—blacksmith, potter, and spinner—and visit the dungeon's museum of torture. Afterward, feast your eyes on a jousting match and your appetites on roasted chicken (which you're allowed to eat with your hands).

### Congo River Golf (ages 4 to 13)

**4777 West Highway 192 (between mile markers 12 and 13, next to Sam's Club), Kissimmee; (407) 396-6900. Open 10:00 a.m. to midnight daily. Admission is $10.45 for adults for one course, $14.50 for both; children 10 and under $2.00 less. Paddleboat rides are $10 for a three-passenger boat.**

Two eighteen-hole courses have different levels of play, but both are set amid giant waterfalls and mysterious caves. There's an arcade, an exhibit of twenty-five hungry gators to feed, and a paddleboat ride.

## Kissimmee **Trivia**

- How do you correctly pronounce Kissimmee? Home-folks like to say Kiss-SIM-ee by day, and KISS-i-me by night.
- *Gasoline Alley* comic strip creator Frank King lived in Kissimmee for twenty-five years and drew inspiration for his cartoon scenes from local streets and buildings.
- Rodeo was brought to town by Milt Hinkle, bodyguard to Teddy Roosevelt and acquaintance of Wyatt Earp, Annie Oakley, Pancho Villa, and Geronimo.

### Lakefront Park (ages 2 to 12)

**250 Lakeshore Boulevard, Kissimmee; (407) 847-2388; www.kissimmeeparksandrec .com.**

This is a great place for a picnic lunch and family exercise on the lake; a marina rents fishing boats. Buy an ice-cream cone from the caboose stand, burn it off on the playground, and walk up Monument Avenue to give the kids a painless geography lesson at *Monument of States,* a 1940s sculpture composed of geological contributions from every state (except Hawaii and Alaska, which didn't join the Union until later).

### Pioneer Center (ages 4 to 13)

**750 North Bass Road, Kissimmee; (407) 396-8644. Open 10:00 a.m. to 4:00 p.m. Saturday, 1:00 to 4:00 p.m. Sunday; call for hours Thursday and Friday. Requested donation is $2 per adult, $1 per child.**

Escape the futuristic madness of the local amusement parks with a step back in time. The museum maintains a bygone Kissimmee personality with its two late-1800s Cracker houses, old country store, and boardwalk into an eight-acre nature preserve. Picnic under one-hundred-year-old oak trees.

### Green Meadows Farm (ages 2 to 10)

**1368 South Poinciana Boulevard, Kissimmee (5 miles south of Highway 192); (407) 846-0770; www.greenmeadowsfarm.com. Open 9:30 a.m. to 5:30 p.m. daily. Two-hour tours run continually until 4:00 p.m. Admission is $19 for adults and children ages 2 or older, $17 for Florida residents, $15 for seniors.**

Some 300 farm animals call Green Meadows home. The kids (and you!) can pet 'em, milk 'em, ride 'em, and feed 'em. In this ultimate petting farm, kids mingle with the geese, sheep, donkeys, pigs, and goats. Price includes pony, miniature train, and tractor-pulled hayrides.

### Horse World (all ages)

**3705 South Poinciana Boulevard, Kissimmee; (407) 847-4343. Open 9:00 a.m. daily. Ride for $39 to $69, plus tax (10 percent senior discount). Children age 5 or under can ride with an adult for $16.95 on basic ride.**

Here you can take bridle in hand. Trails thread through 750 acres of woodlands and are suitable for riders of all levels. Toddlers can enjoy pony rides and farm animals.

### Skyscapes Balloon Tours (ages 6 to 13)

**P.O. Box 452953, Kissimmee 34745; (407) 856-4606. Rides are $185 for adults, $125 for children ages 10 to 15; 9 and under free with each paying adult. Not recommended for children under 5.**

Watch the sunrise on a forty-five-minute to one-hour float above the earth. Your sky journey ends with a traditional champagne toast and "First Flight" certificate. Advance reservations of at least two weeks suggested.

# On a **Budget**

- **Florida Museum of Natural History,** Gainesville, free admission
- **Morningside Nature Center,** Gainesville, free admission
- **Kelly Park,** Apopka, admission $1 for adults, free for children
- **Downtown Disney's LEGO Imagination Center,** Walt Disney World Resort, free admission
- **Disney's BoardWalk,** Walt Disney World Resort, free admission

## Osceola County Stadium and Sports Complex (ages 5 to 13)
1000 Bill Beck Boulevard, Kissimmee (off East Highway 192); (321) 697-3200. Tickets range $17 to $20.

The Houston Astros go into spring training here during March.

## Reptile World Serpentarium (ages 3 to 13)
5705 East Irlo-Bronson Memorial Highway, St. Cloud; (407) 892-6905. Open 9:00 a.m. to 5:30 p.m. Tuesday through Sunday, closed Monday; closed in September. Admission is $5.75 for adults, $4.75 for children ages 6 to 17, $3.75 for ages 3 to 5.

Watch demonstrations with cobras and other poisonous snakes.

## Where to Eat

**Magic Mining Steaks and Seafood.** 7763 West Irlo-Bronson Highway, Kissimmee; (407) 396-1950. Theme restaurant with choo-choo train and game room. Dinner. $$

## Where to Stay

**Holiday Inn Family Suites Resort.** 14500 Continental Gateway, Lake Buena Vista, exit 67 east from I-4; (407) 387-KIDS or (877) 387-KIDS; www.hifamilysuites .com. This property has taken the Kid-Suites concept to new heights with two-bedroom suites, bunk beds and their own electronic entertainment in the kids' room, a cute train station theme, interactive pool gizmos, and complimentary breakfast buffet. Besides KidSuites you can rent Cinema-suites (also "big" with families), Fitness Suites, and Business Suites. $$–$$$

## For More Information

**Kissimmee–St. Cloud Convention and Visitors Bureau.** P.O. Box 422007, Kissimmee 34742-2007; (407) 847-5000 or (800) 327-9159; www.floridakiss.com.

# Winter Haven

From Kissimmee, take I-4 west and turn south on Highway 27. Turn west on either Route 544, 542, or 540 and travel about 5 miles to Winter Haven.

## Splash Island Water Park (all ages )
**6000 Cypress Gardens Boulevard, Winter Haven; (863) 324-2111. Open daily. Included with admission to Cypress Gardens Adventure Park; $44.95 for adults, $39.95 for seniors and children ages 3 to 9; 2 and under free. Parking is $10 for cars, $12 for RVs.**

This water park joins forty rides from carousels to coasters, wildlife, and the just opened Bugsville for small fry with the famed gardens that featured Southern belles.

## Where to Stay
**Grenelefe Golf and Tennis Resort.** 3200 Route 546, Haines City; (863) 422-7511; www.grenelefe.com. One thousand acres with three golf courses, twenty tennis courts, four pools, 850 suites and rooms, three restaurants, a full-service lake marina, and fitness club and trail. Supervised kids' program. $$–$$$$

## For More Information
**Greater Winter Haven Area Chamber of Commerce.** 401 Avenue B Northwest, Winter Haven 33882; (863) 293-2138 or (800) 871-7027; www.winterhavenfl.com.

# Lake Wales

Along Highway 27 headed south.

Orange blossoms scent the air along heaving hillsides—yes, that's right, hills in Florida! Neatly plaited orchards envelope the pretty little town of Lake Wales, which lassos the body of water that gives it its name. For a scenic view of the water and its lakeside mansions and park, follow Lakeshore Boulevard.

## Historic Bok Sanctuary (ages 5 to 13)
**3 miles north of Lake Wales near the intersection of Highway 27 and Route 60; 1151 Tower Boulevard; (863) 676-1408; www.boksanctuary.org. Open 8:00 a.m. to 6:00 p.m. daily (gates close at 5:00 p.m.). Admission is $10 for adults, $3 for children ages 5 to 12; under 5 free.**

A trip to Bok Tower reaches an altitude of 298 feet. (In Florida, that's considered a mountain!) Exotic blossoms perfume leaf-muted pathways. Squirrels chatter atop towering oaks. Carillons chime classical music. Lush greenery stirs the soul. Here, in 1929, Dutch immigrant Edward Bok built a 205-foot carillon tower to show his appreciation for the beauty he felt America had brought into his life. He planted the grounds around the "singing tower" in thousands of magnolias, camellias, azaleas, ferns, oaks, palms, pines, and plants from as far away as Asia. Best time to go is spring, when the flowers are blooming. More than 120 different wild bird species call the 157 acres home, including wood ducks. The fifty-seven-bell carillon tower, listed on the National Register of Historic Places, rings out classical harmonies every half hour starting at 10:00 a.m.

### Spook Hill (all ages)
**Between North Avenue and Burns Avenue.**

The kids will think it's fun to drive to North Avenue and Fifth Street, where mysterious forces seem to power your car uphill. Hokey, but entertaining.

### Lake Wales Depot Museum (ages 8 to 13)
**325 South Scenic Highway; (863) 678-4209. Open 9:00 a.m. to 5:00 p.m. Monday through Friday and 10:00 a.m. to 4:00 p.m. Saturday. Admission is free or by donation.**

The history of the area, including the building of the railroad that settled inland Florida, can be reviewed here. The museum is housed in three buildings, one of them the city's first structure, next to a historic railroad car.

### Chalet Suzanne Country Inn and Restaurant (ages 7 to 13)
**Off Highway 27; 3800 Chalet-Suzanne Drive; (863) 676-6011 or (800) 433-6011; www.chaletsuzanne.com.**

No trip to Lake Wales is complete without a stop here. Have a peek at the quaint Old-world restaurant, inn, gift shops, and ceramic studio. Tours can be arranged through the soup cannery, where the restaurant's trademark dishes are packaged. Its signature romaine soup was sent into space with *Apollo 16*.

### Lake Kissimmee State Park (all ages)
**East of town off Route 60; 14248 Camp Mack Road; (863) 696-1112. Open 7:00 a.m. to sunset daily. Park entrance is $4 per vehicle of eight persons or fewer, $1 per extra passenger, cyclist, or pedestrian.**

Reenactors play the part of cow hunters in a circa-1870 cow camp from 9:30 a.m. to 4:30 p.m. weekends and holidays. Bald eagles, squirrels, ospreys, sandhill cranes, alligators, and deer inhabit the 5,000-acre lake and the land that surrounds it. Spend the day hiking, fishing, canoeing—even stay the night in the sixty-site campground.

## Where to Stay

**Westgate River Ranch.** Off Route 60, 25 miles east of Lake Wales; 3200 River Ranch Road, River Ranch; (863) 692-1321. Tennis, horseshoes, badminton, golf, fitness equipment, pools, tennis, horseback riding, rodeos, barbecues, hayrides, and a petting coral. Stay in your own recreational vehicle, or in an efficiency, hotel room, suite, or cottage. There's also a nine-hole golf course. $–$$

## For More Information

**Lake Wales Chamber of Commerce.** 340 West Central Avenue, Lake Wales 33853; (863) 676-3445; www.lakewales chamber.com.

# Sebring

About a forty-minute drive from Lake Wales on Highway 27.

### Twelve-Hour Endurance Race (ages 10 to 13)

**Sebring International Raceway, 113 Midway Drive; (863) 655-1442.**

Sebring's claim to fame is its annual race for world sports cars each March.

### Highlands Hammock State Park (all ages)

**West of Sebring off Highway 27; 5931 Hammock Road; (863) 386-6094. Open 8:00 a.m. to sunset daily. Park entrance is $4 per vehicle of eight persons or fewer, $1 per extra passenger, cyclist, or pedestrian.**

Far lovelier and a lot less noisy than the raceway, Highlands Hammock State Park gets its name from its ridge elevation. Hikers and cyclists get close to nature in cypress swamps and hardwood hammocks where alligators, otters, bald eagles, deer, and endangered scrub jays hide. You can rent a bike there or hop aboard a tram for a tour. It has picnic grounds, playgrounds, and camping.

## Where to Stay

**Kenilworth Lodge.** 836 Southeast Lakeview Drive; (863) 385-0111 or (800) 423-5939. Historic landmark. Pool and complimentary breakfast. Kids stay **free** with parents. $–$$

## For More Information

**Greater Sebring Chamber of Commerce.** 309 South Circle, Sebring 33870; (863) 385-8448; www.sebringflchamber .com.

## Annual Events

**Florida Strawberry Festival.** Plant City; (813) 752-9194. Strawberry shortcake and country music highlight this eleven-day February-to-March event.

**Kissimmee Bluegrass Festival.** Kissimmee; (813) 783-7205. Three days of fiddling, bluegrass, and gospel music and barbecue in early March.

**Florida High School Rodeo.** Kissimmee; (407) 933-0020. Bull riding, calf roping, bareback riding, and more, two days late in May.

**Kids Festival.** Silver Springs; (352) 236-2121. Two days in mid-July of games and child-oriented fun.

**Halloween Horror Nights at Universal Studios.** Orlando; (407) 363-8000. Seventeen nonconsecutive days of special spook shows, haunted houses, mystery mazes, and roaming monsters and mutants.

**Mickey's Very Merry Christmas Party.** Walt Disney World Magic Kingdom; (407) 824-4321. Holiday goodies, fireworks, and a special night parade with snow; early in December.

# More Things to See and Do
## in Central Florida

- **Retirement Home for Horses,** Gainesville; (386) 462-1001
- **Expo—The Children's Museum of Gainesville,** Gainesville; (352) 378-5492
- **Matheson Museum,** Gainesville; (352) 378-2280
- **Gainesville Raceway,** Gainesville; (352) 377-0046
- **Micanopy Historical Society Museum,** Micanopy; (352) 466-3200
- **Silver River Museum and Environmental Education Center,** Ocala; (352) 236-5401
- **Alexander Spring Creek,** Ocala National Forest; (352) 669-3522
- **Audubon Center for Birds of Prey,** Maitland; (407) 644-0190
- **Bradlee-McIntyre House,** Orlando; (407) 332-0225
- **Boggy Creek Airboat Rides,** Orlando; (407) 344-9550
- **Fun Spot Action Park,** Orlando; (407) 363-3867
- **Titanic: The Exhibition,** Orlando; (407) 248-1166
- **Trainland,** Orlando; (407) 363-9002
- **Sleuth's Mystery Dinner Shows,** Orlando; (407) 363-1985
- **Pirate's Cove Adventure Golf,** Orlando; (407) 352-7378
- **Disney's BoardWalk,** Walt Disney World Resort; (407) W-DISNEY
- **Downtown Disney,** Walt Disney World Resort; (407) W-DISNEY
- **Fantasia Gardens Miniature Golf,** Walt Disney World Resort; (407) 824-4321
- **Shell World,** Kissimmee; (407) 396-9000
- **Kissimmee Go-Karts,** Kissimmee; (407) 396-4800
- **Arabian Nights,** Kissimmee; (407) 239-9223 or (800) 553-6116

# West Central
# Florida

The stretch of Gulf shoreline from the so-called Big Bend south to Sarasota and its environs undergoes many mood swings. At its northern reaches, mangrove coast replaces barrier island beaches, meaning less development and a more natural setting. Midway down begins the parade of islands that trickles down the coast to the southern tip of Florida. With the pretty islands in their sandy skirts come

## TopPicks for Family Fun in West Central Florida

1. Spying animals and whooshing on roller coasters at Busch Gardens, Tampa

2. Feeling hurricane-force winds and other scientific phenomena at the Museum of Science & Industry, Tampa

3. Enjoying shark and manatee experiences at Mote Marine Aquarium, Sarasota

4. Learning at Great Explorations, The Hands-On Museum, St. Petersburg

5. Seeing what's under the sea at Florida Aquarium, Tampa

6. Exploring circus bygones at the Ringling Estate, Sarasota

7. Walking through a kid-size town at Kid City children's museum, Tampa

8. Canoeing the Peace River, Arcadia

9. Watching manatees at their "salad bar" at Homosassa Springs Wildlife State Park, Homosassa

10. Snorkeling among Spanish-American War fort ruins at Egmont Key State Park, St. Pete Beach

# WEST CENTRAL FLORIDA

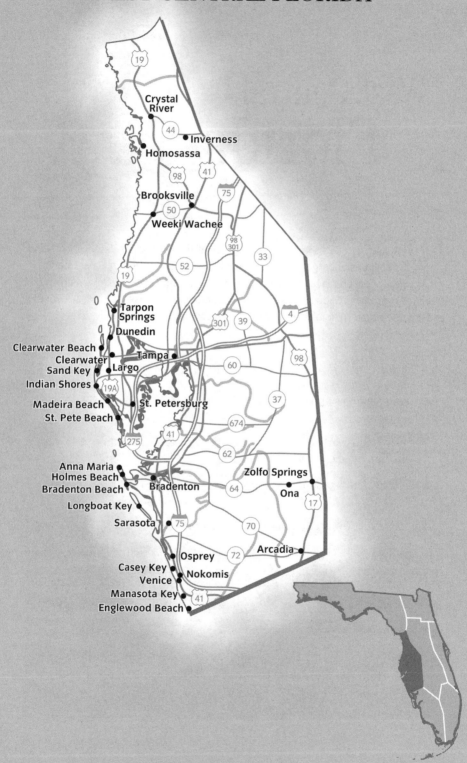

Crystal River

Inverness

Homosassa

Brooksville

Weeki Wachee

Tarpon Springs

Dunedin

Clearwater Beach

Clearwater

Sand Key

Tampa

Largo

Indian Shores

Madeira Beach

St. Petersburg

St. Pete Beach

Anna Maria

Holmes Beach

Bradenton Beach

Zolfo Springs

Bradenton

Ona

Longboat Key

Sarasota

Arcadia

Osprey

Casey Key

Venice

Nokomis

Manasota Key

Englewood Beach

resorts, attractions, and sun-seeking tourists. Big-city Tampa and sister city St. Petersburg form the center of activity along this stretch. To the south, things get more exclusive around Bradenton and Sarasota, then more natural again on their outskirts.

# Crystal River

On Highway 19, about 35 miles west of Interstate 75.

To nature lovers and divers in the know, Crystal River is synonymous with the manatee—that endangered, blimpish, heavyweight darling of Florida marine mammals. The 1,300-pound creatures come each winter to feed on freshwater vegetation in the warm spring waters of aquarium-clear Crystal River, which hosts the largest herd in the state. Snorkelers and divers regularly spot the docile animals.

### Crystal River Archaeological State Park (ages 4 to 13)

**North end of town off Highway 19; 3400 North Museum Point; (352) 795-3817. Museum open 9:00 a.m. to 5:00 p.m.; grounds open 8:00 a.m. to sunset. Entrance fee is $2 per vehicle of eight passengers, $1 per pedestrian or cyclist.**

Above water, you can usually spot the Crystal River's gentle giants from lofty lookouts, such as the one at this fourteen-acre park. Besides manatees, you can see six towering mounds—the highest, 30 feet tall—and artifacts left by ancient civilizations in the museum and throughout the grounds.

### Fort Island Gulf Beach (all ages)

**West of Highway 19 on Route 44; 1600 West Fort Island Trail; (352) 527-7677.**

One of the few Gulf beaches you'll find this far north, it lies off the beaten path. Go for a picnic and a swim. Lifeguards are on duty in the summer.

## Where to Eat

**Oysters.** 606 Highway 19 Northeast; (352) 795-2633. Home-cooked specialties, sandwiches, and kids' menu. Breakfast, lunch, and dinner daily. $–$$

## Where to Stay

**Port Hotel and Marina.** 1610 Southeast Paradise Circle off Highway 19; (352) 795-3111; www.porthotelandmarina.com. On the Crystal River, with bedrooms. $

## For More Information

**Citrus County Tourist Development Council.** 801 Southeast Highway 19; (352) 527-5223 or (800) 587-6667; www.visitcitrus.com.

## Road **Markers**

This tour of west central Florida begins in its northern parts and follows Highway 19 to the beaches of Pinellas County. Traffic on 19 clogs around Port Richey, so avoid it during rush hours. (If you're headed to Tampa, cut over to I-75 north of Port Richey.)

Alternate Highway 19 branches off 19 at Tarpon Springs and continues south close to the coast. At Clearwater, where Route 60 intersects, turn west to reach the beaches. Route 699, a scenic coastal drive, threads the islands together. Most of the way it's four lanes, and traffic flows fairly well. Pinellas Bayway/Route 682 (toll road) connects Route 699 to Interstate 275. Take this north to get to downtown St. Petersburg and Tampa.

South of there, this book's tour follows the parallel path of I-75 and Highway 41 to Bradenton, Sarasota, and their islands—with a few side trips here and there. If you're headed directly to Bradenton-Sarasota from Tampa's west shores, take I-275 south through St. Petersburg—it's quickest and most scenic.

# Weekend Getaway: Withlacoochee State Forest and Brooksville

Take Route 44 southeast to Highway 41. The town of Brooksville is located at the intersection of Highways 41 and 98.

### Withlacoochee State Forest (all ages)

**The Withlacoochee State Forest Headquarters is located on Highway 41, north of Brooksville; 15019 Broad Street, Brooksville; (352) 754-6777 or (352) 754-6896 (for camping and recreational information). The visitor center is at 15003 Broad Street; (352) 754-6896; www.fl-dos.com.**

Florida's second-largest state forest, Withlacoochee's 120,000 acres are divided into six tracts, with three main campgrounds and various recreation areas. You'll find picnic areas, a boat ramp, nature trails, canoeing, snorkeling, and camping. The 46-mile paved Withlacoochee State Trail (352-394-2280) follows an old train route through the park and accommodates bikers and hikers.

# Wilderness-Wary **Kids**

I love the span of rare wilderness around Crystal River, where one can go for a long stretch without seeing another car. But wilderness does not always sit well with young kids. My son, who has been raised on an island outside the city, at age four nonetheless was bothered that we didn't see any other cars. It seemed to scare him. Pointing out the BEAR CROSSING signs didn't help. And to make matters worse, we couldn't find a McDonald's restaurant in town after town. Try preparing young children for forest forays to lessen the potential fear factor. —*C.K.W.*

### Nobleton Canoe Rental (ages 6 to 13)
**Off I-75 exit 62, right outside the state forest northern entrance; 29196 Lake Lindsey Road, Nobleton; (352) 796-7176, (352) 796-4343, or (800) 783-5284; www.nobleton canoes.com. Open 9:00 a.m. to 5:00 p.m.; closed Tuesday. Shuttle and two- to five-hour trips cost $35 to $45 for two to three people.**

Canoe or kayak the blackwater Withlacoochee River on trips ranging from five to thirteen persons. The scenery is gorgeous. Explore the offshoot waterways and bays to discover the richest wildlife. Parks along the way provide pit stops. It also rents pontoon boats and fishing boats, and gives airboat rides.

### Rogers' Christmas House & Village (all ages)
**103 Saxon Avenue, Brooksville; (352) 796-2415 or (877) 312-5046. Open 9:30 a.m. to 5:00 p.m. daily. Admission is free.**

Get in the holiday spirit any day of the week or year (except Christmas Day, of course). Just look for the signs. Five clustered cottages are stuffed like Christmas stockings with yuletide goodies. The Storybook Land cottage makes a big impression with toys inspired by fairy tales and kid stories. As of press time, litigation is pending that will determine the future of Rogers'. Call for more information.

### Fort Cooper State Park (all ages)
**Off Highway 41 south of Inverness; 3100 South Old Floral City Road, Inverness; (352) 726-0315. Open 8:00 a.m. to sunset. Entrance is $2 per carload of eight people or fewer, $1 per cyclist or pedestrian.**

The park is named for a Seminole War site since destroyed and hosts an annual reenactment of the war. A nature trail—where you might chance to spot deer, fox, rabbits, owls, and herons—and a nice sandy beach rim Lake Holathlikaha. Facilities are extensive: five primitive campgrounds, picnicking, swimming, canoe rentals, fishing, horseshoes, volleyball courts, and a playground.

## Where to Eat and Stay

See the Crystal River and Homosassa listings for dining and lodging options.

# Homosassa

South of Crystal River about ten minutes on Highway 19.

### Homosassa Springs Wildlife State Park (all ages)

**Off Highway 19, 4150 South Suncoast Boulevard; (352) 628-5343. Open 9:00 a.m. to 5:30 p.m. daily (ticket sales close at 4:00 p.m.). Admission is $9 plus tax for visitors ages 13 and older, $5 for children ages 3 to 12.**

Where fresh water and salt water intermingle, aquatic life is diverse. See the diversity from an underwater observatory. Here, you're in the fishbowl, and the marine life swims free. From the floating observatory, you can listen to manatees talking underwater via telephones and watch them chomp away at their "salad bar." In the park's virgin Florida forest, you'll see local fauna both caged and roaming free: turtles, bobcats, black bears, deer, ospreys, and other birds. A boat ride tours you around the watery premises, and a children's education center holds, among other curiosities, a live two-headed turtle. Daily educational programs demonstrate the habits of alligators, crocodiles, snakes, and manatees.

## Manatee **Facts**

- Marine mammals and members of the elephant family
- Adults average 10 feet in length and weigh 800 to 3,500 pounds
- Vegetarians, they eat 80 to 500 pounds daily of sea grasses, hydrilla, water hyacinths, and water lettuce
- Gentle, nonaggressive, and slow moving
- Enemies: man, propellers, and red tide
- Endangered status: fewer than 3,000 survive today in Florida waters

## Yulee Sugar Mill Ruins Historic State Park (all ages)

**South of the park on County Road 490, west of Homosassa Springs; (352) 795-3817. Open 9:00 a.m. to 5:00 p.m. daily. Admission is free.**

Here, the state has preserved relics from Florida's sugar production era. The crumbling mill structures provide a lovely background for a picnic, sheltered by time-dignified live oaks. Explore at your leisure along a self-guiding path.

## Where to Eat

**Emily's Family Restaurant.** Highway 19 North; Cardinal Street, Homosassa Springs; (352) 628-6559. From burgers to sirloin steaks, it's no-frills American cooking. Kids' menu. Breakfast, lunch, and dinner daily. $–$$

## Where to Stay

**Homosassa Riverside Resort.** Hall's River Road off Highway 19; 5297 South Cherokee Way; (352) 628-2474. Motel with marina overlooking the Homosassa River. $$–$$$

## For More Information

**Citrus County Chamber of Commerce, Homosassa Branch.** 3495 South Suncoast Boulevard (P.O. Box 709); Homosassa Springs 34447-0709; (352) 628-2666; www.citruscountychamber.com.

# Top Family **Resorts**

1. **Innisbrook Resort,** Tarpon Springs

2. **The Colony,** Longboat Key

3. **Saddlebrook Resort,** Tampa

4. **Holiday Inn Tampa Busch Gardens,** Tampa

5. **Tradewinds Sirata Beach,** St. Pete Beach

6. **Holiday Inn Hotel & Suites,** Longboat Key

7. **Don CeSar Beach Resort & Spa,** St. Pete Beach

8. **Radisson Suites Resort of Sand Key,** Clearwater Beach

# Weeki Wachee

About fifteen minutes south of Homosassa on Highway 19.

## Weeki Wachee Springs Waterpark (ages 2 to 9)
Intersection of Highway 19 and Route 50; 6131 Commercial Way, Spring Hill; (352) 596-2062 or (877) GO-WEEKI; www.weekiwachee.com. Open 10:00 a.m. to 4:00 p.m. daily, with extended summer hours. Admission is $22.95 for adults, $16.95 for seniors, $15.95 for children ages 3 to 10, plus tax. (Prices are subject to change according to season.)

Since 1947, the springs' famous mermaids have been staging underwater mermaid shows, which appeal to kids with stories of Pocahontas, the Little Mermaid, and other kid heroes. You watch from the comfort of an underwater theater with windows onto the clear spring waters. Other shows involve exotic birds and birds of prey, plus there's a river cruise. The former Buccaneer Bay waterpark has been folded into Weeki Wachee, offering springs beach swimming, bumper boat rides, and flume slides in summer and some holidays. Canoe and kayak rentals are available. As of press time, litigation is pending that will determine the future of the park. Call ahead before your visit for more information.

## Where to Stay

**Comfort Inn Weeki Wachee.** 9373 Cortez Boulevard; (352) 596-9000 or (800) 228-5150. Pool and **free** continental breakfast. $–$$

## For More Information

**Hernando County Welcome Center.** 30305 Cortez Boulevard, Brooksville 34602; (352) 754-4405 or (800) 601-4580; www.co.hernando.fl.us/visit.

**Office of Tourism Development.** 26 South Brooksville Avenue, Suite B, Brooksville 34601; (352) 540-4323.

# Tarpon Springs

Take Alternate Highway 19 off Highway 19 north of town, about 35 miles south of Weeki Wachee.

Highly seasoned by its Greek influences, Tarpon Springs is a throwback to the Old World. The Greek community of spongers that settled here in the early 1900s still holds sway; its culture centers around the old sponge docks on Dodecanese Boulevard, off Alternate Highway 19 at the north end of town.

Dodecanese Boulevard represents the more touristy aspects of Tarpon Springs. It's a good place to sample Greek food and pastries, but for a less commercialized look at the town and its Greek heritage, head south on Alternate Highway 19. Downtown Tarpon Springs, at Route 582 (Tarpon Avenue), is a designated National Historic District where vintage structures house antiques shops, cafes, and galleries.

### Tarpon Springs Aquarium (all ages)

At the west end of the sponge docks; 850 Dodecanese Boulevard; (727) 938-5378; www.tarponspringsaquarium.com. Open 10:00 a.m. to 5:00 p.m. Monday through Saturday, noon to 5:00 p.m. Sunday. Admission is $5.75 for adults, $5.00 for seniors, $3.75 for children ages 3 to 11.

Watch from any of three window views as a diver hand-feeds sharks in the 120,000-gallon tank at this family-run aquarium. Other tanks let you feed and pet stingrays, face up to a moray eel, and observe piranhas.

### Island Wind Tours (ages 5 to 13)

600 Dodecanese Boulevard; (727) 934-0606. Tours begin at $10 for adults, $5 for children 6 to 10, and free to those 5 and under.

From the docks, you can depart on excursions to pristine Anclote Key State Preserve for a half day of secluded beaching or an hour of watching birds, dolphins, and manatees. Other tour boats docked in the vicinity stage sponge-diving demonstrations.

### St. Nicholas Greek Orthodox Cathedral (all ages)

348 North Pinellas Avenue; (727) 937-3540. Admission is free.

This replica of St. Sophia Cathedral in Constantinople, Turkey, is open to visitors from 10:00 a.m. to 4:00 p.m. Stained-glass windows and painted icons (which are said to weep on occasion) carry Greek inscriptions. Gilded frames, silver plating, and marble adorn the interior. Anchoring the town's historic district, the cathedral's onion dome and tower dominate the Tarpon Springs skyline. During services you must wear appropriate dress.

## Pinellas **Suncoast**

For information contact the St. Petersburg/Clearwater Area Convention and Visitors Bureau, 14450 Forty-sixth Street North, Clearwater 33762; (727) 464-7200 or (800) 352-3224; www.floridasbeach.com.

Pinellas County encompasses a long stretch of Gulf coastline, from Tarpon Springs to St. Pete Beach, encompassing also the metropolises of Clearwater and St. Petersburg. Known as the Pinellas Suncoast, its islands rank as some of Florida's sunniest and most popular destinations. The business of tourism for the entire coast falls under the auspices of the bureau listed above. Towns and communities have their own visitor bureaus and chambers of commerce as well, which are listed with each town.

## On a **Budget**

- **Rogers' Christmas House & Village,** Brooksville, free admission
- **St. Nicholas Greek Orthodox Cathedral,** Tarpon Springs, free admission
- **Jolley Trolley,** Clearwater Beach, fare $1.25 per person
- **Heritage Village and Pinewood Cultural Park,** Largo, free admission
- **Suncoast Seabird Sanctuary,** Indian Shores, free admission (or by donation)
- **Tampa Electric's Manatee Viewing Center,** Apollo Beach, free admission
- **Manatee Village Historical Park,** Bradenton, free admission
- **DeSoto National Memorial Park,** Bradenton, free admission

### Simply Kayaking (all ages)

**(727) 481-0184; www.simplykayaking.com. Call to reserve a two-hour guided trip. Departure times are dependent on weather and tides. $49 per person.**

Snacks, water, and a CD of digital photos to commemorate your cruise of serene bayous are included in the price. Single, double, and three-person kayaks are available.

### Fred Howard Park (all ages)

**Go west on Klosterman Road (Route 880) to the south and follow the signs to the park.**

For family recreating, you can't beat this park with its 150 acres of beautiful beach, oak-canopied picnic facilities, playgrounds, and windsurfing west of the docks.

## Where to Eat

**Costa's Restaurant.** 521 Athens Street; (727) 938-6890. Authentic Greek seafood and other specialties. $–$$

**Hellas Restaurant.** 785 Dodecanese Boulevard; (727) 943-2400. Cry "opa!" as flaming cheese begins your Greek meal in view of the Anclote River. Adjoining bakery tempts with baklava and other sweets. Lunch and dinner daily. $–$$

## Where to Stay

**Innisbrook Resort and Golf Club.** 36750 Highway 19, North Palm Harbor; (727) 942-2000 or (800) 456-2000; www .innisbrookgolfresort.com. A golfing and tennis focus with schools to teach both. Fine kids' program centered around a playground, nature preserve, waterpark pool, and miniature golf course. Luxury condo and hotel accommodations. $$–$$$$

## For More Information

**Tarpon Springs Chamber of Commerce.** 11 East Orange Street, Tarpon Springs 34689; (727) 937-6109; www .tarponsprings.com.

# Dunedin

A half hour south of Tarpon Springs on Highway 19.

The community of Dunedin is still patterned in the plaids of its Scottish heritage, but these days it is more visited for its terrific state parks and its downtown historic antiques shopping district.

### Honeymoon Island State Park (all ages)

**North of Dunedin; 1 Causeway Boulevard; (727) 469-5942. Open 8:00 a.m. to sunset daily. Park entrance is $5 per vehicle with up to eight passengers, $2 for a single passenger, and $1 for extra passengers, bicyclists, and pedestrians.**

Spend the day fishing, following hiking trails to osprey habitat, or having a picnic. (There's also a snack shop and a new interactive nature center.) The beach isn't so great—it's rocky, even though the staff regularly cleans up—especially when compared with the one at Caladesi Island State Park, a ferry ride away from Honeymoon (see below).

### Caladesi Island State Park (all ages)

**1 Causeway Boulevard; (727) 469-5942 for park information; (727) 734-1501 for ferry schedule. Ferries depart from Honeymoon Island for Caladesi Island every hour on the hour beginning at 10:00 a.m. (On busy weekends, the ferry runs every half hour.) Passengers are assigned a four-hour return time but are allowed to cross back earlier. The last trip leaves from Honeymoon Island at 4:00 p.m. Round-trip ferry fare from Honeymoon Island is $9 for adults, $5.50 for children ages 4 to 12. Private boaters can dock for the day or overnight ($4 fee for a boatload of up to eight persons).**

One of the most outstanding, pristine beaches in the United States and a regular on top-ten lists, Caladesi is worth the cost of ferry and admission. The sand is soft as a feather pillow. With its playground, nature trail, concessions, and picnic area, the park provides a day's worth of entertainment on its own.

### Hammock Park (all ages)

**1900 San Mateo Drive; (727) 298-3271. Admission is free.**

The eighty-five-acre preserve has nature trails, picnic shelters, and a playground.

### Downtown Dunedin (ages 6 to 13)

**Brochure available from the Dunedin Chamber of Commerce, 301 Main Street, Dunedin 34698; (727) 733-3197. Open 8:30 a.m. to 4:30 p.m. Monday through Friday.**

Take a 15-block historic walking tour. Many of Dunedin's historic buildings have been restyled as antiques shops, which attract collectors, especially for the springtime Antiques Fair. Most of the shops are open daily.

### Dunedin Historical Museum (ages 8 to 13)

**349 Main Street; (727) 736-1176. Open 10:00 a.m. to 4:00 p.m. Tuesday through Saturday. Suggested donation is $2 for adults.**

The downtown tour takes in Dunedin's old train depot, which houses a collection of railroad and pioneer day memorabilia, photographs, and artifacts.

### Annual Highland Games (ages 4 to 13)

**(727) 733-6240. Call for dates.**

The games pay homage to Dunedin's heritage. Competitions include piping, drumming, hammer throw, and *clachneart* (stone of strength).

### Pinellas Trail (ages 5 to 13)

**(727) 464-4751.**

Passing right through the middle of town, the 37-mile paved pathway gives joggers, skaters, and cyclists a clear path between Tarpon Springs and St. Petersburg along an old railroad route.

### Knology Park (ages 5 to 13) ⬤

**373 Douglas Avenue; (727) 733-9302. Tickets cost $10 to $20.**

Baseball fans visiting in March and early April should plan on catching the Toronto Blue Jays in spring training here.

## Top Family **Beaches and Parks**

1. **Caladesi Island State Park,** Dunedin

2. **Pier 60 Park,** Clearwater Beach

3. **Pass-A-Grille Beach,** Pass-A-Grille

4. **Siesta Key County Beach,** Siesta Key

5. **Egmont Key,** Fort DeSoto Park

## Where to Eat

**Kelly's . . . For Just About Anything.**
319 Main Street; (727) 736-5284. Casual
restaurant with excellent food, offering
everything from burgers to fancy salads for
Mom and terrific gooey desserts. It sits
just off the Pinellas Trail, so you can eat,
and then take the kids to air out along the
quiet, safe trail on foot, bicycles, or skates.
Breakfast, lunch, and dinner daily. $–$$

## Where to Stay

**Holiday Inn Express.** 975 Broadway
(Alternate Highway 19); (727) 450-1200.
Great for kids because it backs up to the
Pinellas Trail and has a pool, **free** conti-
nental breakfast, and fun-decorated
rooms. $–$$

## For More Information

**Greater Dunedin Chamber of Com-
merce.** 301 Main Street, Dunedin 34698;
(727) 733-3197.

# Clearwater and Clearwater Beach

South of Dunedin 4 miles on Alternate Highway 19. To get to Clearwater Beach, turn
west on Route 60.

Clearwater is a sprawling, metropolitan extension to St. Petersburg. Clearwater
Beach occupies a barrier island to the west and heads a succession of linked islands
that runs about 30 miles down the face of Clearwater and St. Petersburg.

### Celebration Station (all ages)
**24546 Highway 19 North, Clearwater; (727) 791-1799; www.celebrationstation.com.
Open 10:00 a.m. to 11:00 p.m. Monday through Thursday, 10:00 a.m. to midnight Friday and Saturday, and noon to 11:00 p.m. Sunday. Rates vary according to activities.**

A playground for the whole family, it has a spread of miniature golf, batting cages,
bumper boats, go-karts, games, shows, and a pizza parlor.

### Clearwater Marine Aquarium (ages 4 to 13)
**Turn right off Memorial Causeway onto Island Way at Island Estates and follow the
signs to 249 Windward Passage, Clearwater; (727) 447-0980 or (888) 239-9414;
www.cmaquarium.org. Open 9:00 a.m. to 5:00 p.m. Monday through Friday, 9:00 a.m.
to 4:00 p.m. Saturday, and 11:00 a.m.to 4:00 p.m. Sunday. Admission is $9.00 for
adults, $6.50 for children ages 3 to 12. Two-hour boat tours cost $26 for adults, $17
for children ages 3 to 12.**

Kids will enjoy the daily dolphin shows (at noon, 2:00, and 4:00 p.m.) and a touch tank,
and learning interactive techniques at this research and rehab facility. Aquariums

contain exotic fish, and recovering dolphins, otters, and huge sea turtles swim around in tanks. Marine biologists guide its Sea Life Safari Cruises (727-462-2628 or 800-444-4814).

## Pier 60 Park (all ages)

**Intersection of Causeway and Gulfview Boulevards; (727) 462-6466. Parking costs $1 per hour. Open twenty-four hours. Admission to the fishing pier is $6.30 for adults, $5.00 for children under age 10; 50 cents if sightseeing.**

Clearwater Beach has some of the best beaches of all the Suncoast. They're wide, white, plushly sandy, and full of family things to do, especially Gulfview, where a nightly sunset celebration convenes on Pier 60 with jugglers, clowns, magicians, face painters, and musicians. It's also a great place for fishing. The playground is way cool in many ways—it's sheltered from the sun by a tin roof, and it has the newest in play equipment and interactive fountains. Volleyball is the sport of Clearwater Beach, site of major beach volleyball tournaments. Much of the volleyball action takes place at Pier 60, a full-service beach with lifeguards and concessions for food, beach supplies, and water-sports rentals.

## Jolley Trolley

**Office at 483 Mandalay Avenue, Clearwater Beach; (727) 445-1200. Pickups every thirty minutes daily. Fare is $1.25 each, 60 cents per senior.**

It travels around Clearwater Beach and Clearwater.

## Captain Memo's Pirate Cruise (ages 4 to 13)

**Clearwater Marina; 25 Causeway Boulevard, Slip 3, Clearwater Beach; (727) 446-2587; www.pirateflorida.com. Fares (including beverages) are $33 for adults, $28 for seniors and juniors ages 13 to 17, $25 for children ages 3 to 12, $10 for children under 3 (tax is additional).**

Clearwater Marina harbors any number of options for exploring nearby islands and waters. A good one for young seafaring adventurers, Captain Memo's sets sail aboard a vessel of swashbuckling allure four times daily for sightseeing and partying. Kids wear pirate hats, engage in water-pistol battles, get their faces painted, and dance the macarena. Cannons fire at passing watercraft. It's all kinds of fun.

## Sand Key Park (all ages)

**Parking is by meter at 25 cents for twenty minutes.**

The town of Clearwater Beach continues onto Sand Key, across the south-end bridge. Often listed among Florida's top beaches, Sand Key Park is a family favorite with lots of green areas for picnicking and playing. The wide, sugar-sand beach is patrolled by lifeguards and offers water-sports rentals.

## Where to Eat

**Frenchy's Rockaway Grill.** 7 Rockaway Street off Gulfview Boulevard, Clearwater Beach; (727) 446-4844. Colorful furnishings, sunset views, casual fare, and beach location. Lunch and dinner daily. $–$$

**Gondolier Pizza Italian Restaurant.** 674 South Gulfview Boulevard, Clearwater Beach; (727) 441-3353. Relaxed, 160-seat restaurant specializes in lovely lasagnas, ravishing ravioli, and all sorts of pizza, too. Breakfast, lunch, dinner; open until midnight, seven days a week. $–$$

## Where to Stay

**Marriott Suites of Sand Key.** 1201 Gulf Boulevard, Clearwater Beach; (727) 596-1100 or (800) 228–9290. Across the street from Sand Key Park with kid-proofed family suites and a clubhouse for kids' activities. A macaw named Lisa is available for tuck-ins. Microwave ovens and small refrigerators in the suites, waterfall swimming pools, and beach shuttle. $$$

**Sea Stone Resort.** 445 Hamden Drive, Clearwater Beach; (727) 441-1722 or (800) 444-1919; www.seastoneresorts.com. On the bayside, near the beach. $$–$$$$

## For More Information

**St. Petersburg/Clearwater Area Convention and Visitors Bureau,** 14450 Forty-sixth Street, Suite #108, Clearwater 33762; (727) 464-7200 or (877) 352-3224; www.floridasbeach.com.

# West Central **Climes**

In the northern reaches of this region, the average year-round temperature is 70 degrees. Winter temperatures average 60.1 degrees, and summer temperatures 82.4 degrees. Crystal River, for instance, averages 294 days of sunshine.

Sunshine is such a constant around St. Petersburg, in the middle part of this region, that it made the *Guinness Book of World Records* with a 768-day run of consecutive sunny days, from February 8, 1967, to March 17, 1969. It averages 361 sunshiny days a year and a temperature of 73 degrees. Summer highs reach 90.3 degrees; winter lows, 49.5.

Summers mean thunderstorms and the rare hurricane. Winters are cool and dry.

# Sand Key

Just south of Clearwater Beach on Route 699.

A number of small resort and residential communities string along Sand Key south of the town of Clearwater Beach. Indian Rocks Beach is a picturesque town with small public beach accesses and reasonably priced restaurants suited to the family.

If you take a left on Sixteenth Avenue and a right on Bay Palm Boulevard, you'll wander into the historic heart of Indian Rocks Beach.

### Pinewood Cultural Park (ages 7 to 13)

**12175 125th Street North, Largo; (727) 582-2100. Florida Botanical Gardens open daily 7:00 a.m. to 7:00 p.m.; Heritage Village and Gulf Coast Museum of Art open 10:00 a.m. to 4:00 p.m. Tuesday through Saturday, noon to 4:00 p.m. Sunday. Village and gardens free. Admission to art museum (12211 Walsingham Road) is $8 for adults, $7 for seniors, $4 for children ages 7 to 18; 6 and under free.**

Spend a day immersed in history, nature, and art. Two bridges and three separate entrances lead to this twenty-one-acre park, which includes a village of living history, multicolored themed gardens, and a new museum featuring outdoor sculpture and contemporary Florida artists. At Heritage Village, tour guides dress the part of twentieth-century pioneers and lead you through family homes, a one-room schoolhouse, general store, blacksmith shop, and more than a dozen other historic structures.

### Suncoast Seabird Sanctuary (all ages)

**18328 Gulf Boulevard, Indian Shores; (727) 391-6211. Open 9:00 a.m. until dark daily. One-hour tours are conducted at 2:00 p.m. every Wednesday. Admission is free, but donations are appreciated.**

While "doing the beaches," you must stop in to deliver best wishes to recovering patients of the feathered variety. It's right on the beach, and it's usually flocked with pelicans. In the cages you'll find hawks, sandhill cranes, owls, pelicans, and a variety of other injured birds on the mend.

### John's Pass Village and Boardwalk (all ages)

**150 John's Pass Boardwalk, Madeira Beach; (727) 394-0756; www.Johnspass.com.**

Madeira Beach, also known as Mad Beach, is where the action happens. Most of it centers around John's Pass. Here, an angling charter industry has grown into a shopping and restaurant district with a ramshackle fish-house motif. It boasts its catches of grouper, a large Florida fish with tasty white meat. Snag one on a deep-sea fishing charter. Eat it and other local seafood in the village's many restaurants and at the annual John's Pass Seafood Festival in October.

### Hubbard's Sea Adventures (ages 4 to 13)

150 John's Pass Boardwalk, Madeira Beach; (727) 398-6577 or (800) 755-0677; www .hubbardsmarina.com. Cost for excursions is $16.82 to $26.90 for adults, $8.41 to $13.45 for children ages 3 to 11. Tax is additional.

Take sunset, dolphin watch, Shell Key barbecue, and Egmont Key excursions aboard a deck boat for fun and informative narrative. Snorkel gear rentals are available. Boats have restrooms and covered seating.

## Where to Eat

**Crabby Bill's.** 401 Gulf Boulevard, Indian Rocks Beach; (727) 595-4825. A local favorite serving fish-house fare on long picnic tables for lunch and dinner daily. $–$$

**Friendly Fisherman Seafood Restaurant.** 150 John's Pass Boardwalk, Madeira Beach; (727) 391-6025. View of bay waters and just-caught fish. Breakfast, lunch, and dinner daily. $$

## For More Information

**Tampa Bay Beaches Chamber of Commerce.** 6990 Gulf Boulevard, St. Pete Beach 33706; (727) 360-6957 or (800) 944-1847; www.tampabaybeaches.com. Represents the little towns sprinkled along the barrier islands along the Gulf of Mexico, from Sand Key in the north to St. Pete Beach in the south.

# St. Pete Beach

South of Sand Key and Treasure Island along Route 699.

### Pass-A-Grille Beach (all ages)

Gulf Way between First and Twenty-first Avenues. Parking in the area is metered at 25 cents for fifteen minutes.

The village of Pass-A-Grille spreads a great beach. The facilities are minimal, but the sand and water are extremely user-friendly.

### Gulf Beaches Historical Museum (ages 6 to 13)

115 Tenth Avenue; (727) 552-1610. Open 10:00 a.m. to 4:00 p.m. Saturday and Sunday during summer. From September to May, it's open Thursday, Friday, and Saturday 10:00 a.m. to 4:00 p.m., and 1:00 p.m. to 4:00 p.m. Sunday. Admission is **free.**

When you're ready to take a break from the beach, browse the bygones through photos and memorabilia. Or play a little shuffleboard in the park nearby.

## Merry Pier (all ages)

**Pass-A-Grille Way; (727) 360-1348; www.shellkeyshuttle.com about the Shell Key shuttle. The shuttle departs from the pier three times daily. Fare is $22 for adults, $11 for children ages 12 and under, plus tax. Parking is $2.**

On the bay side, you can catch a ten-minute shuttle to Shell Key, an unbridged key with no facilities, but lots of seashells and wildlife. You can also catch a fishing or sunset cruise charter, rent a fishing boat, or drop a hook from the pier, which is **free** and equipped with all the necessities.

## Fort DeSoto Park (all ages)

**Southeast of St. Pete Beach (follow the signs); 3500 Pinellas Bayway South, Tierra Verde; (727) 582-2267 for the campground; www.fortdesoto.com. Open sunrise to sunset. There's a 35-cent toll to get to the park.**

Campers will love it here. It has a nattily maintained campground within a wildlife sanctuary that occupies five keys. The 1,136-acre county park's namesake fort, which never saw battle, was built for the Spanish-American War. Next to it, a fishing pier juts out 1,000 feet into the Gulf. Another in the bay measures 500 feet. The park has two beaches with nice picnic areas and playgrounds. You can watch traffic into deep Tampa Bay from the fort, pier, and beach. Swift currents make swimming dangerous in parts. North Beach is popular with shellers.

## Egmont Key State Park (all ages)

From Fort DeSoto Park, you'll spy a small, slender island, site of a sister fort during the Spanish-American War. This fort is sliding into the sea, creating one of the coast's foremost snorkeling sites. There's no bridge to the island, but a ferry from Fort DeSoto Park and several charters out of St. Pete Beach make trips. The beach is luxuriously long and perfect for swimming and shelling. Some still-intact fort ruins give the kids something to explore on land. There are also nature trails that lead to a still-functioning lighthouse that dates back to 1858.

# Battle **Facts**

During the Spanish-American War, Tampa Bay was deemed a strategic military post. Col. Teddy Roosevelt set up headquarters for his Rough Riders at the ornately luxurious Tampa Bay Hotel, and the town became the staging point for 30,000 American troops. Forts were built on Mullet Key (at today's Fort DeSoto Park) and Egmont Key, but nary a shot was fired in battle.

## Where to Eat

**Skidder's Restaurant.** 5799 Gulf Boulevard; (727) 360-1029 or (727) 367-7825. Friendly restaurant popular among tourists and locals alike, specializing in pizzas as well as more complex dishes like steak Diane glamorous with satiny gravy; finish with rice pudding. Open for breakfast, lunch, and dinner. $–$$

**Wharf Seafood Restaurant.** 2001 Pass-A-Grille Way; (727) 367-9469. Locals' haunt serving fish, shrimp, crab cakes, and crab claws for lunch and dinner daily. $–$$

**Woody's Waterfront Cafe & Beach Bar.** Corey Avenue and Sunset Way; 7308 Sunset Way; (727) 360-9165. Off the beaten path, casual, and waterfront. Burgers and seafood baskets. Lunch and dinner daily. $$

## Where to Stay

Rooms are plentiful up and down the strip.

**Don CeSar Beach Resort & Spa.** 3400 Gulf Boulevard; (727) 360-1881 or (800) 282-1116; www.doncesar.com. At the island's south end, the most noticeable landmark is this vintage bubblegum-pink palace. It has a good kids' program, a great beach with water sports galore, two swimming pools, and an old-fashioned ice cream parlor. A good time to visit is when the resort hosts its sandcastle building contest in late June or early July. $$$–$$$$

**Sirata Beach Resort and Conference Center.** 5300 Gulf Boulevard; (727) 363-5100 or (800) 344-5999; www.sirata.com. Part of a three-resort complex on St. Pete Beach under the TradeWinds umbrella that shares facilities, this one is the most family-suited with its own Island Cafe providing a kids' play space. Daily kids' program; 380 rooms and one-bedroom suites. $$–$$$$

# St. Petersburg

From St. Pete Beach, head east on Pinellas Bayway/Route 682 (toll) to I-275, which travels through St. Petersburg. Interstate 175 and Interstate 375 peel off and skewer the downtown area. The trip from St. Petersburg to I-75 crosses the Skyway Bridge, a suspended work of art especially impressive when lit at night. The bridge that it replaces has been turned into the World's Longest Fishing Pier.

Downtown St. Petersburg hugs Tampa Bay on a peninsula that faces its sister city, Tampa. An old city once known for its elderly population, St. Petersburg has been rejuvenated in recent years. In its sprightly new form, it has much to offer family visitors along its waterfront.

### Salvador Dali Museum (ages 8 to 13)

**Exit 22 off I-275 at 1000 Third Street South; (727) 823-3767; www.salvadordalimuseum .org. Open 9:30 a.m. to 5:30 p.m. Monday through Saturday (extended to 8:00 p.m. on Thursday) and noon to 5:30 p.m. Sunday. Admission is $15.00 for adults; $13.50 for seniors, $10.00 for students with identification, $4.00 for children 5 to 9, and free for children 4 and under. Thursday after 5:00 p.m. admission is $5.00.**

Downtown's most impressive treasure, it is home to the world's largest collection of original works by its namesake surrealist artist, he of melting clocks fame. Some of his works extend from floor to ceiling, others are small preliminary pencil sketches. Special exhibits complement permanent ones.

### Tropicana Field (ages 4 to 13) 

**1 Tropicana Drive; (727) 825-3250 or (888) FAN-RAYS. The Tampa Bay Devil Rays regular single-game tickets range from $8 to $210; spring training tickets are $7 to $20. Parking is free. Kids will enjoy the cool kid page at the Devil Ray Web site, www.devil rays.com.**

Major league baseball's Tampa Bay Devil Rays hosts fans here in air-conditioned comfort, April through September. A play area relieves monotony for the too-small-to-appreciate. The Devil Rays play spring training games nearby every March at Al Lang Stadium (822 Second Avenue; 727-893-7490).

### St. Petersburg Museum of History (ages 4 to 13) 

**335 Second Avenue Northeast; (727) 894-1052; www.spmoh.org. Open 10:00 a.m. to 5:00 p.m. Tuesday through Saturday, noon to 5:00 p.m. Sunday, and noon to 7:00 p.m. Monday. Admission is $6 for adults, $5 for seniors, $3 for those 7 to 17, and free for those 6 and younger.**

With a vintage airplane hanging from the ceiling and period clothes you can "try on," it has plenty to offer family members. The airplane is a replica of the circa-1910 Benoist airboat—the first recorded airplane to fly a commercial route by crossing from Tampa to St. Petersburg. To try on the costumes, you stand behind glass pull-out displays and see yourself in the mirror. Other vignettes realistically depict life throughout the history of St. Petersburg.

### The Pier (all ages)

**800 Second Avenue Northeast; (727) 821-6443; www.stpete-pier.com. Open 10:00 a.m. to 9:00 p.m. Monday through Thursday, 10:00 a.m. to 10:00 p.m. Friday and Saturday, and 11:00 a.m. to 7:00 p.m. Sunday. Pier Aquarium open 10:00 a.m. to 8:00 p.m. Monday through Saturday, noon to 6:00 p.m. Sunday. Admission to the Pier is free; parking is $3. Admission to the Pier Aquarium is $5.00 for adults, $4.00 for seniors and students 7 and older; 6 and under free. On Sunday, admission is $2.50 for all.**

The Pier is a hub of local activity, with charters and rental boats departing from its docks and land tours taking off from its approach. Around the outside perimeter, fishermen cast, just as they did from its six predecessors since 1899. Today, kids enjoy fishing or feeding the pelicans, and they can wear themselves out on rented bikes. At the Pier Aquarium on the second floor kids can become an "Official Fish Feeder" during the 3:00 feedings and touch sea horses and hermit crabs. Exhibits include "Nemo," other exotic fish, and huge tanks full of marine life.

### Great Explorations, The Hands-On Museum (all ages)
**1925 Fourth Street North; (727) 821-8992; www.greatexplorations.org. Open 10:00 a.m. to 4:30 p.m. Monday through Saturday and noon to 4:30 p.m. Sunday. Admission is $8 for seniors, $9 ages 1 and older; under 1 free.**

Kids will like this fast-forward, entertaining, and highly stimulating museum. They can make their own cartoons via computer animation, test a real lie detector, or wear themselves out on a climbing wall. A less frenzied play area is set aside for children six and younger. "I Can Construct," a new two-story tree house featured on several TV shows, introduces interactive activities related to construction, architecture, and engineering.

## Pinching Pennies **at the Pier**

After a morning at a special *Titanic* exhibition at St. Petersburg's Florida International Museum, our wallets looked thin. Two kids, souvenirs, and treats on the trip up had taken their titanic toll. We were hungry and not quite ready to hit the road back home, so we hit the Pier instead. A lot of what the kids loved most at the futuristic upside-down pyramid structure was free or inexpensive. We passed on the motion simulator ride ($5 each) and opted for a ride from the parking lot to the Pier on a free tram and a ride on the glass elevator to the open-air fifth floor (where we could not only pinch pennies but also pitch pennies, as many had, onto a roof below). Up there, 50 cents each bought us a magnified view of Tampa's skyline and bay watercraft traffic. We ordered lunch from the food court, where each could satisfy individual hunger cravings, and visited the second-floor aquarium, which suggests a $1 per person donation. We window-shopped at boutiques specializing in cartoon toys and hats and were on our way down the quarter-mile-long walk, where the kids ran off the last of their steam before the long ride home.

—*C.K.W.*

# Smart **Travel**

- Traveling families should always be on their guard against crime, but especially in and around large cities such as St. Petersburg and Tampa. Keep doors locked always when driving and when getting out at gas stations and rest stops to safeguard against carjacking and theft. Avoid travel at night, especially in dimly lit and unfamiliar areas.

- In summer, plan dry outdoor activities for mornings. By afternoon you'll be looking for water, air-conditioning, and an umbrella.

- Many resorts throughout Florida let kids under a certain age stay **free** with parents. Be sure to indicate the number of children in your family and their ages when you're making reservations.

- If traveling with toddlers, ask to have your room childproofed when making your reservation. If the hotel or resort does not have a childproofing kit or plan, request that matches be removed and ask for a room on the ground floor if there are open balconies. Bring your own childproof outlet plugs. And don't forget the night-lights.

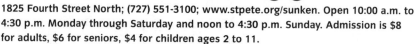

## St. Petersburg Historic Sunken Gardens

1825 Fourth Street North; (727) 551-3100; www.stpete.org/sunken. Open 10:00 a.m. to 4:30 p.m. Monday through Saturday and noon to 4:30 p.m. Sunday. Admission is $8 for adults, $6 for seniors, $4 for children ages 2 to 11.

Down a sinkhole in the middle of the city, you'll find cool, quiet respite amid thriving plant life at Sunken Gardens, a tourist attraction since 1935. See butterflies, birds, and bird and reptile shows three times daily. Garden tours available.

## Science Center (ages 5 to 13)

7701 Twenty-second Avenue North; (727) 384-0027; www.sciencecenterofpinellas.com. Open 1:00 to 4:00 p.m. Monday through Friday. Admission is $5 per person and includes self-guided tours, planetarium shows, and the Environmental Learning Zone.

This is a neighborhood, Mr. Wizard kind of place where kids learn about marine science, animals, astronomy, chemistry, and archaeology. A touch tank with marine life; a room with small animals, birds and reptiles, and alligators; and a sixteenth-century Native American village are some of the exhibits kids can explore.

## Boyd Hill Nature Park (all ages)

1101 Country Club Way South; (727) 893-7326. Open 9:00 a.m. to 8:00 p.m. Tuesday through Thursday, 9:00 a.m. to 6:00 p.m. Friday, 7:00 a.m. to 6:00 p.m. Saturday, and 11:00 a.m. to 6:00 p.m. Sunday. Admission is $2 for adults, $1 for children ages 3 to 17; tram tour is $1 extra.

Add nature lessons to your family picnic at this park, tucked away in south St. Petersburg. Lizards and squirrels scamper while kids conquer the tree-house-like playground, explore the nature center, and bike or hike trails. Ask for the butterfly checklist and make a game of spotting different species. A daily tram tour departs at 1:00 p.m.

## Where to Eat

**Cha Cha Coconuts.** The Pier, 800 Second Avenue Northeast; (727) 822-6655. Colorful, panoramic view from the Pier's fifth floor, sandwiches, and seafood for lunch and dinner daily. $–$$

**The Pier Food Court.** 800 Second Avenue Northeast; (727) 895-4460. Bakery goods, pizza, steaks, burgers, and ice cream, all reasonably priced and above standard fast-food fare. Often you're entertained by minstrels. Open daily. $

**Skyway Jacks.** 2795 Thirty-fourth Street South; (727) 866-3217. Popular, old-fashioned diner, homemade Southern-style eats. The kids will like the big chicken out front and the chocolate chip pancakes. Breakfast and lunch. $

## Where to Stay

**Renaissance Vinoy Resort.** 501 Fifth Avenue Northeast; (727) 894-1000; www.renaissancehotels.com. Grand historic hotel with plush rooms, marina, tennis courts, swimming pools, golf, and fitness center. $$$–$$$$

## For More Information

**St. Petersburg/Clearwater Area Convention and Visitors Bureau.** 14450 Forty-sixth Street, Suite 108, Clearwater 33762; (727) 464-7200 or (877) 352-3224; www.floridasbeach.com.

# Tampa

Continuing through St. Petersburg, I-275 crosses Tampa Bay on the Howard Frankland Bridge, plunging into Tampa's core.

The west coast's biggest town, Tampa is a megacenter of transportation, commerce, and communication, as well as tourism. Visitors often combine a trip to the Pinellas Suncoast with a visit to Tampa, and vice versa, to get a taste of the best Florida has to offer: culture, year-round sports, amusement parks, and beaches. There's even some outdoor adventure to be had in Tampa.

This tour loops to the northern and western parts of the city before heading to the vibrant, revitalizing downtown area. From the west side of downtown, Highway 92 will take you across the Gandy Bridge to St. Petersburg and on to I-275 south.

### Legends Field (ages 5 to 13)

**4330 North Dale Mabry Highway; (813) 879-2244 or (800)-96YANKS. Tickets range from $3 to $5.**

Tampa is big on sports—major-league type—most of which are found in northwest Tampa. The new Yankees complex seats 10,000 for March exhibition games and off-season rookie and semiprofessional baseball. It replicates New York's Yankee Stadium.

### Raymond James Stadium (ages 5 to 13)

**3501 West Tampa Bay Boulevard; (813) 673-4300.**

This is home to National Football League's Tampa Bay Buccaneers (813-879-2827; www.tampasportsauthority.com) in fall and winter.

### Lowry Park Zoological Garden (ages 2 to 11)

**1101 West Sligh Avenue; (813) 935-8552; www.lowryparkzoo.com. Open 9:30 a.m. to 5:00 p.m. daily. Admission is $16.95 for adults, $15.95 for seniors, $12.50 for children ages 3 to 11. River Odyssey ecotour (offered Wednesday through Sunday) not included.**

The latest addition to these fifty-six acres of exotic and native animals in their natural habitats is a colony of "happy feet" penguins from southwest Africa. Kids can feed a giraffe, ride a camel, and pet a goat or a stingray. Exhibits include such endangered animals as manatees, Florida panthers, Sumatran tigers, and an Indian rhinoceros.

### Kid City (ages 2 to 12)

**Next to Lowry Park; 7550 North Boulevard; (813) 935–8441. Open 9:30 a.m. to 2:30 p.m. Monday through Thursday, 9:30 a.m. to 5:00 p.m. Frriday and Saturday, and noon to 5:00 p.m. Sunday. Admission is $5 for ages 1 and older.**

Toddlers love the darling little park with its miniature outdoor town. Indoor hands-on exhibits teach about using your hands.

## Recipe for a **Tampa Cuban Sandwich**

Mind you, this differs from a Miami Cuban sandwich.

Take one loaf Cuban bread, baked with a palm leaf laid on top. Fill with roast pork, baked ham, Genoa salami, cheese, pickles, and mustard. Nothing else. Toast in a special Cuban sandwich press.

## Busch Gardens (all ages)

3000 Busch Boulevard; (813) 987-5082; www.buschgardens.com. Hours vary by season and by day; call for a schedule. Admission is $61.95 for adults, $51.95 for children ages 3 to 9 (tax is additional). Parking is $9 for cars, $10 for recreational vehicles, trucks, and campers.

The attractions grow grander as you head east. Busch Gardens, one of Florida's top family attractions, is an all-day affair with monstrous adventure rides and African animals wandering 300 acres. The park is divided into nine different African-themed areas—such as Morocco, the Congo, Egypt, and Timbuktu—with shops and restaurants to go along with the animals, shows, and rides. You can view the entire grounds by skyride or train. Especially interesting are the Myombe Reserve gorilla and chimp area. Some of the rides get you moderately wet to drenched, so you may wish to bring extra clothes and rent a locker. A lovable tot's playland is dragon-themed. Edge of Africa devotes fifteen acres of land to habitats for African animals, which visitors can view close up and from afar. Truck tours of the Serengeti start at an extra $33.99 per person (must be over five years of age; make reservations once in the park). The newest ride is the "floorless" SheiKra, a dive coaster where 200 feet up, a 90-degree straight drop gives an unobstructed view at 70 mph. Too thrilling? Try the Cheetah Chase, a family ride made for that first coaster experience.

## Adventure Island (ages 3 to 13)

Next door to Busch Gardens; 4500 Bougainvillea Avenue; (813) 987-5600; www .adventureisland.com. Hours vary by season and day. It closes November through February and is open weekends only in fall and spring. Admission is $35.95 for adults, $33.95 for children ages 3 to 9. (Tax is additional.) Combination tickets for one day each at Busch Gardens and Adventure Island are $79.95 and $65.95, plus tax. Parking is $6.

As far as water theme parks go, it's a splash above most. Splash Attack lets small ones get wet and get even with water artillery. Key West Rapids twists and contorts you along 700 feet of climbs and drops. It joins a full menu of fun: the Endless Surf pool, Caribbean Corkscrew, Wahoo Run, and Tampa Typhoon, to name a few. The park fills up early with families who come to grab picnic tables and shade, but only coolers of less than 16-quart size are allowed. Snack bars and cafes are also on-site.

## Museum of Science & Industry (MOSI) (ages 4 to 13)

4801 East Fowler Avenue; (813) 987-6100, (800) 995-MOSI, or (877) 987-IMAX; www .mosi.org. Open 9:00 a.m. to 5:00 p.m. daily. Admission (including one IMAX movie) is $19.95 for adults, $17.95 for seniors, $15.95 for children ages 2 to 12.

MOSI, the largest science center in the southeastern United States, gives you a feel for tornadoes, the birthing process, and hurricanes. Kids In Charge, a challenging interactive children's science center for ages twelve and under that opened in 2006, was largely planned by kids ages ten to seventeen. Some 450 other exhibits deal with

Florida's environment and natural history, health, flight, and space in a creative, interactive manner, using computer and other games. IMAX domed screen shows and a planetarium will enchant the entire family with 180-degree views of volcanoes, the planets, and the Amazon rain forest. Explore a butterfly garden and stroll more than 3 miles of backwoods trails. This is one of Florida's most high-tech interactive museums.

## Canoe Escape (ages 5 to 13)

**9335 East Fowler Avenue, Thonotosassa; (813) 986-2067 or 44-TAMPA; www.canoe escape.com. Open 9:00 a.m. to 5:00 p.m. weekdays and 8:00 a.m. to 5:00 p.m. weekends. Self-guided trips start at $22.50 per person (two-person minimum); $42 and up per solo kayak.**

Canoeing on the Hillsborough River is a great way to explore local ecology. Ibises, alligators, ospreys, and herons course among the gigantic oaks and cypress trees. Canoe Escape provides outfitting and shuttle service for two-hour to full-day excursions.

## Hillsborough River State Park (ages 5 to 13)

**Take Highway 301 north to Thonotosassa; 15402 Highway 301 North, Thonotosassa; (813) 987-6771. Open 8:00 a.m. to sunset daily. Park entrance is $4 per vehicle of eight persons or fewer, $1 per extra passenger, cyclist, or pedestrian.**

It holds memories of Florida's long and painful Seminole Indian conflicts during the 1800s at the Fort Foster living history site (winter only). For families, it also holds the opportunity within its 3,000 acres for outdoor bonding along its canoe trails, campsites, and nature paths.

## Ybor City 🏛

**Take exit 1 off Interstate 4 West.**

A Latin essence lingers from Ybor City's heyday as a Cuban cigar-making district. The era brought an intermingling of many other cultures, including German, Italian, and Jewish, which is reflected in the district's acclaimed restaurants. The competition is always on to see who makes the best Cuban sandwich. Black bean soup and Cuban coffee are other specialties. The entire 110-block Ybor City district is filled with historic cigar factories and workers' homes, many of them reborn as shops, galleries, and restaurants. Kids will like Game Works, a Steven Spielberg video game land at the Centro Ybor shopping and entertainment venue. For a walking tour visit the chamber of commerce, listed at the end of this section.

## Ybor City Museum State Park (ages 8 to 13)

**1818 East Ninth Avenue; (813) 247-6323. Open 9:00 a.m. to 5:00 p.m. daily. Admission is $3 per person and includes a tour of La Casita House Museum (see below).**

Ybor (EE-bore) City was founded by Vincente Martínez Ybor. This Spanish entrepreneur began the city's cigar industry there in 1886. The political, social, and cultural factors that influenced the district's boomtown era are exposed in a period bakery building, complete with the ovens where the community's supply of Cuban bread was baked. A video, cigar-making exhibits, and gardens complete the tour.

### La Casita House Museum (ages 8 to 13)

**1804 East Ninth Avenue. Open 11:00 a.m. to 3:00 p.m. by tour when docents are available. Combined admission for the Ybor City Museum State Park and La Casita is $3 per person.**

In Preservation Park you can see how cigar factory workers once lived. La Casita, circa 1895, is a furnished "shotgun" cottage (for its straight-through design), one of a group of six in the park's reconstructed streetscape.

### Columbia Restaurant (ages 6 to 13)

**2117 East Seventh Avenue; (813) 248-4961.**

Most noticeable and renowned of Ybor's restaurants is this Latin-Baroque-style jewel. You must have a look at it; you can't miss its rococo tile exterior. Stop in for lunch or dinner any day and marvel at the architecture of its many rooms and the authenticity of its Spanish cuisine. Kids love the dramatic, live flamenco dancers, who perform six nights a week. $$$–$$$$

### TECO Line Streetcar (all ages)

**(813) 254-HART; www.tecolinestreetcar.org. One-way fares are $2 for adults, $1 for seniors, children 17 or younger, and people on Medicare or with disabilities; children who are no taller than the fare box and who are traveling with an adult ride free.**

Not many cities have zippy yellow, fully air-conditioned streetcars that clank their way around, but Tampa invested $53 million in a new 2.3-mile streetcar track linking downtown, the Channelside District, and Ybor City. Opened in October 2002, it boasts eight shiny streetcars, duplicates of the original Birney cars that traversed Tampa until their demise in 1946. This is a fascinating expedition for kids, many of whom have never been on a real streetcar, relatively cheap, and perfect for families who want to leave their cars behind and walk around town. Streetcars go right past the Florida Aquarium and through Ybor City.

### Gasparilla Invasion (all ages)

**(813) 353-8108; www.gasparillapiratefest.com.**

Downtown is the site of the town's best festival, which takes place in February—a re-creation of the legend of local hero, pirate Gasparilla. Invasion Day thunders with the harbor landing of hundreds of swashbuckling pirates aboard the tri-masted *Jose Gasparilla* pirate ship, followed by a boisterous parade along Bayshore Boulevard. Month-long festivities include street dances, foot races, Ybor City's concurring Fiesta Day street festival and illuminated night parade (813-248-3712), and the Florida State Fair at Florida Expo Park (813-621-7821 or, in Florida, 800-345-FAIR).

### Florida Aquarium (ages 4 to 13)

**701 Channelside Drive; (813) 273-4000; www.flaquarium.org. Open 9:30 a.m. to 5:00 p.m. daily. Admission is $17.95 for adults, $14.95 for seniors, $12.95 for children ages 3 to 11. Parking is $4.**

Under its shell-shaped glass dome, exhibit areas showcase the state's different aquarian environments. You can look below the surface of a mangrove estuary to see mullet and snook; above the water line, native owls and vegetation create the effect of the damp environment. Another display demonstrates beach life—waves and all. An interactive addition allows children to dig for beach treasures and build a reef. Awes & Jaws features more than twenty additional species of sharks and rays and hands-on ways to learn about the animals' power and anatomy. Frights of the Forest contains leeches, scorpions, vampire bats, and other under-loved critters. The complex's most colorful section gives you a magnificent window into reef life. Many of the exhibits are conveniently at kid's-eye level.

### St. Petersburg Times Forum (ages 5 to 13)

**Near the Florida Aquarium; 401 Channelside Drive; (813) 301-6500 or (813) 301-2500 for box office; www.tampabaylightning.com.**

The 2004 Stanley Cup champions Tampa Bay Lightning hockey team plays its games at this immense $153 million arena.

### Tampa Theatre (ages 5 to 13)

**711 Franklin Street; (813) 274-8981; www.tampatheatre.org. Requested donation for one-hour tour (held Wednesday and Saturday at 11:30 a.m.) is $5 per person.**

In the heart of downtown, it's the old, not the new, that dazzles. You shouldn't miss this ornately bedecked gem. It has been restored to its 1926 grandeur and stages films, concerts, and other special events. Guided tours and open houses allow you into its Gothic interior. Tours include a mini-concert and film. Rumor has it the theater comes with its own resident ghost, which has been featured on national TV.

### Henry B. Plant Museum (ages 8 to 13)

**401 West Kennedy Boulevard; (813) 254-1891; www.plantmuseum.com. Open 10:00 a.m. to 4:00 p.m. Tuesday through Saturday, noon to 4:00 p.m. Sunday. A donation of $5 per adult, $2 per child under age 12, is requested January through November.**

Your little ones are bound to be intrigued at the sight of the skyline-dominating building: It looks like something out of *Aladdin*, with its silver minarets and ornate profile. Built in 1891 by its namesake as a railroad luxury hotel, the Moorish-Byzantine-style landmark is today maintained in its original splendor on the campus of the University of Tampa. Period pieces furnish the Grand Salon, Solarium, Guest Room, and others.

# Mr. Fink, **the Afterlife Projectionist**

Foster "Fink" Finley was Tampa Theatre's projectionist for twenty-five years, until his death in 1970. Not willing to give up his job in the after-life, Fink has been accused of slamming doors and fooling around in the projection booth, causing his first replacement to quit. Other manifestations involve keys: Fink likes to jiggle them and turn them in keyholes for workers opening up the theater. The phenomena once drew the attention of a nationally known parapsychologist, who visited with a crew from NBC and registered otherworldly activity around the theater's stage.

### Tampa Electric's Manatee Viewing Center (all ages)
**Big Bend and Dickman Roads, I-75 exit 47 south of Tampa in Apollo Beach; (813) 228-4289; www.manatee-teco.com. Open daily 10:00 a.m. to 5:00 p.m. November through April. Admission is free.**

Watch manatees during their migration to warmer waters in winter. An observation platform, educational displays, and a video familiarize visitors with the behavior of Florida's "gentle giants."

## Where to Eat

**La Tropicana.** 1822 East Seventh Avenue; (813) 247-4040. While in Ybor, do as the Cubans do: Take the family out for Cuban sandwiches, black beans and rice, and other local specialties at this Latin quarter fixture. Lunch and dinner daily. $

**Mel's Hot Dogs.** 4136 East Busch Boulevard; (813) 985-8000. Classic Chicago-style dog, bagel dog, bacon dog, corn dog, and many others. Lunch and dinner daily. $

## Where to Stay

**New Clarion Hotel of Tampa.** 2701 East Fowler Avenue; (813) 971-4710 or (800) 4-CHOICE; fax (813) 977-0155 . Close to the city's major kids' attractions and popular with families because of its suites, food court, and pirate ship water playground. $$–$$$

**Saddlebrook Resort.** 5700 Saddlebrook Way, Wesley Chapel; north of Tampa; (813) 973-1111 or (800) 729-8383; www.saddle brookresort.com. A destination in itself, especially for golfers and sports lovers. Thirty-six holes of golf, three swimming pools (including its central Super Pool), forty-five tennis courts, volleyball, basketball, lawn games, a fitness center, a spa and sauna, a kids' program, and a variety of dining options. $$–$$$$

## For More Information

**Tampa/Hillsborough Convention and Visitors Association.** 400 North Tampa Street, Suite 2800, Tampa 33602; (813) 223-1111 or (800) 826–8358; www.visit tampabay.com.

**Ybor City Chamber of Commerce.** 1800 East Ninth Avenue, Tampa 33605; (813) 248-3712; www.ybor.org.

## Florida **Trivia**

**Trivia for Bladers** Bayshore Boulevard, touted as the world's longest continuous sidewalk, is perfect for in-line skating, offering scenic skate-by views of the waterfront and its lovely old homes. However, be careful crossing the street, as Tampa is among the nation's most dangerous cities for pedestrians.

# Day Trip: Ona, Zolfo Springs, and Arcadia

From I-75, a triangular side trip east of Bradenton via Route 64 (known here as the Florida Cracker Trail) sneaks you into some unusual, back-road Florida attractions.

### Solomon's Castle (ages 4 to 13)

**Turn right on Route 665 and continue to 4533 Solomon Road, Ona; (863) 494-6077; fax (863) 993-0755; www.solomonscastle.com. The castle is open 11:00 a.m. to 4:00 p.m. Tuesday through Sunday. It closes Monday and between July 1 and October 1. Admission is $10 for adults, $4 for children ages 12 and under. The Boat in the Moat restaurant is open the same hours.**

Behold a most unexpected sight rising out of the cow pastures and orange groves—a full-size castle made completely out of recycled materials, mostly cast-off aluminum offset newspaper plates. The creator and king, Howard Solomon, is a whimsical fellow with a quick humor and a castle full of stained-glass windows, bizarre sculptures, and other oddities. Have lunch in the pirate ship he built next to his castle.

### Pioneer Park (all ages)

**Continue along Route 64 to juncture of Route 17 in Zolfo Springs; (863) 735-0330. Park entrance is free.**

Here is a pleasant spot where you can explore buildings from the past, picnic, camp, and canoe or fish in the Peace River.

### Arcadia (all ages)
**About 20 miles south of Zolfo Springs on Route 17.**

Best known for its biannual rodeos in March and July, Arcadia is worth a visit even when the rodeos are not in session because of its lovely old architecture and numerous antique shops. Pick up a self-guided historic tour guide from the chamber of commerce.

### Peace River State Canoe Trail (ages 6 to 13)

Contact Canoe Outpost, on Route 661 outside Arcadia, 2816 Northwest County Road 661, Arcadia; (863) 494-1215 for outfitting and livery service. Open at 8:00 A.M. daily. Cost per canoe for two people on day trips, with shuttle, is $40. Extra person costs $10, except kids age 12 and under, who go **free.**

Day and overnight trips on the scenic Peace River, shuttle service, and camp gear rentals are available.

### Watermelon Festival (all ages)

DeSoto Park, west of Arcadia on Route 70; (863) 494-4033.

What could be more fun than spitting watermelon seeds—with permission? Seed spitting and watermelon eating are just two of the events at the Memorial Day weekend event.

## Where to Eat and Stay

See Bradenton or Sarasota listings for dining and lodging options.

## For More Information

**DeSoto County Chamber of Commerce.** 16 South Volusia Avenue, Arcadia 34266; (863) 494-4033; www.desoto chamber.net.

# Bradenton

From Tampa, follow I-75 south about 5 miles from the I-275 intersection. From Arcadia, follow Route 70, then take I-75 north to the Bradenton exit, number 224.

In the 1800s, the Bradenton area was settled by sugar planters. Today it's known as the doorstep to sunny vacation isles. Route 64 drops you into downtown Bradenton, which is slowly restoring and reviving its past days of grandeur. Old Main Street, the city yacht basin, and Waterfront Park form the backbone of the downtown district.

### Gamble Plantation Historic State Park (ages 6 to 13)

Route 301 near the interstate; 3708 Patten Avenue, Ellenton; (941) 723-4536; www .floridastateparks.org/gambleplantation. Visitor center open 8:00 a.m. to 4:30 p.m. (closed 11:45 a.m. to 12:45 p.m.) Thursday through Monday. Visitors can view the home by tour only at 9:30 and 10:30 a.m. and on every hour between 1:00 and 4:00 p.m. Admission to the visitor center is **free;** entry to the mansion is $5 for adults and $3 for children ages 6 to 12.

The sugar days left their residue most notably here. Built circa 1840 in Greek Revival style out of local oyster shell, sand, and, some believe, molasses, its eighteen stately columns welcome visitors to an era "gone with the wind." Abandoned in 1856, the mansion was rescued from neglect in 1925 by the United Daughters of the Confederacy, who declared it a Civil War shrine for sheltering Confederate secretary of state Judah P. Benjamin when on the lam after the war. A museum in the visitor center tells the story of the property through the eras.

### McKechnie Field (ages 5 to 13)

**Ninth Street and Seventeenth Avenue West; (941) 748-4610. Tickets are $6 to $9.**

It is the site of the Pittsburgh Pirates' spring exhibition games, played mostly in March.

### Pirate City (ages 5 to 13)

**1701 Twenty-seventh Street East; (941) 747-3031. Practice 8:00 a.m. and 12:30 p.m. daily.**

You can catch the Pirates at practice during exhibition season.

### Manatee Village Historical Park (ages 4 to 13)

**Corner of Fourteenth Street and Route 64; 604 Fifteenth Street East; (941) 741-4075. Open 9:00 a.m. to 4:30 p.m. weekdays and 1:30 to 4:30 p.m. Sunday. The park closes on Saturday year-round and also on Sunday during July and August. Admission is free.**

Several buildings with local historical significance form the preserved community in its pleasant, oak-shaded park setting. The County Courthouse is the oldest building, completed in 1860. Others include a church, Cracker farmhouse, one-room schoolhouse, smokehouse, boat works, and general store. A museum of artifacts, photographs, and hands-on exhibits for children resides in the general store. The Stephens House is stocked with period kitchen items, furniture, and farm implements. Staff dress for the times to enhance the feel of authenticity.

### South Florida Museum (ages 4 to 13)

**201 Tenth Street West; (941) 746-4131; www.southfloridamuseum.org. Open 10:00 a.m. to 5:00 p.m. Tuesday through Saturday, noon to 5:00 p.m. Sunday in May, June, and August through December. Open daily January through April and July. Closed Thanksgiving, Christmas Day, and New Year's Day. Admission is $15.95 for adults, $13.95 for seniors, $11.95 for children ages 4 to 12, children under age 4 are free when accompanied by a paying adult.**

The museum focuses on southwest Florida's natural and cultural history with life-size dioramas and dramatic exhibits. See fossil, bird, and shell collections, along with full-scale replicas of a sixteenth-century manor house. Other exhibits address Native American, Spanish conquistador, and Civil War days, and include Discovery Place, a childrens' hands-on activity center. The brightest star of the museum is Snooty the manatee, the oldest manatee born in captivity, who celebrated his fifty-fifth birthday in 2003 with two young manatee friends residing temporarily at the aquarium. Summer brings space camp and other children's activities to the museum.

### DeSoto National Memorial Park (ages 4 to 13)
**Seventy-fifth Street Northwest, north of Route 64, P.O. Box 15390, Bradenton 34280; (941) 792-0458; www.nps.gov/desoto/index.htm. Open 9:00 a.m. to 5:00 p.m. daily. Admission is free.**

Hernando DeSoto is the local trademark historical figure. He supposedly first came ashore at the mouth of the Manatee River, where the United States has established its out-of-the-way DeSoto National Memorial Park. Displays, a re-created Indian village, an audio-narrated interpretive trail, and in-season living history guides recall the life and times of the sixteenth-century explorer and unfettered Florida.

### Florida Heritage Festival (all ages)
**(941) 747-1998.**

In April the entire county celebrates its past during Florida Heritage Festival. A reenactment of DeSoto's 1539 landing highlights the events.

## Where to Eat
**Mattison's Riverside at Twin Dolphin Marina.** 1200 First Avenue West; (941) 748-8087. Floribbean cuisine indoors and outside. Riverfront view. Lunch and dinner Tuesday through Sunday; closed Monday. $$–$$$

## Where to Stay
Most folks, when vacationing in the vicinity, head to Anna Maria Island (see page 170) or Longboat Key (page 171) for resort accommodations.

**Holiday Inn Riverfront.** 100 Riverfront Drive; (941) 747-3727; www.holiday-inn.com/bradentonfl. Lovely Spanish-motif hotel on the river with restaurant, pool, and 153 rooms and suites. $$–$$$

## For More Information
**Bradenton Area Convention and Visitors Bureau.** P.O. Box 1000, Bradenton 34206; (941) 729-9177 or (800) 4-MANATEE; www.flagulfbeaches.com.

# Anna Maria Island

Continue on Route 64 over the Anna Maria Island Causeway, about thirty minutes from downtown Bradenton.

A beachy, relaxed island, it holds three separate communities. Anna Maria lies northernmost. Most of its attractions round its northern tip.

Gulf Drive (Route 789) is the best one to take south, through the more commercial and upscale community of Holmes Beach and its popular beaches, and Bradenton Beach, at the island's south end.

## Bayfront Park (all ages)
**Northeast end of Bay Boulevard.**

The Anna Maria City Pier extends 700 feet into Anna Maria Sound at the northeast end of the island and has food and bait concessions. The park, one of the island's most secluded, fronts the bay with picnic facilities, a playground, and recreational opportunities. It affords a magnificent view of St. Petersburg's Sunshine Skyway Bridge.

## Anna Maria Island Historical Society Museum (ages 8 to 13)
**402 Pine Avenue; (941) 778-0492. Open 10:00 a.m. to 1:00 p.m. Tuesday through Thursday and Saturday, June through October; 10:00 a.m. to noon the rest of the year. Closed Monday, Friday, and Sunday. Admission is free or by donation.**

The town's past is preserved at a 1920s icehouse. Inside, you'll browse among photographs, maps, records, books, a shell collection, a turtle display, and vintage videos. Have a chuckle at the old jail next door.

## Manatee County Park
**Gulf Drive, Holmes Beach.**

This is the island's hot spot in more ways than one. Families love it here because of all the facilities: playground, picnicking, lifeguard, snack bar, fishing pier, restrooms, and showers.

## Coquina Beach
**Gulf Drive, Bradenton Beach.**

Equally popular Coquina Beach wraps around the pass and provides beachgoers with lifeguards, picnic areas, concessions, boat ramps, good snorkeling, a playground, a mangrove nature trail, and lots of shady Australian pine trees.

## Where to Eat

**Melinda's Café.** 5315 Gulf Drive, Holmes Beach; (941) 778-0411. Lunch on home-made soups, sandwiches, and salads every day but Monday. Open 7:00 a.m. to 4:00 p.m. for breakfast and lunch. $-$$

**Rotten Ralph's.** Galati Yacht Basin, 902 Bay Boulevard South, Anna Maria; (941) 778-3953; www.rottenralphs.com. View of the marina and bay, Old Florida–style ambience indoors and out, fresh seafood. Lunch and dinner daily. $-$$$

**The Sandbar.** On the beach at 100 Spring Avenue, Anna Maria; (941) 778-0444. Deck (best for families) or indoor seating with offerings casual to gourmet. Lunch and dinner daily. $$-$$$

## Where to Stay

**Rod & Reel Resort.** 877 North Shore Drive, Anna Maria; (941) 778-2780; www.rodandreelmotel.com. Small, quiet bay-side retreat with modern efficiencies. $-$$

**Seaside Inn and Beach Resort.** 2200 Gulf Drive North, Bradenton Beach; (941) 778-5254 or (800) 447-7124; www.seaside resort.com. Small charming property (ten rooms and suites) on the beach. $$-$$$

## For More Information

**Anna Maria Island Chamber of Commerce.** 5313 Gulf Drive North, Holmes Beach 34217; (941) 778-1541; fax (941) 778-9679; www.annamariaislandchamber .org.

# Longboat Key

A short bridge on Route 789 spans the pass from Anna Maria Island to Longboat Key.

A much more exclusive island, Longboat Key's northern end is nonetheless family friendly with a public beach access, affordable accommodations, and the casual fish-house restaurants of the community known simply as the Village. To get to the Village, turn east off Gulf of Mexico Boulevard (Route 789) onto Broadway Street.

If you drive around the neighborhood of the Village, which was Longboat Key's original settlement, you'll probably spot a peacock or two, part of a colony of wild peacocks that have made themselves at home here. Look on roofs.

Back on Route 789, cyclists ride the 12-mile-long island along the paved bike path. The view is of majestic homes and meticulously manicured, blossomy yards.

## Where to Eat

**Mar-Vista Dockside Restaurant & Pub.** 760 Broadway Street; (941) 383-2391. Genuine Old Florida atmosphere, fresh seafood by the boatload, and island attitudes. Lunch and dinner daily. Kids' menu. $$-$$$

**Moore's Stone Crab Restaurant.** 800 Broadway Street; (941) 383-1748. Lodge-style, Southern-fried dining on the water. Lunch and dinner daily. Kids' menu. $$

## Where to Stay

**The Colony Beach & Tennis Resort.**
1620 Gulf of Mexico Drive; (941) 383-6464
or (800) 282-1138; www.colonybeach
resort.com. Premier destination resort
with self-catering suites, complimentary
kids' program, and fabulous beach and
restaurants. It's the number-one rated
tennis resort in the United States, with
twenty-one hard and clay courts, two lit for
night play. $$$$

## For More Information

**Longboat Key Chamber of Commerce.** Whitney Beach Plaza, 6854 Gulf of
Mexico Drive, Longboat Key 34228; (941)
383-2466; fax (941) 383-2466; www.long
boatkeychamber.com

# Sarasota

Continue down Route 789.

As you cross the next bridge to a new cluster of islands, the address changes to Sarasota. City Island, just north and east of the bridge from Longboat Key, protects Sarasota's environmental soul. The following three attractions concentrate on the area's flora and fauna.

On the west side of Route 789, or John Ringling Parkway, Lido Key holds some very nice beaches that attract sun lovers in throngs. Tucked into the island's bayside crook, St. Armands Key is the site of the famous shopper's arena known as St. Armands Circle. Here you get your first inkling of the great impact one man had on Sarasota. That man was John Ringling, circus mogul. Though Sarasota tries at times to forget the raucousness of its circus era—thirty-odd years during which the "Greatest Show on Earth" wintered in town—the memories lurk everywhere. In the park areas around St. Armands Circle, you'll find classic statues, reminders of Ringling's love of art, and plaques commemorating some of the circus's greatest performers. Also of interest to kids are the shopping center's various ice cream and candy shops.

### Sarasota Bay Walk (ages 4 to 13)

1550 Ken Thompson Parkway (left off Route 789), City Island. Admission is **free.**

This quiet, self-guided tour of the bay, estuaries, lagoons, and upland gives lessons about coastal ecology along boardwalks and shell paths.

### Mote Marine Laboratory and Aquarium (all ages)

1600 Ken Thompson Parkway; (941) 388-2451 or (800) 691-MOTE; www.mote.org. Open
10:00 a.m. to 5:00 p.m. daily. Admission is $15 for adults, $10 for children ages 4
through 12, under 4 **free.**

The highly respected facility specializes in the research and rehabilitation of marine mammals. Kids especially love its 135,000-gallon shark tank, stocked with sharks and fish typical of the area, such as grouper, snook, jewfish, pompano, and snapper. Aquariums, a ray touch tank, and a separate touch tank hold more than 200 varieties of common and unusual species. A mollusk tank holds a rare preserved giant squid. In a separate building, visitors can watch recovering whales, dolphins, manatees, or whatever happens to be a guest patient at the time and visit with the two resident manatees, Hugh and Buffett. Quench your thirst at the old-fashioned soda fountain in the retro 1950s-style Deep Sea Diner.

### Sarasota Bay Explorers (ages 4 to 12)

**Mote Marine Aquarium, 1600 Ken Thompson Parkway; (941) 388-4200. Cruises depart daily from behind Mote at 11:00 a.m., 1:30 p.m., and 4:00 p.m. Boat tickets cost $26 for adults, $22 for children ages 4 to 12. Combination tickets for Mote and the cruise are $35 and $28. Reservations are recommended.**

A pontoon tour of bay waters between City Island and Siesta Key, it features a trawl-net toss, binocular-ogling at rookery islands, and naturalist narration. The Nature Safari is a new tour that takes kids ages six to twelve on a "wade and walk" journey to seek a variety of marine life in shallow water. Custom and kayak tours are also available.

# Water Wonder **Adventure**

All but one young boy nudged forward to crowd around the trawl net as it was drawn into the bow of Sarasota Bay Explorers' boat. He stayed seated, instead, at the back of the boat, next to Captain Tom. "He prefers motors," his grandmother explained to me with a knowing nod. "A city boy."

The city boy effectively resisted petting a cowfish, squeezing a sponge, and eying a baby tilefish that was finning around in a plastic bug catcher. Yawn, bo-o-o-ring. But squeals of delight over one particular net catch collared his attention. He edged closer a couple of seats to see what all the commotion was about. As he watched, the boy's eyes grew with the size of the Atlantic puffer fish as the guide stroked its belly. When the guide plopped the creature into the cylindrical aquarium on deck, it floated around on top of the water like a balloon, slowly deflating and defying even the most disinterested to ignore the wonders of marine-world nature.  —C.K.W.

### Sarasota Ski-A-Rees Show (ages 4 to 13)

City Island, behind Mote Marine; (941) 388-1666; www.skiarees.com. 2:00 p.m. Sunday. Admission is free.

Amateur performances in the bay.

### Tony Saprito Fishing Pier (ages 4 to 13)

Ringling Causeway Park.

As you cross the Ringling Causeway to the mainland, stop here for some rod-and-reeling. A bait store across the road provides whatever you've neglected to bring with you.

### Van Wezel Performing Arts Hall (ages 5 to 13)

777 North Tamiami Trail; (941) 953-3366; www.vanwezel.org.

Downtown Sarasota is known for its theaters and art galleries. Most is high-brow stuff, opera and experimental. For something more kid-friendly, head to the monthly Saturday kids' show, November through April. The hall itself, in the shape of a purple scallop shell, exudes a bit of circus razzamatazz and Big Top drama.

### G. Wiz (ages 3 to 13)

Blivas Science and Technology Center, 1001 Boulevard of the Arts; (941) 906-1851; www.gwiz.org. Open 10:00 a.m. to 5:00 p.m. Monday through Friday, 10:00 a.m. to 6:00 p.m. Saturday, and noon to 6:00 p.m. Sunday. Admission is $9 for adults, $8 for seniors, $6 for ages 3 to 18. Free admission for the first Wednesday of the month 5:00 to 8:00 p.m.

One would expect Sarasota's version of a hands-on museum to be brighter, artsier, edgier than the rest—and it is. Two floors of exhibits have the kids doing everything from sprint racing to creating cartoons. The cool outdoor playground makes a fun outing on its own. The museum continually grows with state-of-the-art exhibits.

### Ed Smith Stadium (ages 6 to 13)

East of Highway 41; 2700 Twelfth Street; (941) 954-SOXX.

Catch some Cincinnati Reds spring training action.

### Sarasota Jungle Gardens (all ages)

3701 Bay Shore Road; (941) 355-5305; www.sarasotajunglegardens.com. Open 9:00 a.m. to 5:00 p.m. daily. Admission is $12 for adults, $11 for seniors, and $8 for children ages 3 to 12.

It gives the kids a place to stretch their legs while enjoying exotic and predatory bird and reptile shows, a mounted butterfly collection, a jungle-themed playground, a small petting zoo, monkeys, flamingos, swans, wallabies, and other animals. Mom and Dad will enjoy the peace of lush vegetation in a sixteen-acre garden setting.

### Sarasota Classic Car Museum (ages 7 to 13)

5500 North Tamiami Trail; (941) 355-6228; www.sarasotacarmuseum.com. Open 9:00 a.m. to 6:00 p.m. daily. Admission is $8.50 for adults, $7.65 for seniors, $5.75 for kids 13 to 17, $4.00 for children ages 6 to 12.

Fun for kids and parents, it displays more than one hundred antique, celebrity, and classic cars, including John Lennon's Mercedes-Benz and Rolls Royces that belonged to circus king John Ringling, patriarch of Sarasota. By tour, you can see a collection of old player pianos, phonographs, music boxes, hurdy-gurdies, and record albums. The kids will especially get a kick out of the museum's first exhibit, a precursor to today's video arcades. Its old-timey games still take nickels and dimes.

### John and Mable Ringling Museum of Art (ages 8 to 13)

Ringling Estate, 5401 Bay Shore Road; (941) 351-1660; www.ringling.org. Open daily 10:00 a.m. to 5:30 p.m. Admission fees allow admittance to all Ringling attractions: $15 for adults, $13 for seniors, $5 for Florida students and teachers (with identification); 5 and under free. Admission to the art museum is free for everyone on Monday, by provision of Ringling's will. Audio tour $5.

Just off Tamiami Trail lies Sarasota's preeminent attraction, the sixty-six-acre bay-front estate that John Ringling left to the state upon his death. The art museum is responsible for giving Sarasota its reputation for the artistic. Designated as the State Art Museum of Florida, it specializes in late Medieval, Renaissance Italian, and Spanish baroque works. The most impressive exhibit flaunts a collection of five original Rubens tapestries. Definitely too highbrow for youngsters (and for adults bored by religious paintings), it does have hands-on activities Saturday and Sunday from 1:00 to 3:00 p.m.

### Ringling Museum of the Circus (ages 4 to 13)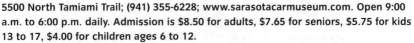

Ringling Estate, 5401 Bay Shore Road; (941) 351-1660; www.ringling.org. Open daily 10:00 a.m.to 5:30 p.m. Admission fees allow admittance to all Ringling attractions: $15 for adults, $13 for seniors, $5 for Florida students and teachers (with identification); 5 and under free. Tour reservations are suggested; call (941) 358-3180.

The kids are likely to enjoy most the property's circus museum, especially the calliopes, costumes, oversized clowns' props, wagons, and circus grounds model. Kids love the miniature circus where tiny figures portray a typical day in circus life during the 1920s and 1930s.

### Cà D'Zan (ages 7 to 13)

**Ringling Estate, 5401 Bay Shore Road; (941) 351-1660; www.ringling.org. Open daily 10:00 a.m. to 5:30 p.m. Admission fees allow admittance to all Ringling attractions: $15 for adults, $13 for seniors, $5 for Florida students and teachers (with identification); 5 and under free. Tour reservations are suggested; call (941) 358-3180.**

You must peek into Ringling's incomparable "House of John" (*Cà D'Zan* in Italian) palace. Using the Doge's Palace in Venice as a model, Ringling spared no expense building a monument to success and excess in the 1920s. Baroque, Gothic, and Renaissance elements contribute to an overall look of breathtaking opulence and ornateness throughout the thirty-room, $1.5 million mansion that John built, which has undergone a seven-year, $16 million renovation. Also on the grounds, you can visit the rose garden, three gift shops, and Banyan Cafe.

### Bayfront Park (ages 6 to 13)

**Bayfront Drive, downtown Sarasota.**

Shop here for adventure charters in Sarasota's waters—everything from sightseeing to shark fishing. Merely stroll along the docks and take your pick. There is also an open-air restaurant in the park.

### Siesta Key County Beach (all ages)

**Midnight Pass Road at Beach Way Drive, Siesta Key.**

South of downtown Sarasota, cross via Route 72 to Siesta Key, home of the whitest sand beaches south of the Florida Panhandle. Its silky white sands are plush and an active family's dream come true. The park holds picnic tables, volleyball nets, tennis courts, a fitness trail, ball fields, a soccer field, playgrounds, lifeguards, and rental and food concessions. The parking lot, large as it is, fills early in high season, so get there top of the morning.

### Historic Spanish Point (ages 8 to 13)

**500 North Tamiami Trail, Osprey; (941) 966-5214; www.historicspanishpoint.org. Open 9:00 a.m. to 5:00 p.m. Monday through Saturday and noon to 5:00 p.m. Sunday. Admission is $9 for adults, $8 for Florida residents and seniors, $3 for children ages 6 to 12. Tram tours $3 extra.**

It occupies eras from 2150 B.C. through A.D. 1918. Within its thirty acres on Little Sarasota Bay, you can explore a prehistoric Indian shell mound, pioneer homestead, late Victorian home, old cemetery, reconstructed chapel and citrus packinghouse, and archaeological exhibit. By the end of the ninety-minute tour, you become well acquainted with the pioneering Webb family and Sarasota matriarch Bertha Palmer. Local actors give living-history performances Saturday and Sunday during the winter season (January to mid-April). Guided walking tours are available daily and tram tours by reservation Monday through Friday.

### Oscar Scherer State Park (all ages)

**1843 South Tamiami Trail, Osprey; (941) 483-5956. Open 8:00 a.m. to sunset daily. Park entrance is $4 per vehicle of eight persons or fewer, $1 per extra passenger, cyclist, or pedestrian.**

Go here for wilderness camping, canoeing, and getting back to nature. River otters and alligators inhabit the waters; threatened scrub jays, bobcats, and bald eagles inhabit the land. Campers are secluded in a setting of palmettos, pines, lovely moss-draped oaks, and creek. The nearly 1,400-acre park also offers picnicking, hiking, freshwater swimming, and fishing opportunities. In October, Oscar Scherer Day is a Sunday filled with living history, craft demonstrations, guided walks, food, and live music.

### Casey Key & Nokomis Beach

**Take Blackburn Point Road west off South Highway 41.**

For a scenic detour, follow the skinny, snaky road that threads through lovely Casey Key, a refuge for well-heeled escapists for several decades. At the island's south end, Nokomis Beach has more than pretty views to offer families, namely fun-filled beaches and great fishing. Bustling Nokomis Beach and its sand volleyball courts lie at the junction of Albee Road. Keep heading south to North Jetty Park, which is a little more out of the mainstream but still with lots to do. It has a picnic area, restrooms, lifeguards, and concessions, and, most important, throngs of fish in the narrow pass that separates it from Venice Beach to the south.

## Where to Eat

**Old Salty Dog.** 1601 Ken Thompson Parkway; (941) 388-4311. Near Mote Marine, on the water. Seafood and sandwiches. Lunch and dinner daily. $–$$

**Phillippi Creek Village Oyster Bar.** 5353 South Tamiami Trail; (941) 925-4444. Famous for its combo seafood steamer pots, but the sandwiches and other seafood items are tops, too. Sit inside an old Southern-style fish house or creekside on the patio or floating dock. Lunch and dinner daily. $–$$$

## Where to Stay

**Lido Beach Resort.** 700 Ben Franklin Drive; (941) 388-2161 or (800) 441-2113; www.lidobeachresort.com. Near the public beach entrance, with pool and outdoor restaurant. Kitchens or kitchenettes in rooms. $$–$$$$

## For More Information

**Sarasota Convention and Visitors Bureau.** 655 North Tamiami Trail, Sarasota 34236; (941) 957-1877 or (800) 522-9799; www.sarasotafl.org.

## Weekend Getaway:
## Myakka River State Park

Inland about 9 miles on Route 72; 13207 Route 72, Sarasota; (941) 361-6511 for park information; (941) 365-0100 for tour information. Open 8:00 a.m. to sunset daily. Park entrance is $5 per vehicle with up to eight passengers, $3 for a single passenger, and $1 for extra passengers, bicyclists, and pedestrians. One-hour boat and tram tours cost $10 for adults, $6 for children ages 6 through 12.

Myakka River State Park affords opportunity for camping, canoeing, and communing with nature in 35,000 acres of forest and wetlands. A 25-foot-high boardwalk lets you explore wildlife at treetop level. It's fun to tour the park via tram or boat or to take a guided walk. Canoe and bike rentals are also available.

# Venice

About five minutes south of Nokomis on Highway 41.

Don't pass this small town by—it has more to offer than meets the eye. Its best features lie west of Highway 41, in the vicinity of West Venice Avenue. Follow it through a charming shopping district and neo-Mediterranean-style neighborhood to get to the beaches, known near and far for their abundance of shark's teeth.

Stop at one of the local stores for a book about collecting shark's teeth and a "Florida snow shovel"—a screen scoop used to sift the shark's teeth from the sand. The chamber of commerce hands out basic information and sometimes specimens.

### Venice Little Theatre For Young People (ages 5 to 13)
140 West Tampa Avenue; (941) 488-1115.

It provides off-season theatrical instruction (ages eight to sixteen) and Christmas and springtime performances for youngsters.

### Brohard Park and Venice Fishing Pier (all ages)
1600 South Harbor Drive; (941) 316-1172. Admission to the pier is $1 for adults, 50 cents for children.

Head where collecting and beaching are best. At 750 feet, the pier is one of the state's longest.

### Sharks Tooth & Seafood Festival (all ages)

Sharky's on the Pier restaurant is headquarters for this annual bash held in April. Get your picture taken in the mouth of a shark, look at mounds of shark's teeth and other fossils, browse among crafts booths, and eat your fill of shark shish kebob and other local seafood specialties.

### Caspersen Beach (all ages)
**South of Brohard Park on Harbor Drive; (941) 316-1172.**

This is more secluded than Brohard Park, but with most of the same amenities: picnic areas, dunes walkovers, restrooms. You can walk to Manasota Beach from here, 1 mile away. (By car, it takes close to a half hour to reach.)

# The Great Shark's Tooth **Adventure**

The shark's spiky incisor poked into my arm, not breaking the skin but prompting a startled "youch!" It was only my son, testing the sharpness of the shark tooth sample he had gotten at the Venice Chamber of Commerce. We were in quest of Venice's highly reputed shark's teeth pickings, the result of an ancient offshore shark graveyard. Armed with a child's sand sifter and beach shovels, we began scooping at the surf line on Caspersen Beach. I had been told that all you need do is plunge your hand into the pebbly sand and you'll come out pulling teeth. The sand was not exactly pebbly, and the suspicious lack of other hunters soon sent us northward to the area around Venice Pier.

Things looked more hopeful there. More shells, pebbly stuff, lots of serious hunters wielding their Florida snow shovels. Aaron, at age four, had by then, of course, lost interest. He was having fun catching love bugs, which were considerably more plentiful and less elusive. I gave him a sand flea culled from the surf with my trusty toy colander, and two pointy-looking pebbles that could have been shark's teeth, and he was happy—but hungry.

We ate lunch at—where else?—Sharky's on the Pier. Inside the door of the popular restaurant, a box of sand studded with shark's teeth held a miniature Florida snow shovel. Aaron fished and came up with a handful. Our best catch of the day!   —C.K.W.

## Where to Eat

**Sharky's on the Pier.** 1600 South Harbor Drive (P.O. Box 267), Venice 34284; (941) 488-1456. On the pier with indoor and outdoor seating. Lunch and dinner daily. $$

**Snook Haven Retreat.** Exit 191 off I-75; 5000 East Venice Avenue; (941) 485-7221. Rural and casual on the Myakka River with canoe rentals and Sunday barbecues. Lunch and dinner daily. $–$$

## Where to Stay

**Hampton Inn and Suites Venice.** 881 Venetia Bay Boulevard; (941) 488-5900; fax (941) 488-6746; www.hamptoninnvenice .com. Nice hotel located near local attractions. $–$$

## For More Information

**Venice Area Chamber of Commerce.** 597 Tamiami Trail South, Venice 34285-1908; (941) 488-2236; www.venice chamber.com.

# Manasota Key and Englewood Beach

South of downtown Venice, turn south on Route 776. Turn west on Manasota Beach Road.

The island's northern section, which lies in Sarasota County, holds a wildlife preserve, discreet mansions blocked from view by natural vegetation, ancient Amerindian mounds, and public beaches. The south end is more inviting to families, with affordable resorts and active beach parks.

### Manasota Beach (all ages)

8570 Manasota Beach Road. Open 8:00 a.m. to 8:00 p.m. daily.

The northernmost beach has lots of amenities, including lifeguards, picnic pavilions with grills, volleyball, and a boat launch. By foot, this beach lies about a mile south of Venice's Caspersen Beach.

### Middle or Blind Pass Beach (all ages)

3 miles to the south at 6725 Manasota Beach Road. Open 8:00 a.m. to 8:00 p.m. daily.

This one feels less cramped by sand erosion and is prettily landscaped.

### Chadwick Park Beach (all ages)

Beach Road (Route 776), Englewood Beach. Open 6:00 a.m. to 11:00 p.m. daily. Parking is $1.

Located right where the south bridge meets the Gulf, it is convenient also because of its recreational and picnic facilities. There are volleyball and basketball courts, play areas, and food concessions, but no lifeguards. Shops, restaurants, and water-sports rentals are located nearby. It gets to be a high school hangout in the evening.

## Oyster Creek Regional Park (all ages)
**6791 San Casa Drive, Englewood; (941) 475-3904.**

The new park has a public swimming pool, nature trails to explore, a rink for skating, tennis courts, and baseball fields. Even dogs will find a section all their own.

## More Things to See and Do in West Central Florida

- **The Manatee Toy Co.,** Crystal River; (352) 795-6126
- **Old Mill House Gallery and Printing Museum,** Homosassa; (352) 628-1081
- **Wild Bill's Airboat Tours,** Inverness; (352) 726-6060
- **Nabor Doll Factory and Museum,** Homosassa; (352) 382-1001
- **Captain Bligh's Landing,** Clearwater Beach; (727) 443-6348
- **Florida International Museum,** St. Petersburg; (727) 822-3693 or (800) 777-9882
- **Tampa Museum of Art,** Tampa; (813) 274-8130
- **Marie Selby Botanical Gardens,** Sarasota; (941) 366-5731

## Where to Eat

**Lock & Key Restaurant and Pub.** 2045 North Beach Road, Englewood; (941) 474-1517. Casual indoor/outdoor dining with a waterfront view. Voted Englewood's best restaurant ten years in a row. Kids' menu. Open daily for lunch and dinner. $–$$

## Where to Stay

**Weston's Resort.** 985 Gulf Boulevard, Englewood Beach; (941) 474-3431. Eighty-three-unit beach-to-bay property with fishing dock, boat slips and rentals, two swimming pools, tennis courts, barbecue grills, and shuffleboard. Studio efficiencies to three-bedroom apartments. $–$$$

## For More Information

**Englewood Area Chamber of Commerce.** 601 South Indiana Avenue, Englewood 34223; (941) 474-5511 or (800) 603-7198; www.englewoodchamber.com.

## Annual Events

**Epiphany.** Tarpon Springs; (727) 937-3540. On January 6 the Greek town's young men dive for the cross; a Greek celebration follows. **Free.**

**PAL Sailor Circus.** Sarasota; (941) 361-6350; www.sailorcircus.org. Students from grades three to twelve perform professional circus feats during a two-week season March to April and over the Christmas and New Year's holidays.

**Children's Art Festival.** Sarasota; (941) 355-5101. For one day mid-March, families can enjoy hands-on art activities and musical and dramatic performances.

**Manatee Heritage Days.** Bradenton; (941) 741-4070. The month of March is devoted to the celebration of local history and traditions throughout the county. **Free.**

**Festival of States.** St. Petersburg; (727) 898-3654. During March and April parades, school bands, kids' art displays, clown school, and baseball clinics.

**Suncoast Offshore Grand Prix.** Sarasota; (941) 371-2827. A national attraction, with powerboat racers from around the world in June. **Free.**

**John's Pass Seafood Festival.** Madeira Beach; (727) 398-5994. For one weekend late in October, enjoy seafood and kids' attractions such as the Catch Tank, a costume contest, and haunted house. **Free.**

**Sarasota Medieval Fair.** Hunsader Farms, Bradenton; (888) 303-FAIR; www.sarasotamedievalfair.com. Watch thirteenth-century knights in full armor joust for ladies faire on two weekends in November. A marketpace offers trinkets and food.

**Santa Parade and Snow Fest.** St. Petersburg; (813) 274-8615. The first weekend of December brings snowball fights, ice-skating, a parade, kids' games, and a visit from St. Nick. **Free.**

# Southwest
# Florida

As Florida's last region to be settled and developed, southwest Florida manages to maintain more natural decorum than its other coastal counterparts. Greater thought and care went into community and resort planning, so the focus remained on wildlife and its habitat. Once a playground for wealthy adventurers

## TopPicks for Family Fun in Southwest Florida

1. Seeing the (electric) light at the Edison-Ford Winter Estates, Fort Myers

2. Experiencing a thunderstorm and hurricane at Imaginarium: Hands-On Museum and Aquarium, Fort Myers

3. Watching the big cats snacking at the Zoo at Caribbean Gardens, Naples

4. Interacting with nature at the Conservancy of Southwest Florida's Natural Science Museum and Naples Nature Center, Naples

5. Kayaking through J. N. "Ding" Darling National Wildlife Refuge, Sanibel Island

6. Hiking through ancient forest at Corkscrew Swamp Sanctuary, Naples

7. Experiencing the world of shells at Bailey-Matthews Shell Museum, Sanibel Island

8. Petting a snake at Calusa Nature Center and Planetarium, Fort Myers

9. Getting out on the water with Grande Tours, Placida

10. Paddling into nowhere along the Wilderness Waterway canoe trail, Everglades National Park

# SOUTHWEST FLORIDA

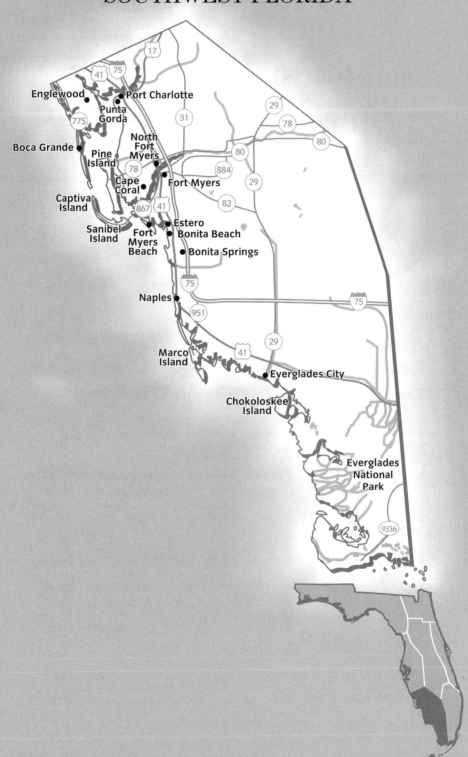

in the early part of the last century, it still holds itself highly exclusive in parts. For families this may mean steeper prices, but also more opportunity for water adventures and nature discovery away from the crowds and the lights. Those with young kids especially favor the Gulf of Mexico's lazy waves over the frothy challenge of Atlantic Ocean breakers on the East Coast.

This route begins on the west shores of quiet Charlotte County, south of Sarasota County and off the well-trod path. It continues through old towns, unblighted countryside, highly touted resort communities such as Sanibel Island and Naples, and new urban development, ending at the west coast access to the Florida Everglades. The lower Gulf Coast tour takes occasional back-road stabs at southwest Florida's more hidden inner parts.

# Boca Grande and Vicinity

From Englewood, follow Route 776 to Route 775. Cape Haze, access point to Palm Island, lies along this route. Gasparilla Island, home to Boca Grande, lies to the west on Route 771. Causeway toll is $3.50.

The historic town of Boca Grande begs to be explored. A longtime escape destination for the nation's wealthy, it remains exclusive, while its reputation for tarpon fishing adds a maritime flavor. The Gasparilla Inn, grande dame of southwest Florida, still reserves rooms for the Vanderbilts each winter. An old circa-1910 depot and a 1928 movie theater now hold shopping centers. Restaurants range from fun and casual to spiffy.

## Grande Tours (ages 5 to 13)

**12575 Placida Road (P.O. Box 281), Placida 33946; (941) 697-8825; www.grandetours .com. Kayak rentals start at $25 for two hours. Ecotours cost $50 for a two-and-a-half-hour kayak tour. Don Pedro Island Shuttle is $19 per person.**

Naturalist-interpreted deck boat and kayaking excursions tour the Myakka River and Charlotte Harbor Aquatic Preserve. Sea Life Excursion features seine net pulling to collect and study marine life. Don Pedro Island Shuttle cruises to a barrier island for shelling, fossil hunting, and swimming at an 8-mile-long beach with facilities and grills; you bring your own food and drink. The staff specializes in fishing trips for the kids.

## Rum Bay Restaurant

**Palm Island, Palm Harbor Island Resort Reception Area; 7092 Placida Road, Cape Haze; (941) 697-0566. Ferry costs $4 per passenger. Reservations required.**

You can begin an adventure in lunching at the ferry landing for Rum Bay Restaurant. The chugalug ferry departs hourly, and the trip takes less than fifteen minutes. The restaurant is part of an exclusive getaway island resort with a family-friendly attitude. The tropical restaurant also serves dinner and is known for its baby back ribs. $$–$$$

# Road **Markers**

Interstate 75 zips you along the coast's eastern edge, connecting to Alligator Alley, the aptly named arterial that crosses the Everglades to reach Fort Lauderdale. Highway 41, also known as Tamiami Trail, meanders—often clogs—as it makes its way through towns and cities. It also penetrates Everglades territory south of I-75 and hits the east coast at Miami.

The region's northern destinations require back-road treks off the main arterials. Directions appear under each destination.

### Loose Caboose

The Depot Mall, Park Avenue, Boca Grande; (941) 964-0440.

Stop in for a dip or two of homemade ice cream or a fruit smoothie.

### Boca Grande Bike Trail (ages 5 to 11)

The best way to explore Gasparilla Island is by bike. A 7-mile bike path follows the trail of the old railroad that once shipped phosphate from inland Florida to Boca Grande's deep port. Don't miss riding under the tree canopy on Banyan Street. Have a gape at the gracious Gasparilla Inn on Fifth and Palm Streets, where the Vanderbilts and their ilk have come to winter since the 1910s. Keep a watchful eye out for iguanas, a colony of which lives on the island. Motorized golf carts are also allowed on the path.

### Island Bike 'n Beach (ages 5 to 11)

333 Park Avenue, Boca Grande; (941) 964-0711. Open daily. Rates range from $7 an hour to $59 a week.

Rent bikes and golf carts here.

### Boca Grande Lighthouse Museum and Gasparilla Island State Park (all ages) 🏕️

Gulf Boulevard; (941) 964-0060; www.barrierislandparkssociety.org. Parking is $2 per car. Museum open 10:00 a.m. to 4:00 p.m. Wednesday through Sunday June through October and daily November through May. Admission is free or by donation.

The park around this hundred-year-old lighthouse provides a good place for a picnic and swim. Stay out of the waters in Boca Grande Pass; they're deep and swift. Inside, look at photographs, artifacts, and exhibits depicting the island's multifaceted past.

**The Boca Grande Fishing Guides Association** (ages 10 to 13)
www.fishingboca.com.

Boca Grande Pass is a mecca for tarpon fishing in spring and summer. To hook up with a charter, contact this group. Be prepared to dig deep into your pockets, especially if you're among those who try for the purse in the World's Richest Tarpon Tournament in July. Top prize: $150,000.

## Where to Eat

**South Beach.** 777 Gulf Boulevard, Boca Grande; (941) 964-0765. Squatting right on the beach, this is a great place for casual lunches sandwiched into sunning time. Seafood and sandwiches. Also open for lunch and dinner daily. $$$

## Where to Stay

**The Innlet.** 1251 Twelfth Street East (P.O. Box 248), Boca Grande 33921; (941) 964-2294. Pool, restaurant, and play area; boat-accessible location. $$–$$$

**Palm Island Resort.** 7092 Placida Road, Cape Haze; (941) 697-4800 or (800) 824-5412; www.palmisland.com. Luxury beach villa accommodations, five pools, eleven tennis courts, restaurants and bar, island store, full-service marina, boat rentals, charter service, nature trail, bicycle and water-sports equipment rentals, and kids' program. $$$$

## For More Information

**Boca Grande Chamber of Commerce.** P.O. Box 704, Boca Grande 33921; (941) 964-0568; www.bocagrandechamber.com. Information center at Courtyard Plaza at island's north end.

# Port Charlotte and Vicinity

Along Highway 41 at exits 167 and 170 off I-75. From Boca Grande, follow Route 771 northeast; Highway 41 is about a thirty-minute drive away.

Port Charlotte is a new town that grew up around Highway 41 with little character. To bypass it, take Collingswood Boulevard off Route 776. Turn left on Edgewater Drive and continue to Highway 41 at the south end of town.

**Fish Cove Adventure Golf** (ages 4 to 13)
4949 Tamiami Trail, Port Charlotte; (941) 627-5393. Open 10:00 a.m. to 11:00 p.m. daily. Admission for eighteen holes of golf is $8.50 (plus tax) for ages 13 and older, $7.50 for seniors, $6.50 for ages 5 to 13.

Two eighteen-hole putt-putt golf courses.

### Port Charlotte Beach (all ages)

South end of Port Charlotte at the east end of Harbor Boulevard; (941) 627-1628. Open 8:00 a.m. to 5:00 p.m. Parking is 50 cents an hour. Admission to swimming is $2.50 (plus tax) for persons 18 and older, $1.50 for ages 3 to 18.

Clustered around the man-made beach, a variety of facilities and activities will keep the family entertained for an entire day. Bring a picnic lunch or buy from the concessions. Play volleyball, basketball, tennis, or horseshoes. There's also a playground, boat ramps, a fishing pier, and a swimming pool.

## For More Information

**Charlotte County Chamber of Commerce.** 2702 Tamiami Trail, Port Charlotte 33952; (941) 627-2222; fax (941) 627-9730; www.charlottecountychamber.org

# Punta Gorda

South of Port Charlotte across the Peace River, about ten minutes along Highway 41. Downtown Punta Gorda lies close to exit 164 off I-75.

Across the wide mouth of the Peace River lies the old waterfront and historic downtown area of Punta Gorda. Gilchrist Park runs along the river on Retta Esplanade and has picnicking, a playground, a tennis court, and bike paths. The restored buildings of old cattle town Punta Gorda line Marion Avenue, 1 block south of Retta Esplanade. Walking tour guides are available at the chamber of commerce, located in the historic city hall building.

### Charlotte County Historical Center (ages 4 to 10)

22959 Bayshore Road, Charlotte Harbor; (941) 629-7278; www.charlottefl.com/historical. Open 10:00 a.m. to 5:00 p.m. Monday through Friday, 10:00 a.m. to 3:00 p.m. Saturday. Admission is free.

Its exhibits teach informally about local natural history, ecology, and history. One gallery is devoted to African animals, another holds dress-up costumes. Other exhibits rotate in and out.

### Ponce de Leon Historical Park (all ages)

**West end of Marion Avenue. Admission is free.**

Here, supposedly, the infamous conqueror and seeker of eternal youth breached west coast shores in 1513. The monument for such a momentous event is humble, the centerpiece for a remote waterfront park that holds picnic facilities, a nature observation boardwalk, and a nature refuge.

### Peace River Wildlife Center (all ages)

**3400 West Marion Avenue; (941) 637-3830. Open 11:00 a.m. to 4:00 p.m. daily for public tours; 8:00 a.m. to 5:00 p.m. daily, the center is open for people to bring in wildlife. A donation of $5 for adults and $3 for children is requested.**

Adjacent to Ponce de León Historical Park, it conducts tours among cages of baby opossums, taped-together gopher tortoises, and other rescued and recovering animals.

### King Fisher Fleet (ages 5 to 13)

**Fishermen's Village shopping center, Maud Street, at 1200 West Retta Esplanade; (941) 639-0969; www.kingfisherfleet.com. Fares range from $9.95 to $24.95 for adults, half price for children under age 12.**

The best place to go for nature-hunting and island-hopping boat excursions.

### Charlotte Harbor Aquatic Office (ages 5 to 13)

**10941 Burnt Store Road. Hours vary. Admission is free.**

It conducts guided tours (in season) around 4 miles of nature trails through pine and palmetto flatlands, hammocks, and marshes where alligators and bobcats live. Educational exhibits teach about local wildlife. Bring bug repellent.

## On a **Budget**

- **Charlotte Harbor Aquatic Office,** Punta Gorda, free admission
- **Manatee Park,** Fort Myers, $1 per hour parking
- **Naples Fishing Pier,** Naples, free admission
- **Collier County Museum,** Naples, admission free or by donation
- **Key Marco Museum,** Marco Island, free admission

### Babcock Wilderness Adventures (ages 4 to 13)

**Route 31; 8000 State Road; (800) 500-5583; www.babcockwilderness.com. Admission is $17.95 for adults, $10.95 for kids ages 3 to 12.**

East of town, wilderness still prevails. Route 31 is a tranquil drive along undeveloped lands. If you're planning on being in the area, call ahead to arrange a tour of Babcock. Prepare for a time warp back into Old Florida, naturally intact. Ninety-minute swamp buggy tours plow you through the farm country and wetlands of 90,000-acre Crescent B Ranch and Telegraph Cypress Swamp to see alligators, cattle, deer, relocated bison, turkeys, and panthers. Bike tours lasting three hours are another mode of exploring. A prop shack chronicles the partial filming of the movie *Just Cause*, starring Sean Connery, at the site.

## Where to Eat

**Harpoon Harry's.** Fishermen's Village, 1200 West Retta Esplanade; (941) 637-1177; www.smugglers.com. River view, casual dining: sandwiches, seafoods, steaks. Lunch and dinner daily. $–$$

## Where to Stay

**Fishermen's Village Villas.** 1200 West Retta Esplanade #58; (941) 639-8721 or (800) 639-0020. Spacious time-share apartments above Fishermen's Village shopping arcade (well soundproofed). Swimming pool, clay tennis courts, bicycles, and full-service marina. $$

## For More Information

**Charlotte County Chamber of Commerce.** 326 West Marion Avenue, Suite 112, Punta Gorda 33950, (941) 639-2222, fax (941) 639-6330; 2702 Tamiami Trail, Port Charlotte 33952; www.charlotte countychamber.org.

# North Fort Myers and Cape Coral

You can continue down Route 31 or take Highway 41 or I-75 South to reach North Fort Myers, about a half hour south of Babcock. Cape Coral lies to the west along Pine Island Road (Route 78).

### Shell Factory (ages 4 to 13)

**2787 North Tamiami Trail, North Fort Myers; (239) 995-2141 or (800) 282-5805; www .shellfactory.com. Open 9:00 a.m. to 8:00 p.m. daily. Admission to Shell Factory is free; to bumper boat rides, $5 each; to nature park, $10 for adults, $8 for seniors, $6 for ages 4 to 12. Minigolf costs $5 for nine holes.**

Look for the gigantic conch shell. It marks a shopping and unusual entertainment complex that features Florida souvenirs, a small wild animal zoo, bumper boat rides, a stuffed African animal collection, and aquariums. The bazaar is filled with small gift shops, whose merchandise ranges from tacky to tasteful. Seashells are the focus.

### Fossil Expeditions (ages 7 to 13)

**213 Lincoln Avenue, Lehigh Acres; (239) 368-3252; www.fossilexpeditions.com. Four- to five-hour day trips with professional guides start at 9:30 or 10:00 a.m. depending on chosen site. $75 for adults, $65 for children ages 12 and under.**

Screen-wash for shark's teeth and bones of mammoths, camels, sabertooth cats, and other fossils at Peace River or Creek sites. Guides show how and where to look, and how to preserve finds to last another million years.

### Cape Coral Historical Museum (ages 6 to 13)

**Off Pine Island Road at 544 Cultural Park Boulevard, Cape Coral; (239) 772-7037. Open 1:00 to 4:00 p.m. Wednesday, Thursday, and Sunday. Closed July and August. A donation of $1.00 per adult is requested.**

Its exhibits concentrate on the young town's social and natural history, including one devoted to the burrowing owl, something of a Cape Coral icon.

### Greenwell's Bat-A-Ball and Family Fun Park (ages 4 to 13)

**35 Northeast Pine Island Road, Cape Coral; (239) 574-4386. Open 10:00 a.m. to midnight daily depending on action. Admission to the park is free; pay by the activity. Fee for minigolf is $6.50 for persons ages 12 and older, $5.50 for children ages 6 to 11 and seniors, $3.00 for ages 5 and younger. Second game is $3.00 for all ages. Race cars cost $4.00 to $6.50 for six minutes.**

Named after the city's favorite sports son, Red Sox baseball player Mike Greenwell, it lets the kids spend some energy in the batting cages, at miniature golf (on a course in slightly shabby condition), in the video arcade, and on the go-karts.

### Sun Splash Family Waterpark (all ages)

**400 Santa Barbara Boulevard, Cape Coral (go south off Pine Island Road); (239) 574-0557; www.sunsplashwaterpark.com. Admission is $14.95 for guests 48 inches or taller, $12.95 for children under 48 inches and older than 3, $4.95 for those 2 and under (tax not included). From mid-March to the end of September, the park opens generally at 10:00 a.m. Hours and days of operation vary according to time of year. Closed October to June.**

For cool refreshment on hot days, head to Sun Splash. There's something wet in store for all ages, from tot-size water slides to high-speed tube drops. The inner-tube river ride is fun for everyone. Snacks and lockers are available. No food or coolers are allowed inside the gates, but there are tables for picnics outside.

## Where to Eat

**Iguana Mia.** 1027 Cape Coral Parkway, Cape Coral; (239) 945-7755. Mexican food in a fun atmosphere. Look for the unsightly green building. Kids' menu. $–$$

## Where to Stay

**Casa Loma Motel.** 3608 Del Prado Boulevard, Cape Coral; (239) 549-6000 or (877) 227-2566. If you're looking for an affordable place close to Cape Coral's family attractions, this one fits the bill. It sits on a canal and has a cheery pool waterside. $–$$

## For More Information

**North Fort Myers Chamber of Commerce.** 3323 North Key Drive, Suite D-1, North Fort Myers 33903; (239) 997-9111; www.northfortmyerschamber.org.

**Cape Coral Chamber of Commerce.** 2051 Cape Coral Parkway, Cape Coral 33904; (239) 549-6900 or (800) 226-9609; www.capecoralfl.com.

# Lee Island **Coast**

Lee Island Coast Visitor and Convention Bureau, 2180 West First Street, Suite 100, Fort Myers 33901; (239) 338-3500 or (888) 231-6933; www.lee islandcoast.com.

A clever play on words, Lee County markets itself as the Lee Island Coast. Its visitor bureau handles a large territory, including North Fort Myers, Cape Coral, Pine Island and out-islands (and part of Gasparilla Island), Fort Myers, Sanibel and Captiva Islands, Fort Myers Beach, Estero, Bonita Beach, and Bonita Springs. Individual chambers of commerce are listed under each destination.

It comes by its "island" moniker honestly. Lee County contains more than one hundred barrier and coastal islands with 50 miles of white-sand beaches.

According to legend, this region was the kingdom of eighteenth-century pirate Gasparilla, attributed with good breeding and keen ransoming techniques. He is credited for naming Captiva Island after his kidnap victims and Gasparilla Island after himself.

# Pine Island and Out-Islands

Follow Pine Island Road 15 miles west of Highway 41.

To poke into a fascinating pocket of untainted Florida island life, take Pine Island Road to the World's Most Fishingest Bridge, which crosses into the town of Matlacha (matt-la-SHAY) on Pine Island. You'll feel the difference in temperament as you continue through the town, past pastel Cracker-box guest houses, ramshackle fish markets, teeny shops, and seafood restaurants. Next comes preserved mangrove forest, followed by a foray into tropical agriculture and the historic Cracker-shack world of Pineland, with its tiny post office and looming Indian mounds.

### Gulf Coast Kayak Company (ages 6 to 13)
**4530 Pine Island Road, Matlacha; (239) 283-1125. Kayak rentals start at $30 for a half-day single. Three-hour nature tour is $45 per person; reservations required.**

To explore Pine Island's well-maintained natural pleasures, sign up here. It offers morning nature and manatee tours into the Matlacha Aquatic Preserve and other local natural areas.The tour guide is a naturalist and instructor.

### Museum of the Islands (ages 5 to 13)
**Stringfellow Road at 5728 Sesame Drive, Pine Island Center; (239) 283-1525; www .museumoftheislands.com. Open 11:00 a.m. to 3:00 p.m. Tuesday through Saturday and 1:00 to 4:00 p.m. Sunday, November 1 through April 30; 11:00 a.m. to 3:00 p.m. Tuesday, Thursday, and Saturday, May 1 through October 31. Admission is $2 for adults, $1 for children. Group tours are available by appointment.**

It enshrines eras past and present with vignettes portraying the Calusa Indians, pioneers, and fishermen.

### Tropic Star Cruises (ages 5 to 13)
**Pineland Marina, 13921 Waterfront Drive, Pineland; (239) 283-0015; www.tropicstar cruises.com. Fares for cruises that run from 9:30 a.m. to 4:00 p.m. are $30 for adults and $17 for children ages 2 to 11. Cabbage Key only: $25.**

Board a water taxi to exotic unbridged islands to the north.

### Cayo Costa State Park (all ages)
**P.O. Box 1150, Boca Grande 33921; (941) 964-0375. Accessible only by boat. Admission to the park is $1 per person.**

This park is one of the most popular unbridged island destinations of southwest Florida. You'll love it if you favor secluded beaches. At the northern end, the almost entirely natural island provides a picnic ground for day-trippers and rustic cabins and tent sites for overnighters. There's no drinking water or electricity on the island.

There *are* mosquitoes—lots of them. Avoid hot, still days if you plan on attacking the island's trails through subtropic jungle to historic sites such as a pioneer cemetery. Shuttles and boat rentals are also available from Captiva Island.

## Cabbage Key Inn

**Cabbage Key, accessible only by boat. P.O. Box 200, Pineland 33945; (239) 283-2278.**

If you're out on the water, lunch on Cabbage Key is a must. It's served in a historic inn built by novelist Mary Roberts Rinehart in the 1930s as a wedding gift to her son. Some say Jimmy Buffett was inspired to write "Cheeseburger in Paradise" here. He's one of millions who have taped an autographed dollar bill to the inn's wall. After lunch, have a walk around the small island's short nature trail. The inn is open for lunch and dinner daily. $$–$$$$

## Where to Eat

**Waterfront Restaurant.** South end of Pine Island. 2131 Oleander Street, St. James City; (239) 283-0592; www.water frontrestaurant.com. Casual, on the water, and the kids can play hangman on the butcher-paper tablecloths while waiting for their grouper fish sandwiches or foot-long Waterdoggies to arrive. Open daily for lunch and dinner. $–$$

# Fort Myers

Across the river from North Fort Myers via Highway 41 or Business 41.

Across the river from Cape Coral, Fort Myers has a lot to offer family travelers in its museums and historic attractions. It serves as gateway to the coast's highly reputed island playgrounds.

## Edison-Ford Winter Estates (ages 6 to 13) 🏛 🌸

**2350–2400 McGregor Boulevard; (239) 334-3614; www.edison-ford-estate.com. Continuous tours of both the Edison and Ford estates 9:00 a.m. to 5:30 p.m. daily. Admission to both homes and museum is $20 for adults, $11 for children ages 6 to 12. For the lab and museum only, $11.00 for adults, $4.50 for children.**

Fort Myers's most venerable attraction sits right on the river and takes you into the home and workplace of a genius. The tour guides are enthusiastic and deliver fun anecdotes about the famed lightbulb inventor. On the ninety-minute walking tour, you'll be amazed at how many other things Edison invented. He owned 1,000 patents on everything from the phonograph to the movie camera. One of the best parts of the tour is the botanical gardens surrounding Edison's home. He was an avid botanist, and his outstanding collection of tropical plants proves it. Many he gathered looking for a cheaper way to produce rubber for his friend Harvey Firestone, who also wintered in Fort Myers. The tour continues on to the winter home of Edison's friend and next-door neighbor, none other than Henry Ford, whose estate is not quite as impressive because of the Fords' simple tastes. Thomas Edison, you'll soon discover, remains the patron saint of Fort Myers, with a college, mall, and all kinds of things named for him. Each year the town celebrates his legacy with the Edison Pageant of Light Festival, which culminates in a lighted night parade. It goes on for two weeks in early February.

## Centennial Park (all ages)
**Downtown on Edwards Drive.**

It fronts the river with playgrounds, a fitness trail, picnic pavilions, and a fishing pier. It's the site of open-air concerts and special festivals.

## Imaginarium: Hands-On Museum and Aquarium (all ages)
**Dr. Martin Luther King Jr. Boulevard and Cranford Avenue (P.O. Box 2217), Fort Myers 33902; (239) 337-3332. Open 10:00 a.m. to 5:00 p.m. Monday through Saturday, noon to 5:00 p.m. Sunday. Admission is $8 for ages 13 and up, $7 for seniors, $5 for children ages 3 to 12 when accompanied by an adult.**

The facility takes over the city's old waterworks and is clever in how it uses that as a theme. Everything is bright, colorful, and kid-fascinating (parent-fascinating, too). A Hurricane Experience chamber "blows 'em away," and a see-through mechanical body demonstrates how body parts work. Tots can crawl through a maze or play in a tiny house with cutaways showing building techniques. Older kids can "Be a Meteorologist" by selecting thunderstorm, hurricane, or tornado, then watching themselves broadcast on location via closed-circuit monitor. A movie theater shows animated features, aquariums and a touch tank display local and reef water life, a kid-size bank venue teaches about the world of financing, and an exhibit in the form of a car shows the effects of chemical abuse. Its gift shop sells a superb selection of child enrichment books and science-related games.

## Southwest Florida Museum of History (ages 5 to 13)
**2300 Peck Street at Jackson Street; (239) 332-5955. Open 10:00 a.m. to 5:00 p.m. Tuesday through Saturday. Admission is $9.50 for adults, $8.50 for seniors, $4.00 for children ages 3 to 12.**

It holds forth in a historic railroad depot. Displays take you back to the days of the prehistoric Calusa Indians with scale models, vignettes, graphic depictions, and historical IQ games. Outdoors, you can tour an early-1900s replica of a local Cracker house and the world's last and longest Pullman private railcar, circa 1930. Children will enjoy the hands-on switchboard and locomotive cab, the climb-aboard fire truck, and the baseball room.

## Recipe for an **Island**

Stick one torpedo-shaped mangrove pod into a sandbar. Bake in Florida sun for many years.

Mangroves are Florida's island builders. Their leggy, barnacle-crusted roots capture silt, sediment, leaves, and other muck, which eventually creates solid ground—and, in time, a new island.

### City of Palms Park (ages 6 to 13)
Edison Avenue at Jackson Street; 2201 Edison Avenue; (239) 334-4700; www.redsox.com.

The Boston Red Sox play their spring exhibition season (March and April) here.

### Manatee Park (ages 5 to 13)
10901 Route 80; (239) 694-3537. Park open 8:00 a.m. to 8:00 p.m.; visitor center open 9:00 a.m. to 4:00 p.m. daily, November through March. Parking is $1 per hour or $5 a day.

This is the place to take the kids in winter to spot manatees, the teddy bears of the water world. The sixteen-acre passive recreational park provides a manatee viewing area, interpretative exhibits, a nature boardwalk, a canoe and kayak launch, a fishing pier, and picnic facilities. It also serves as a rescue and release site for injured and rehabilitated manatees.

## Till the Cows **Come Home**

Fort Myers built itself as a cow town, where cow hunters such as Jake Summerlin became millionaires and legends. Today's lovely, royal-palm-lined McGregor Boulevard was once a dirt path that cows followed to the shipping port at Punta Rassa. The Thomas Edisons had to erect a picket fence to keep the free-roaming animals out of their garden. In 1886 the city widened the path as a gift to Edison. He later planted the boulevard's trademark palms.

City matron Tootie McGregor paid to have it paved in 1912 and requested that cattle be barred from the road. That, however, required a state law, which didn't pass—thanks to the powerful cattle lobby—until the 1950s.

## Calusa Nature Center and Planetarium (ages 4 to 11)

3450 Ortiz Avenue; (239) 275-3435; www.calusanature.com. Museum and trails open 9:00 a.m. to 5:00 p.m. Monday through Saturday, 11:00 a.m. to 5:00 p.m. Sunday. Call for schedule at planetarium. Admission to the museum is $8 for adults, $3 for children ages 3 to 12. Admission to the planetarium is included.

It offers a 2-mile wildlife trail, Seminole Indian village, native bird aviary, and live animal exhibits. Staff demonstrate snake and alligator behaviors daily. The planetarium hosts a variety of presentations, using telescopes, laser lights, and astronomy shows.

## Six Mile Cypress Slough Preserve

Six Mile Cypress Parkway at Penzance Crossing; (239) 432-2004. Open daylight hours daily. Admission is free; parking costs $1 an hour, or $5 per day.

Boardwalks meander through 9 miles of wetlands ecology.

## Lakes Regional Park (all ages)

7330 Gladiolus Drive; (239) 432-2000 for park information; (239) 432-2017 for marina; (239) 267-1905 for train information. Open 8:00 a.m. to 6:00 p.m. daily. Parking is $1 an hour or $5 a day. Train rides run 10:00 a.m. to 2:00 p.m. Monday through Friday, 10:00 a.m. to 4:00 p.m. Saturday, noon to 4:00 p.m. Sunday. Cost is $4 for persons over 6 years old, $1 for children ages 5 and under.

Outdoor days are well spent at this 277-acre complex of bike trails, playgrounds, picnic areas, food concessions, paddleboats, canoes, and a fitness trail. You can ride a model train for fifteen minutes around a village and the woods, a precursor of a railroad museum that's trying to grow there. The train runs daily. There's also a beach, but alligators and algae keep it from being a safe place to swim. Fishing is permitted.

## Castle Miniature Golf (ages 5 to 13)

7400 Gladiolus Drive; (239) 489-1999. Open 10:00 a.m. to 10:00 p.m. Monday through Friday and 11:00 p.m. on the weekend. Admission is $9.75 for adults, $8.75 for children ages 12 and under.

An eighteen-hole course located convenient to Lakes Park.

## Lee County Sports Complex (ages 6 to 13)

Near the intersection of Daniels Parkway; 14100 Six Mile Cypress Road; (941) 768-4270 or (800) 33-TWINS for Twins tickets; (941) 768-4210 for Miracles. Twins tickets range from $10 to $35; Miracles, $5 to $8.

Fort Myers is turning into Baseball Town, U.S.A., because, besides the Red Sox, it hosts the Minnesota Twins spring league here. Also, from April through August, the Miracle Professional Baseball team, a member of the Florida State League, competes here.

## Top Family **Beaches and Parks**

1. **Delnor-Wiggins State Park,** Vanderbilt Beach

2. **Tigertail Beach,** Marco Island

3. **Lighthouse Beach,** Sanibel Island

4. **Barefoot Beach Preserve,** Bonita Beach

5. **Lover's Key State Park,** Bonita Beach

6. **Bowman's Beach,** Sanibel Island

7. **Cayo Costa State Park,** Cayo Costa

## Where to Eat

**La Casita.** 15185 McGregor Boulevard; (239) 415-1050. If your family values authentic Mexican cuisine, bring them to this adorable and Crayola-bright setting. Kids' menu. Open lunch and dinner hours daily; serves breakfast all day. $$

## Where to Stay

**Holiday Inn Historic District.** 2431 Cleveland Avenue, Fort Myers; (239) 332-3232 or (800) 315-2621. Near Edison-Ford winter homes. Pool. 122 completely renovated rooms. Kids under 10 **free.** $$–$$$

**Sanibel Harbour Resort & Spa.** East of the Sanibel Causeway at 17260 Harbour Pointe Drive; (239) 466-4000 or (800) 767-7777. Mom and Dad can be coddled at the spa, while kids are cared for in the extensive Kids Klub program. Tennis facilities are world-class, and most of the rooms have a water view. $$$–$$$$

## For More Information

**Greater Fort Myers Chamber of Commerce.** 2310 Edwards Drive, P.O. Box 9289, Fort Myers 33902; (239) 332-3624 or (800) 366–3622; fax (239) 332–7276; www.fortmyers.org.

## Top Family **Resorts**

1. **South Seas Plantation,** Captiva Island

2. **Best Western Pink Shell Resort,** Fort Myers Beach

3. **Sundial Beach Resort,** Sanibel Island

4. **Marriott's Marco Island Resort,** Marco Island

5. **Palm Island Resort,** Cape Haze

6. **Radisson Suite Beach Resort,** Marco Island

7. **Naples Beach Hotel & Golf Club,** Naples

# Sanibel and Captiva Islands

From Highway 41 or I-75's exit 131, head west on Daniels Parkway. Take a left on Summerlin Road (Route 867) and continue about twenty minutes to Sanibel Island (toll $3). To continue to Captiva, go right on Periwinkle Way once you reach Sanibel, then right on Tarpon Bay Road and left on Sanibel-Captiva Road.

At least a day on Sanibel Island is required visiting for those traveling through the area. It's among the most expensive of the area's destinations, but its beautiful shelling beaches and natural attractions make it worth the price. As you cross the causeway, watch for windsurfers, especially on breezy days. They put on a colorful show.

Tiny Captiva lies across a narrow, bridged pass from Sanibel. Twisty Captiva Drive runs scenically beneath vegetation canopies and along the sand-flounced, aquamarine Gulf of Mexico.

## Lighthouse Beach (all ages) 🏕️ 🐟 🏛️
**South end of Periwinkle Way; (239) 472-9075. Parking is $2 an hour.**

Sanibel's beaches are maintained in a natural, low-impact state, meaning little development and facilities. This one is the most family accommodating with its nature trail, fishing pier, and historic site—the circa-1884 Sanibel lighthouse. The beach wraps around the island's south end to front both the Gulf and bay. Swimming is treacherous near the pass.

# Lessons in the **Sand**

We looked like overzealous interior designers determined to duplicate Mother Nature's clever decorating scheme. Clenching paint swatches, we scanned the beach intently, picking up bits and shells and comparing them studiously with the color scale on our swatch. Regrouped, the six adults and two children exhibited our findings in an "art gallery" delineated in the sand and learned about the creatures connected with our beach-accessorized artifacts.

Participants filled the gallery with grasses, shells, fishing line, egg cases, debris, and other quizzical-looking objects. Emily, six, from Michigan, found a mermaid's purse. The naturalist showed the group turtle grass—salad, she said, for island tortoises. The animal that once lived in the reddish scallop shell, she explained, had a hundred eyes and could swim sideways.

Other fascinating facts and fun are part of SCCF's beach walk experience. It is geared to children and adults alike.

## Periwinkle Park (ages 2 to 7)

Periwinkle Way, Sanibel Island; (239) 472-1433. Open daily. Admission is free.

It has sites for tents and RVs, but you must reserve well in advance, especially for the winter-to-spring season. If you don't stay there, take a bike ride through and have a peek at the park's exotic bird aviaries. Some 600 feathered friends live here, including flamingos and toucans.

## Billy's Rentals

1470 Periwinkle Way, Sanibel Island; (239) 472--5248.

Sanibel's 23 miles of bike paths provide an adventurous way to explore main streets and backwoods, where marsh rabbits scurry roadside. In-line skaters also favor the paved trail. Here's a good place to rent bicycles, surrey bikes, and other equipment for family biking, as well as scooters and beach gear. Rentals by hour, day, or week.

## Sanibel Historical Village (ages 4 to 13)

950 Dunlop Road, Sanibel Island; (239) 472-4648. Open 10:00 a.m. to 4:00 p.m. Tuesday through Saturday. Closed mid-August to November. A donation of $2 per adult is requested.

It makes for a fun, lightly educational pause from the sun and sand. The village huddles together a pioneer Cracker house-turned-museum, 1920s post office, historic general store, another vintage home, and teahouse.

### Bailey-Matthews Shell Museum (ages 3 to 13)

3075 Sanibel-Captiva Road, Sanibel Island (south of the first mile marker); (239) 395-2233; www.shellmuseum.org. Open 10:00 a.m. to 5:00 p.m. daily. Admission is $7 for visitors age 17 and older, $4 for children ages 5 to 16; under 5 free.

After culling the beach for shells, your youngsters will enjoy learning more about their finds. Especially for them, a Children's Science Lab offers toddlers hands-on learning experiences in colorful reef-motif surroundings. But the touch table is under glass, so really it's just a "look table," and the museum eliminated the find-the-shell sticker game that kids loved. Kids under age seventeen get to pick two free shells. Other aesthetically arranged exhibits and vignettes examine the role of shells in natural and social history.

### Sanibel-Captiva Conservation Foundation (SCCF) (all ages)

3333 Sanibel-Captiva Road (P.O. Box 839), Sanibel Island 33957; (239) 472-2329; www.sccf.org. Mid-October through mid-May the center opens Monday through Friday at 8:30 a.m. and closes at 4:00 p.m. In the off-season, the museum closes at 3:00 p.m. and is usually closed on Saturday. Admission is $3 for visitors age 12 and up.

It has a touch tank in its visitors gallery, a soft, life-size manatee that children can climb, an alligator's jawbone, and wildlife blocks—a great place for preschoolers. Outside, take an easy walk to the bird observation tower and butterfly house to discover more about the local environment. The foundation hosts guided tours, interpretive beach walks, wildlife boat tours, and special children's programs.

### J. N. "Ding" Darling National Wildlife Refuge (ages 5 to 13)

Off Sanibel-Captiva Road; 1 Wildlife Drive, Sanibel Island; (239) 472-1100. The refuge is open sunrise to sunset; the visitor center is open 9:00 a.m. to 4:00 p.m. May through December, 9:00 a.m. to 5:00 p.m. January through April. The visitor center is open Friday, but the refuge drive is not. Admission is $5 per car or $1 per cyclist or walk-in.

The refuge's visitor center teaches about local critters and the refuge's namesake—cartoonist and conservationist "Ding" Darling. The massive refuge encompasses more than 5,000 acres, but you don't really see that much if you simply drive through in your car. The best way to go is by canoe, kayak, or narrated tram (see below). Otherwise, get out and walk the short trails and climb the observation tower. You're likely to spot alligators, manatees, and lots of birds—some of them, like the roseate spoonbill, exquisitely rare. Best time to go is morning, low tide, and sunset, when birds are feeding. The still-developing visitor center contains exhibits on bird migration and mangroves.

### Tarpon Bay Explorers (ages 5 to 13)

**900 Tarpon Bay Road, Sanibel Island; (239) 472-8900; www.tarponbay.com. Open 8:00 a.m. to 6:00 p.m. daily. Last rentals go out two hours before closing. Canoe and kayak rentals start at $30 for the first two hours for a double. Call ahead for tram schedule. Two-hour tram tours cost $12 for adults, $8 for children ages 12 and under.**

It rents canoes and kayaks for paddling through "Ding" Darling Refuge (see above). You can also catch an interpretive tram or guided on-water tour of the refuge from here.

### C.R.O.W. (Care and Rehabilitation of Wildlife) (ages 4 to 13)

**3883 Sanibel-Captiva Road, Sanibel Island; (239) 472-3644. Tours 11:00 a.m. Monday through Friday and 1:00 p.m. Sunday, November through April only. A $5 per adult tour fee is requested.**

This hospital complex duplicates natural habitat to rehabilitate sick and injured wildlife: birds, bobcats, raccoons, rabbits, and otters. Visit by appointment or regularly scheduled tour in season.

### Bowman's Beach (all ages)

**Bowman's Beach Road. Parking is $2 per hour.**

The island's most secluded and shelly beach, it has picnic tables, restrooms, showers, and shady trees, but no lifeguards. Like all of Sanibel's beaches, it is maintained in its natural state.

### Adventures in Paradise (ages 5 to 12)

**Port Sanibel Marina, Fort Myers; (239) 472-8443. Admission for tours starts at $20 for adults, $15 for children.**

Board the pontoon boat for fishing, a sea-life encounter, or a sunset cruise.

### Sweet Water Boat Rentals (ages 3 to 13)

**'Tween Waters Marina, Captiva Drive, Captiva; (239) 472-6336. Rental rates begin at $160 a half day, $275 a full day. Tax and fuel are additional.**

To explore the upper islands or go out fishing on your own, rent a boat for the day.

### New Moon (ages 5 to 13) 

**'Tween Waters Marina, Captiva Drive, Captiva; (239) 395-1782 or (888) 472-7245; www.newmoonsailing.com.**

Capt. Mick Gurley conducts sailing excursions and offers sailing classes for families and children (must be at least eight years old if not accompanied by parents). Lessons and extended sails to the Keys can be arranged. Advance reservations are requested.

### Crab Races (ages 4 to 13)
**Crow's Nest Lounge, 'Tween Waters Resort, Captiva Drive, Captiva; (239) 472-5161. 6:00 p.m. Monday and Thursday.**

These weekly events are a blast. For $3 you rent a hermit crab, which the kids can name, then cheer it on to victory. The announcer of eighteen-plus years is very funny, gives out prizes, and likes to joke with the kids. (There's an all-adult version later in the evening.) Half the pot goes to the United Way.

### Captiva Cruises (ages 5 to 13)
**South Seas Resort Marina, Captiva; (239) 472-5300. Excursion fees range from $20.00 to $45.00, $12.50 to $25.00 for children ages 4 to 12.**

The 150-passenger *Lady Chadwick* and other boats make dolphin, shelling, and luncheon excursions to the upper islands, with seating outdoors or in air-conditioned comfort. It's one of the few ways to see and dine on Useppa Island, where Zane Grey, Hedy LaMarr, and other illuminati of the 1920s reputedly recharged. It is now a private vacation club.

## Where to Eat

Island restaurants, including the very finest, welcome children. Some, such as those listed here, make a more concerted effort to attract families than others.

**The Bubble Room.** 15001 Captiva Drive, Captiva; (239) 472-5558. Fun and whimsical but expensive for dinner and touristy. Go have lunch or one of their sinful desserts and a look at the childhood-nostalgic decorations. $$$

**Hungry Heron Restaurant.** 2330 Palm Ridge Road, Sanibel; (239) 395-2300. A favorite of locals, especially those with kids, because it shows cartoons, has a dinnertime roving magician and lists a long selection of dishes for preteenagers. Service can be slow. Open for lunch and dinner daily and breakfast Saturday and Sunday. $$

**Mucky Duck.** 11546 Andy Rosse Lane, Captiva; (239) 472-3434; www.mucky duck.com. Popular, fun beachside eatery. Go early, put your name in, and spend the hour or so wait on the beach right outside the door, where sunsets are spectacular. Lunch and dinner Monday through Saturday. $$–$$$

## Where to Stay

**Jensen's Twin Palm Cottages & Marina.** Captiva Drive (P.O. Box 191), Captiva Island 33924; (239) 472-5800; www .gocaptiva.com. One- and two-bedroom cottages on the water with a focus on fishing lifestyles. $$–$$$

**South Seas Island Resort.** North end of Captiva; 5400 Plantation Road, Captiva; (239) 472-5111 or (866) 565-5089; www .southseas.com. Spacious beach resort perfect for families. Hotel rooms, suites, villas, cottages, homes. Recreational opportunities include nine-hole golf course and excellent kids' program. A **free** resort trolley transports you around the 330-acre property. $$$–$$$$

**Sundial Beach & Golf Resort.** 1451 Middle Gulf Drive, Sanibel; (239) 472-4151 or (800) 237-4184; www.sundialresort .com. It has the best programs for and attitude about "age-challenged" guests. Touch tank on-site in the environmental center. Kids can dial a bedtime story, go on nature beach walks, or choose from dozens of scheduled activities. Full kitchens, water-sports equipment rentals. $$$–$$$$

## For More Information

**Sanibel-Captiva Islands Chamber of Commerce.** 1159 Causeway Road, Sanibel Island 33957; (239) 472-1080; www .sanibel-captiva.org.

# Fort Myers Beach

From Sanibel Island, follow Summerlin Road (Route 867) about five minutes to San Carlos Boulevard and turn right (west). Cross the high bridge to Estero Boulevard (Route 865), Fort Myers Beach's main drag.

This beach town, situated on Estero Island, is trying to change its image from a spring-break party place to a family destination. Playgrounds are appearing on beaches, and resorts heartily welcome kids. Still, in March and April the college gang swarms in. Fort Myers Beach is water-sports heaven. You can book a Jet Ski tour to see dolphins or head skyward by parasail.

### Getaway Deep Sea Fishing (ages 4 to 13)

**Getaway Marina, 18400 San Carlos Boulevard; (239) 466-3600. Half-day trip (9:00 a.m. to 3:00 p.m.) is $44 for adults, $30 for children 12 and under, and $20 for those not fishing; no reservations necessary.**

Party boat excursions take you into deep waters aboard a 90-foot craft to hook into grouper, shark, mackerel, and other prize catches.

### Fish-Tale Marina (all ages)

**7225 Estero Boulevard; (239) 463-4448. Open 8:00 a.m. to 5:00 p.m. daily. Rental fees begin at $95 for a half day, $200 for a full day. Refueling, collision waiver, and tax are extra.**

Rent a fishing or pontoon boat for a self-guided family water adventure.

# Southwestern **Climes**

Southwest Florida feels the most tropical of Gulf Coast regions. Winter temperatures rarely dip below 70 degrees in the daytime and require little more than sweatshirts (unless you plan on boating; bring warm-weather gear). Summers are sticky and hot, normally showered each afternoon by thunderstorms. Plan to spend a lot of time in the water. On the islands, insulated by water, temperatures stay lower in the summer and higher in the winter.

### Bowditch Point Regional Park (all ages)

**North end of Estero Boulevard; (239) 461-7400. Parking costs $1 per hour.**

A lovely beach, it fronts Estero Bay and the Gulf. This is a nice beach for the family, with playground equipment, picnic tables, grills, hiking paths, and distance from the beach bar scene at so-called Times Square, where the bridge connects to the island.

### Lovers Key State Park (all ages)

**South of Estero Island on Route 865; 8700 Estero Boulevard; (239) 463-4588. Open 8:00 a.m. to sunset daily. Park entrance is $5 per vehicle with up to eight passengers, $3 for a single passenger, and $1 for extra passengers, bicyclists, and pedestrians.**

It makes a great getaway beach destination while offering the convenience of picnicking facilities and nature activities. A tram or footbridge takes you to the beach and over a mangrove estuary. Kayak and bike rentals are available, plus there are camping and food concessions. This is a good place to spot ospreys, collect shells, and have a picnic.

## Where to Eat

As headquarters for a major shrimp fleet, Fort Myers Beach serves the freshest of seafood. Every March it celebrates its briny harvest with the Fort Myers Beach Shrimp Festival. Festivities include a blessing of the fleet, parade, and shrimp boil. For more information call (239) 454-7500.

**Snug Harbor.** 645 San Carlos Boulevard; (239) 463-4343; www.snugharborrestaurant .com. Waterfront dining indoors or out with seafood, salad, and pasta specialties. Lunch and dinner daily. $$–$$$

## Where to Stay

Fort Myers Beach's resorts are generally less expensive than those on neighboring islands.

**Pink Shell Beach & Bay Resort.** 275 Estero Boulevard; (239) 463-6181; www .pinkshell.com. At the island's quieter north end, with modern upscale condos. Twelve acres Gulf to bay, with marina, restaurant, boat tours, a kids' activity program, water-sports rentals, swimming pools, and tennis courts. $$–$$$$

## For More Information

**Greater Fort Myers Beach Chamber of Commerce.** 17200 San Carlos Boulevard, Fort Myers Beach 33931; (239) 454- 7500; fax (239) 454-7910; www.fmb chamber.com.

# Bonita Beach and Bonita Springs

Follow Route 865 for about ten minutes south of Lovers Key.

Route 865, which transports you the 15 miles from Estero Island to Little Hickory Island, passes undeveloped barrier island territory and the key-clotted Estero Bay Aquatic Preserve. The town of Bonita Beach on Little Hickory Island marks the beginning of more developed beachfront. On the mainland, Bonita Springs is metamorphosing from a tomato-growing town to a golfing development mecca between Fort Myers and Naples.

### Bonita Beach Public Beach (all ages)

**South end of Hickory Boulevard; (239) 461-7400. Parking is $1 per hour.**

Older kids especially will like all the fun, games, and excitement—volleyball, windsurfing, hot dog stands, loud music. Lifeguards are on duty.

### Little Hickory Island (all ages)

**26082 North Hickory Boulevard/Route 865, Fort Myers Beach. Open sunrise to sunset. Admission is free; parking is $1 per hour.**

Located in southern Lee County near Bonita Beach, a shelly, white-sand beach combined with a feeling of seclusion is the main attraction at this beachfront park. A ramp runs from the parking lot to the sand, allowing handicapped access, and the shore is wide and clean. Surf fishing is a favorite pastime for visitors here, with locals and tourists alike raving about abundant catches. The beach offers restrooms, picnic tables, and showers.

### Barefoot Beach Preserve (all ages)

**Entrance at Hickory Boulevard and Bonita Beach Road; (239) 353-0404. Open 8:00 a.m. to sunset daily. Parking is $4 a day.**

Food concessions, picnic areas, and a brush with nature mean your family is going to love this 342-acre park.

# Smart **Travel**

- There are plenty of fast-food places in southwest Florida, but if you're looking for something that pleases parents and kids alike, you're in luck here. Few restaurants do not accommodate children in southwest Florida. Naples restaurants as a whole are least conducive to families.

- Call ahead to a restaurant to discover the house policy. Some that do not actually have a kids' menu will fix hamburgers, pasta, or PBJs for small visitors. Ask about high chairs and booster seats.

- Almost any restaurant can be a family restaurant if you're prepared. Bring crackers, straw-sip containers of milk or juice, coloring books and crayons, electronic games—whatever it takes to keep them fed and occupied while you try to act like a normal person out for dinner.

- Although children under age sixteen can fish free in Florida, adults must purchase separate salt- and freshwater licenses.

## Where to Eat

**Anthony's Trattoria.** 8951 Bonita Beach Road (Springs Plaza), Bonita Springs; (239) 947-2202. For good Italian food in a family-friendly setting. Kids' menu. Lunch every day except Sunday; dinner daily. $$–$$$

**Doc's Beach House.** 27980 Hickory Boulevard, Bonita Beach; (239) 992-6444. You barely have to leave the beach to eat here. Downstairs is ultracasual, with outdoor seating; upstairs, enjoy a beach view with air-conditioning. Burgers, hot dogs, chili, and finger foods. Open for breakfast, lunch, and dinner daily. $–$$

## For More Information

**Bonita Springs Area Chamber of Commerce.** 25071 Chamber of Commerce Drive, Bonita Springs 34135; (239) 992-2943; fax (239) 992-5011; www.bonita springschamber.com.

# Estero

North of Bonita Springs on Highway 41 about 15 miles.

### Koreshan State Historic Site (ages 5 to 13)

**Highway 41 and Corkscrew Road (P.O. Box 7), Estero 33928; (239) 992-0311. Open 8:00 a.m. to sunset daily. Park entrance is $4 per vehicle of eight persons or fewer, $1 per extra passenger, cyclist, or pedestrian.**

For an unusual journey to times past, make a northward side trip on Highway 41 to Estero. This historic site commemorates a turn-of-the-twentieth-century religious cult that settled the banks of the Estero River. Koreshans were preoccupied with science and the arts. They theorized that the earth clung to the inside of the world's sphere, and they also planted experimental tropical gardens. You can camp in the grounds where they once made their home. Many of their buildings have been reconstructed, and the rare gardens still flourish.

### Estero River Tackle and Canoe Outfitters (ages 6 to 13)

**20991 South Tamiami Trail; (239) 992-4050. Open 7:00 a.m. to 6:00 p.m. daily. Three-hour rentals cost $22.50 to $27.50 for canoes, $17.50 to $42.50 per person for kayaks.**

Across the street from Koreshan, you can rent a canoe for the 4-mile trip into the park's wildlife asylum. It has a boat ramp on the river and also sells bait and tackle.

### Beachcomber Tours (all ages)

**4765 Estero Boulevard, Fort Myers Beach; (239) 443-7456; www.beachcombertours inc.com. Call for reservations and directions to the marina; pickups also available by arrangement at Koreshan State Park and Lovers Key Resort. All trips cost $30 for adults and $15 for children 12 and under.**

Offers dolphin watch and shelling trips, sunset cruises, Estero River nature tours, and trips to Mound Key.

# Naples

South of Bonita Springs on Highway 41.

A city of contrasts, Naples balances wild and natural attractions with ultracivilized culture and wealth. Naples sits on the doorstep to the Florida Everglades, and its southern neighborhoods most reflect this rugged aspect of its personality.

### Corkscrew Swamp Sanctuary (ages 5 to 13)

**21 miles east of Highway 41 off Immokalee Road; 375 Sanctuary Road; (239) 348-9151. Open 7:00 a.m. to 5:30 p.m. October 1 to April 10, 7:00 a.m. to 7:30 p.m. April 11 to September 30. Admission is $10 for adults, $6 for college students, $4 for children ages 6 to 18.**

In Naples's northern reaches, nesting wood storks and some of the nation's oldest bald cypress trees are the star attractions. The 11,000-acre preserve, operated by the National Audubon Society, features a 2-mile boardwalk that crosses swampland inhabited by rich plant and marine life. You can usually spot an alligator or two and sometimes deer, otters, and wild hogs. A new interactive Audubon visitor center sensitizes guests to the unusual ecosystem.

### Delnor-Wiggins State Park (ages 4 to 13)

**Route 846 at 11100 Gulf Shore Drive North, Naples Park; (239) 597-6196. Open 8:00 a.m. to sunset daily. Park entrance is $5 per vehicle with up to eight passengers, $3 for a single passenger, and $1 for extra passengers, bicyclists, and pedestrians.**

If your family favors beach seclusion and nature over water sports and crowds, spend the day here, just north of Naples. Fishing in the swift pass waters is as rowdy as it gets. Climb the observation tower for excitement. Bring a picnic; tables and grills are provided. Lifeguards are on duty, and beach and kayak rentals and food concessions are available.

### King Richard's Family Fun Park (ages 3 to 13)

**North of Pine Ridge Road (exit 107 off I-75), 6780 North Airport Road; (239) 598-1666. Open 11:00 a.m. to 9:00 p.m. Monday through Thursday, 11:00 a.m. to 10:00 p.m. Friday and Saturday, noon to 9:00 p.m. Sunday. Admission to each attraction is $6.95 per person, and all-day/all-attraction passes are $29.95.**

Pick your fun: water sports (for children up to age ten), laser tag, a rock wall, and extreme go-karts (for persons eighteen and older).

## Sweet Liberty Sailing Catamaran (all ages)

City Dock, 880 Twelfth Avenue South, Naples; (239) 793-3523; www.sweetliberty.com. Reservations required. Sunset cruise each evening departs one and a half hours prior to sunset and is $27 for adults, $15 for children ages 12 and under. Shelling trips (9:30 a.m. to 12:30 p.m.) are $38 for adults, $15 for children ages 12 and under. Sightseeing Naples waterfront (1:30 to 3:30 p.m.) is $27 for adults and $15 for children ages 12 and under.

Enjoy a quiet, smooth, relaxing tour aboard a 53-foot sailing catamaran. There is plenty of room to walk around, inside and outside seating, and two restrooms on board.

## The Conservancy of Southwest Florida (all ages)

Merrihue Drive at 1450 Fourteenth Avenue North; 1 block east of Goodlette Road; (239) 262-0304; www.conservancy.org. Open 9:00 a.m. to 4:30 p.m. Monday through Saturday. Museum admission is $9 for adults and $4 for children ages 3 to 12. Canoe rentals start at $15.

Stroke a snake. Watch a turtle chow down. Name that tree. The Natural Science Museum exhibits, serpentarium, trail walks, and discovery experiences are a natural for kids. They can watch injured and sick animals rehabilitating or sign up for a special hiking, canoe, or boat trip (minimum age six). Canoe and kayak rentals are available. A **free** boat ride takes you through the thirteen-acre Conservancy's mangrove estuary to the Gordon River and a canal where nature suffers at the hands of progress. The center is associated with the Rookery Bay Estuarine Reserve and its programs.

## The Zoo at Caribbean Gardens (all ages)

1590 Goodlette Road; (239) 262-5409; www.napleszoo.com. Open 9:30 a.m. to 5:30 p.m. daily (ticket office closes at 4:30 p.m.). Admission is $18.50 for adults, $17.50 for seniors, $9.95 for children ages 3 to 15, plus tax.

A boat tour, animal shows, and tropical gardens add to the allure of this small zoo. Favorite spots for the kids include Young Explorers Playground Forest. "Meet the Keeper" and multimedia animal shows (video and live) feature Bengal tigers, lions, alligators, dingoes, monitor lizards, and leaping lemurs.

## Naples Fishing Pier (all ages) 

Twelfth Avenue South; (239) 213-3062. Open 9:00 a.m. to sunset. Free, but parking is metered and limited.

Gorgeous white beaches run the length of Naples. The beach around the historic pier is a popular spot, especially for anglers and sunset-gazers. It comes equipped with a bait shop, snack bar, restrooms, and showers. There's no charge, which makes it Florida's largest free fishing pier.

## Lowdermilk Park (all ages)

Gulf Shore Boulevard at Banyan Boulevard. Open 7:00 a.m. to dusk. Parking is metered.

Families are likely to find entertainment at Lowdermilk, where there's volleyball, playgrounds, picnicking, and concessions.

## Palm Cottage and Norris Gardens (ages 8 to 13)

137 Twelfth Avenue South; (239) 261-8164. Open 1:00 to 4:00 p.m. Sunday through Friday in winter, Wednesday and Saturday only in summer or by appointment. Admission is $6 for adults and $3 for children ages 12 and under.

A speck of local history resides here. Built in the 1880s of tabby mortar and Florida mahogany, it was one of the first buildings in southwest Florida to be constructed of local materials. Alternately a home and part of the Naples Hotel, today it houses the Collier County Historical Society and remembers lifestyles of the rich and acclaimed who once visited.

## Collier County Museum (ages 4 to 13)

3301 Tamiami Trail East; (239) 774-8476. Open 9:00 a.m. to 5:00 p.m. Monday through Friday, 9:00 a.m. to 4:00 p.m. Saturday. Admission is free or by donation.

In a lush park setting, it displays a Seminole Indian village, classic swamp buggy, archaeological lab, skeleton of an Ice Age giant ground sloth, re-created nineteenth-century trading post, and steam locomotive from the county's cypress logging era, as well as indoor prehistoric artifacts.

## Florida Sports Park (ages 7 to 13)

Route 951, less than 4 miles south of I-75's exit 101; P.O. Box 990010, Naples 34116; (239) 774-2701 or (800) 897-2701. Tickets cost about $14.50 to $17.00.

Three times yearly the nationally televised Swamp Buggy Races take place here. Swamp buggies are vehicles adapted to the Everglades' marshy terrain; these are speedy, souped-up versions. The races in October feature a downtown parade. The year's Swamp Buggy Queen makes her first appearance at the March race and gets dunked in the mud at every race. (The third race is in May.)

# Where to Eat

Naples is known for its chichi restaurants and daring cuisine. Families are not discouraged, but these places often have no specific kids' menu or other accommodations, especially for the high-chair crowd. Those below have a more relaxed, family atmosphere.

**Remy's Neighborhood Bistro.** 2300 Pine Ridge Road (Target center), Naples; (239) 403-9922. American cuisine with a French twist. Open for lunch and dinner. $

**Riverwalk Fish & Ale House.** Tin City, 1200 Fifth Avenue South; (239) 263-2734. Casual, shanty-style waterfront dining with emphasis on seafood. Kids' menu. Lunch and dinner daily. $$

## Where to Stay

Staying in Naples with a family can be a pricey venture. Yet even its storied luxury resorts are kid friendly.

**Naples Beach Hotel & Golf Club.** 851 Gulf Shore Boulevard North; (239) 261-2222 or (800) 237-7600; www.naplesbeach hotel.com. Fifty-year-old property with eighteen-hole golf course, spa and fitness center, beachfront and water-sports rentals, tennis courts, pool, kids' club, and dining room. There are 315 rooms and efficiencies. $$$–$$$$

**The Ritz-Carlton.** 280 Vanderbilt Beach Road in north Naples; (239) 598-3300 for information; (800) 241-3333 for reserva-

tions; www.ritz-carlton.com. Great beach and a commitment to family travelers. Try booking on the club floor, where all-day complimentary munchies can save on restaurant bills. Kids' programs. $$$$

**Trianon Old Naples.** 955 Seventh Avenue South; (239) 435-9600. Located in a residential area within walking distance of the waterfront and shopping district; 55 guest rooms, 3 large one-bedroom suites, pool, off-street parking. Continental breakfast in the lobby. Gulf beaches are just five minutes away. $$$

## For More Information

**Chamber Center.** 3620 Tamiami Trail North, Naples 34103-3724; (239) 262-6367; www.napleschamber.org.

**Visitor Information Center.** 895 Fifth Avenue South, Naples 34102-6605; (239) 262-6141.

# Marco Island

South of Naples along Route 951 about thirty minutes.

The northernmost of the Everglades' Ten Thousand Islands, Marco Island is nonetheless highly developed. Its golden crescent beach is lined with high-rises and resorts. To get away from all the high-rise glitz, go to the fishing village of Goodland, on the island's northeast side. It's a fun place for lunch and a great place to buy seafood.

### Tigertail Beach (all ages)
**Hernando Drive (take Tigertail Court north off Collier Boulevard). Open 7:00 a.m. to dusk daily. Parking is $3 a day.**

Marco Island's main public access often fills up early. Offshore, a sandbar known as Sand Dollar Island surfaces in low tide. Between it and the beach, tidal pools fill with fish, small shells, and the shorebirds that feed upon them. Behind the beach, a restricted nesting area assures good bird-watching. The park has picnic facilities, food concessions, volleyball, a cool playground divided for two different age ranges, and water-sports rentals.

# Going In-Seine at **Tigertail**

Tide was low, striating Marco Island's beach into fingers of sandbars separated by muck-bottomed tidal pools. Some in the group were well prepared for a foray into sea world minutia. They wore swimwear and surf walkers. Others rolled up their shorts and shirtsleeves or backed away to assume the role of spectator. Aaron, seven, didn't let a pair of Wilson gym shorts and a T-shirt get in his way. He was first to volunteer for the two-person swooping team on one of three small-mesh nets and was immediately drenched.

The first prize was a lizard fish, until that was upstaged by a baby horseshoe crab the size of a quarter. Both went into tubs for "show and tell" later, along with a dwarf sea horse, a pufferfish no bigger than a pinky fingernail, killifishes, a spider crab, sea stars, a ribbonlike pipe fish, a baby spade fish, a live lightning whelk, and its curly-cue egg case. As the sun edged toward the horizon, all gathered around to discuss the finds, which we passed around in plastic bags filled with water. Our guide talked about their habits, habitat, and—with nary a blush—sex lives. We all went away from the beach that evening with a better understanding of what lies below the surface glamour of beachgoing.    —*C.K.W.*

### Marco Island Trolley (ages 4 to 13)

**Park at the chamber of commerce, near the island's north bridge on Collier Boulevard, or catch it at any of its stops; (239) 394-1600. Admission is $25 for adults, $12 for children under age 12.**

This is a great tour of the island. You can get off and reboard as often as you like. One highlight is driving up the steep Indian Hill on the island's north end. You'll learn about the area's history from the drivers, who are generally fun characters.

### Key Marco Museum (ages 7 to 13)

**Corner of Bald Eagle Drive and Waterway Drive in the Association of Realtors building; 140 Waterway Drive. Open 9:00 a.m. to 4:00 p.m. Monday through Friday. Admission is free.**

Marco Island has a proud archaeological history, and digs have unearthed important ancient finds. This museum displays some of the artifacts, as well as photographs and other memorabilia of more modern times.

## Captain's John and Pam Stop

Calusa Island Marina, Goodland; (239) 394-8000; www.stopsmarinecharters.com. Rate is $300 for up to six people for three and a half hours.

Take a backwater ecotour, fishing or shelling from the local fishing capital into Ten Thousand Islands and thereabouts. Modes of transportation include a 26-foot luxury vessel and a 25-foot center console.

## Where to Eat

**Snook Inn.** 1215 Bald Eagle Drive; (239) 394-3313. Waterfront seafood house with twice-weekly seafood buffets open daily. $$$

**Stan's Idle Hour Seafood Restaurant.** 221 West Goodland Drive, Goodland; (239) 394-3041. A favorite stop for waterfront dining and local color. You shouldn't miss Sunday's goings-on. Country music accompanies a strange dance ritual invented here and known as the Buzzard Lope. In January, Stan's hosts the Mullet Festival, a small-town hoedown. Closed Monday year-round and in late summer, otherwise it's open for lunch and dinner. $$

## Where to Stay

**Marco Island Lakeside Inn.** 155 First Avenue, Marco Island; (239) 394-1161 or (800) 729-0216; www.marcoislandlakeside .com. Located just 1 mile from the Marco Island beaches. On-site restaurant (sushi and steaks), heated pool. $$$–$$$$

**Marriott's Marco Island Resort Golf Club & Spa.** 400 South Collier Boulevard; (239) 394-2511 or (800) 438-4373; www .marcomarriottresort.com. Two playgrounds, kids' pool, wide beach, recreation program, shopping arcade, pizza parlor, and restaurants. Each room has a microwave oven, refrigerator, toaster, iron, and ironing board. $$$–$$$$

## For More Information

**Marco Island Area Chamber of Commerce.** 1102 North Collier Boulevard (P.O. Box 913), Marco Island 34145; (239) 394-7549 or (800) 788-MARCO; www.marco islandchamber.org.

# Everglades City and Chokoloskee Island

From Goodland, take Route 92 off the island to Highway 41. Turn right. Take Route 29 from Highway 41 to reach Everglades City.

East of Marco Island, the wilderness of the Everglades and various surrounding national and state parks and refuges begins.

## Gator **Trivia**

- Alligators can live a year without food.
- Alligators are born without a predetermined sex. Incubation temperature differences determine the sex of the babies.
- Feeding alligators causes them to lose fear of humans.
- Fine for feeding an alligator: up to $500 and sixty days in jail.

If you're serious about exploring the vast maze land of the Everglades, Everglades City is a good place to set up base camp. From Everglades City, a causeway takes you to Chokoloskee Island, a throwback to frontier days.

### Collier-Seminole State Park (ages 5 to 13)

**20200 East Tamiami Trail at Route 92, Naples; (239) 394-3397. Open 8:00 a.m. to sunset daily. Park entrance is $4 per vehicle of eight persons or fewer, $1 per extra passenger, cyclist, or pedestrian.**

Come here to camp and canoe in winter. In warm weather the mosquitoes will drive you away, or crazy. For the kids, the 6,400-acre park also holds a nice playground, nature trails, and one of the dredges used to forge Tamiami Trail out of the swamps. If you're not up to canoeing, you can hop on a boat tour (239-642-8898) down the Blackwater River and into the Ten Thousand Islands.

### Everglades National Park Boat Tours (ages 5 to 13)

**National Park Ranger Station, Chokoloskee Causeway, Route 29; (239) 695-2591 or (800) 445-7724. Tours depart daily every thirty minutes, beginning at 9:00 a.m., until 4:30 or 5:00 p.m., depending on what time the sun sets. Tours last about an hour and a half. Cost is $26.50 for adults, $13.25 for kids ages 5 to 12. Canoe rentals are $25.44 a day. Shuttle service is available.**

The national park conducts naturalist-narrated tours through the maze of Ten Thousand Islands and its teeming bird, alligator, and aquatic life. The facility also rents canoes. In season, rangers lead guided canoe tours.

### Ted Smallwood's Store and Museum (ages 7 to 13)

**360 Mamie Street, Chokoloskee Island; (239) 695-2989. Open 10:00 a.m. to 5:00 p.m. daily December through April, 11:00 a.m. to 5:00 p.m. May through November. Admission is $3.00 for adults, $2.50 for seniors, free for children under age 12 when accompanied by an adult.**

Explore the Everglades' wild and woolly era at this old Indian trading post of the early 1900s. Learn how Smallwood's was the site of an outlaw gun-down in 1910 and all about frontier life in the 'Glades through simple vignettes and antique general store products. The view from the back porch may be the best part; the rest is somewhat gloomy and dusty.

### Everglades National Park Wilderness Waterway (ages 7 to 13)

Everglades National Park is accessible from the east (see Southeast chapter) as well as from the west, via Highway 41.

Avid outdoor types can explore the eerily lonesome terrain of the Ten Thousand Islands via the 98-mile Wilderness Waterway canoe trail. (Do this in cool weather.) Canoeists must register with park rangers. You can paddle portions of the trail; the entire length takes at least eight days. Chickee (Indian-thatched) hut landings provide rustic shelter for campers. Several outfitters run guided tours within the park. Canoeists must bring all of their own gear unless outfitted by one of these businesses. A list of canoe rentals, outfitters, and recommended gear, plus necessary charts, guidebooks, and complete information are available from the U.S. Department of the Interior, National Park Service, Everglades National Park, P.O. Box 279, Homestead 33030.

# More Things to See and Do
# in Southwest Florida

- **Ostego Bay Foundation,** Fort Myers Beach; (239) 765-8101
- **Gulfside Park,** Sanibel; (239) 472-9075
- **Golf Safari,** Bonita Springs; (239) 947-1377
- **Everglades Wonder Gardens,** Bonita Springs; (239) 992-2591
- **C.R.E.W. Marsh Trail System,** Naples; (239) 657-2253
- **Coral Cay Adventure Golf,** Naples; (239) 793-4999
- **Gulf Coast Skimmers Water Ski Show,** Naples; (239) 732-0570
- **Golden Gate Aquatic Complex,** Naples; (239) 353-7128
- **Fakahatchee Strand State Preserve,** Naples; (239) 695-4593
- **Big Cypress National Preserve,** Naples; (239) 695-4111, ext. 0
- **Museum of the Everglades,** Everglades City; (239) 695-0008

## Wooten's Everglades Tours (ages 7 to 13)
East of Everglades City, 32330 Tamiami Trail East (Star Route, Box 120), Ochopee; (800) 282-2781.

In the vicinity you'll find any number of swamp buggy and airboat (another craft born of Everglades ingenuity—but noisy) tours, fishing charters, and such. Wooten's is one of the more well-respected names in the business.

## Where to Eat

**Rod & Gun Club.** 200 Broadway, Everglades City; (239) 695-2101. A historic lodge with walls covered in trophy catches and alligator hides, serving Everglades fare—fish, frog's legs, peanut butter pie, and Southern-fried specialties. $$–$$$

## Where to Stay

**Ivey House.** 107 Camellia Street, Everglades City; (239) 695-3299; www.ivey house.com. Not only a casual inn but also headquarters of North American Canoe Tours, which provides a variety of backcountry trips into the Ten Thousand Islands and the Everglades Wilderness Waterway. Lodging and canoe trip prices vary with the details and the season, and lodging is higher during the Seafood Festival (first weekend in February). $–$$

## For More Information

**Everglades Area Chamber of Commerce.** Corner of Highway 41 and Route 29 (P.O. Box 130), Everglades City 34139; (239) 695-3941 or (800) 914-6355.

## Annual Events

**Edison Pageant of Light.** Fort Myers; (239) 334-2999. Taking place late January to early February, it honors former winter resident Thomas Edison with events culmi-

nating in a lighted night parade. Miles of light strings electrify the historic homes, decorated in special holiday garb. **Free.**

**Everglades Seafood Festival.** Everglades City; (239) 695-4100. Three days of music, an artisan fair, and seafood the end of January and first weekend of February. **Free.**

**Native American & Pioneer Heritage Days.** Collier-Seminole State Park, Naples; (239) 394-3397. For three days in late February, the park celebrates the culture of local and nationwide tribes and early Everglades settlers.

**Sanibel Shell Fair and Show.** Sanibel Island; (239) 472-2155. A four-day exhibit early in March that features sea life displays, specimen shells, and shell art.

**Fourth of July Freedom Swim.** Punta Gorda. Participants swim the half-mile stretch across the mouth of the Peace River from Charlotte Harbor to Fishermen's Village while boaters accompany them. Entertainment and fireworks follow.

**Kids Fishing Tournament.** Fishermen's Village, Punta Gorda. Takes place one Saturday in July.

**Old Florida Festival.** Naples; (239) 774-8476. Music, Seminole War reenactments, history camps, and traditional arts and crafts the first weekend of November.

**Sandsculpting Contest.** Fort Myers Beach; (239) 454-7500. One weekend early in November, masters, amateurs, and spectators gather. **Free.**

**Teddy Bear Teas.** Naples; (239) 598-6644. A whimsical December holiday date with stuffed toys.

# Southeast
# Florida

Southeast Florida—home of Miami Beach, Fort Lauderdale, Palm Beach, and other giant resort towns—is the first Florida many get to know. From the north, you first enter Palm Beach County, stretched long and lean along the coast. At northern extremes, this foray into the state's most populated, metropolitan area meets with lightly trodden wilderness. Then the city life begins and doesn't end until 100 miles later, when you've left the Fort Lauderdale–Miami area for the eccentricities of the Florida Keys.

Despite its urban sprawl, however, the south coast's traffic and development are easily left behind with a short drive away from the coast. In the West Palm Beach

# TopPicks for Family Fun in Southeast Florida

1. Driving through Lion Country Safari, West Palm Beach

2. Playing weird science at Museum of Discovery and Science, Fort Lauderdale

3. Watching the primates swing free at Monkey Jungle, Miami

4. Swimming the caves and crannies of Venetian Pool, Coral Gables

5. Biking Shark Valley, Everglades National Park

6. Spending the whole day beached at Crandon Park, Key Biscayne

7. Counting angelfish on the glass-bottom boat ride, Biscayne National Underwater Park

8. Seeing deer in miniature at National Key Deer Refuge, Big Pine Key

9. Celebrating day's end at the bottom of the United States at Mallory Square pier, Key West

# SOUTHEAST FLORIDA

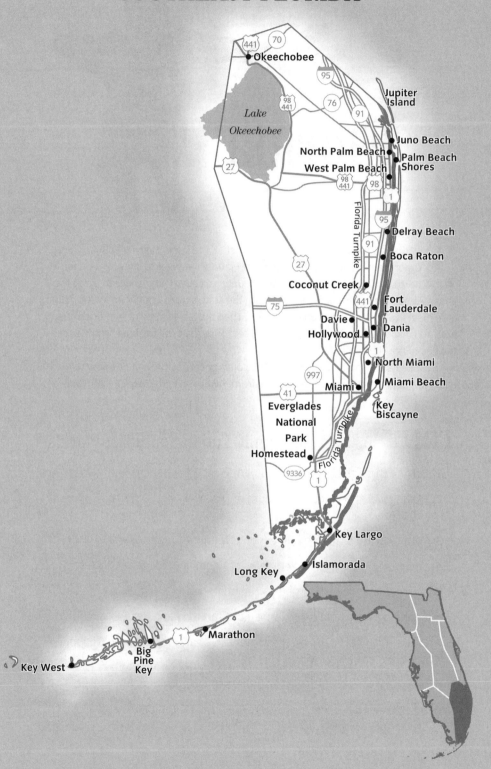

environs, a westward trek takes you to big and fishy Lake Okeechobee and the Loxahatchee National Wildlife Refuge. From Fort Lauderdale and Miami, a half hour gets you to the Everglades and Seminole and Miccosukee Indian territory. This tour will guide you to side trips into Florida's most profound wilderness as it heads to the very last speck of land in the state, Key West.

# Jupiter Island

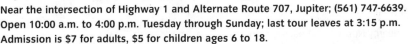

From Highway 1 or Route A1A in Hobe Sound, turn east on Route 707 (Bridge Road).

Jupiter Island hides its privileged residents from the noisy, fun resort world around it. (It's Palm Beach without the reputation.) The drive down Beach Road (Route 707) affords a vision of natural and wealth-driven beauty.

### Jupiter Inlet Lighthouse (ages 7 to 13)

**Near the intersection of Highway 1 and Alternate Route 707, Jupiter; (561) 747-6639. Open 10:00 a.m. to 4:00 p.m. Tuesday through Sunday; last tour leaves at 3:15 p.m. Admission is $7 for adults, $5 for children ages 6 to 18.**

It stands as one of Florida's most scenic lighthouses, built in 1860. Visit the small museum at the base and climb to the top (must be 48 inches or taller) by tour only.

### Jupiter Hills Lighthouse Marina (all ages)

**18261 Southeast Federal Highway, Tequesta; (561) 744-0727. Open daily. Rates for half-day rentals range from $125 to $165.**

Rent a boat for family seabound adventure.

### Canoe Outfitters of Florida (ages 7 to 13)

**Riverbend County Park, on Route 706 (Indiantown Road), about 9 miles west of Highway 1; 9060 West Indiantown Road, Jupiter; (561) 746-7053. Open Thursday through Monday. Package rate for the full trip is $40 to $60 for two people.**

For a slower waterborne pace, take a leisurely canoe or kayak trip on the wild and scenic Loxahatchee River, along with the gators and multitude of birds.

### Loxahatchee River Historical Society (ages 6 to 13)

**805 North Highway 1, Jupiter; (561) 747-6639. Open 10:00 a.m. to 5:00 p.m. Tuesday through Sunday. Admission is $7 for adults, $5 for children ages 6 to 18.**

It occupies a Cracker-style building in Burt Reynolds Park and relates how nature shaped the land's history. Other exhibits the kids will enjoy include pioneer toys, an outdoor Seminole Indian Living History Village, Spanish silver coins, and an 1892 Cracker shack that's being restored.

### Carlin Park (all ages)
**Off Route A1A on Jupiter Beach Road, just north of Route 706.**

This is Jupiter Island's most spectacular and popular recreational area, with food concessions, playgrounds, lots of picnic shelters with grills, lifeguards, and a wide apron of clean sand. Concerts and other special events are held outdoors and in its civic center. North of the Carlin Park access, at Jupiter Beach Park, jetties reaching into the pass make for great fishing.

## Where to Eat

**The Crab House.** 1065 Route A1A, Jupiter; (561) 744-1300. View of the Intracoastal Waterway and Jupiter Lighthouse. Crab, seafood, prime rib, and pasta. Kids' menu. Lunch and dinner daily. $$$

## For More Information

**Jupiter–Tequesta–Juno Beach Chamber of Commerce.** 800 North Highway 1, Jupiter 33477; (561) 746-7111; www.jupiter fl.org.

## Where to Stay

See nearby North Palm Beach for lodging suggestions.

# Juno Beach

Just south of Jupiter on Highway 1 or Route A1A.

To the south, the beaches are bluff lined, necessitating steep stairways to get from Route A1A parking to sea level. The tall dunes successfully cloister the beach from the reality shock inherent in developed areas.

## Road **Markers**

Route A1A and Highway 1 thread together coastal communities with increasing tightness as you head south. Interstate 95 and the Florida Turnpike offer quicker access. The turnpike is best for avoiding rush-hour traffic snarls.

South of Miami, expect slow traffic en route to the Keys, especially on a Friday afternoon, when it seems as if all of Miami is headed there for the weekend.

## Loggerhead Park and Marinelife Center of Juno Beach
(all ages)

14200 Highway 1; (561) 627-8280 (Marinelife Center); www.marinelife.org. The center is open 10:00 a.m. to 5:00 p.m. Monday through Saturday, noon to 3:00 p.m. Sunday. Turtle Walks are $8 per person and take place at 9:00 p.m. and by advance reservation only, and the few slots fill up fast.

Loggerhead Beach has the most to offer among the local beaches. Across the street from the beach access, a nicely groomed park offers tennis, picnicking, a playground area, and the Marinelife Center of Juno Beach. The latter introduces you to maritime fauna and flora with a nature trail and indoor displays on shells, crabs, sharks, and sea turtles. During turtle nesting season (June and July), the center conducts night-time Turtle Walks. In May, it hosts Turtle Time Festival on the beach to promote conservation, with music, food, and children's entertainment.

# North Palm Beach County

Just south of Juno Beach on Highway 1.

### John D. MacArthur Beach State Park (ages 4 to 13)

10900 State Road 703, North Palm Beach; (561) 624-6950. Open 8:00 a.m. to sunset daily. Park entrance is $4 per vehicle of eight persons or fewer, $1 per extra passenger, cyclist, or pedestrian. The nature center, free with park admission, is open 9:00 a.m. to 5:00 p.m. daily.

The area's most naturally intact beach runs for an 8,000-foot stretch on the north end of Singer Island. But there's more than beach to see here. The adventure begins at the nature center, near the park's entrance. You'll find aquariums, wildlife exhibits, historical documents, and an interpretive video. Outside, you walk around a butterfly garden and picnic pavilions, then across a 1,600-foot boardwalk (tram service available) to a nature trail that finally leads to the remote beach known for great snorkeling. Saturday and summer programs teach families about the environment.

### Sailfish Marina and Resort (ages 4 to 13)

Sailfish Marina, 98 Lake Drive, Palm Beach Shores; resort desk (561) 844-1724, water taxi reservations (561) 472-1252; www.sailfishmarina.com. Open daily. Sixty- to ninety-minute water-taxi tours (at 10:00 a.m., noon, and 2:00 and 4:00 p.m.) run $24 for adults, $12 for children under 12.

Palm Beach Water Taxi conducts narrated tours of Palm Beach mansions and yachts and Peanut Island, an Intracoastal island containing a recreational park and maritime museum. Sailing and fishing charters specializing in kingfish, dolphinfish, and sailfish also depart daily from its docks. Families can observe and feed tropical fish in the marina's aquarium. Thursday nights bring local artists and artisans with their marine-themed wares for Sunset at Sailfish. Ask about summer Camp Sailfish. Rooms, efficiencies, and kids' program available. $–$$

## Where to Eat

**Crab Pot.** On the mainland at 386 East Blue Heron Boulevard, Riviera Beach; across the Route A1A bridge from Singer Island; (561) 844-2722. Breezy, funky spot on the Intracoastal. Crab and other seafood. Open daily for lunch and dinner. $$–$$$

## Where to Stay

**Palm Beach Shores Resort.** South end of Singer Island, 181 Ocean Avenue (Route A1A), Palm Beach Shores; (561) 863-4000 or (800) 328-2289. Its Beach Buddies club tantalizes tiny tots with lots of games and toys, plus the program sponsors nighttime parties and off-campus field trips. Tennis, water sports, fishing charters, and a less-traveled beachfront add to the amenities; 257 two-room suites. $$$–$$$$

**PGA National Resort & Spa.** 400 Avenue of Champions, Palm Beach Gardens; (561) 627-2000 or (800) 633-9150. Golf focus. Five eighteen-hole courses, a lake beach, nineteen tennis courts, a European spa, five restaurants, summer tennis and golf programs for kids, and 459 rooms, suites, and villas. $$$–$$$$

# Patriotic **Palm Beach**

Well-heeled Palm Beach dressed in khaki to do its civil duty during World War II. While German U-boats scoured local shores, torpedoing tanks and sometimes sending spies ashore, the ornate Breakers was dressed down to serve as a hospital for servicemen. Lights-out orders were issued to the island's coastal residents.

## For More Information

**Northern Palm Beaches Chamber of Commerce.** 1983 PGA Boulevard, Suite 104, Palm Beach Gardens 33408; (561) 694-2300; www.npbchamber.com. Open 8:00 a.m. to 5:00 p.m. Monday through Friday.

# Palm Beach

From Singer Island, head south on Highway 1 or take scenic Flagler Drive for about ten minutes to West Palm Beach. Cross the Route A1A bridge (Royal Palm Way) into the moneyed world of the nation's social register.

If for no other reason, go to Palm Beach to gawk at the estates on a gold-paved drive down Ocean Boulevard. Hang out at Chuck & Harold's restaurant and see what celebrities you can spy. Stop in at the bookstore next door for a great selection of kids' reads. Window-shop as if price were no object along Worth Avenue.

**Flagler Museum** (ages 9 to 13)
**1 Whitehall Way at Cocoanut Row (P.O. Box 969), Palm Beach 33480; (561) 655-2833; www.flagler.org. Open 10:00 a.m. to 5:00 p.m. Tuesday through Saturday, noon to 5:00 p.m. Sunday. Admission is $15 for adults, $8 for children ages 13 to 18, $3 for children ages 6 to 12; under 6 free.**

Lots of glittery, gilded stuff. Kids and adults love looking at the ornate Whitehall, palatial home of Henry Flagler. Flagler is credited with settling the east coast by improving and building railroads from St. Augustine to Key West. Children are especially impressed with the railway car out back. You can see the home by guided or self tour.

## Where to Eat

**Chuck & Harold's.** 207 Royal Poinciana Way; (561) 659-1440. The place to see and be seen. Open daily for lunch and dinner. $$$–$$$$

**Green's Pharmacy.** 151 North County Road; (561) 832-0304. Locals and wealthy winterers meet at the luncheonette counter or tables. All-American food, hearty breakfasts. Breakfast and lunch daily. $

## Where to Stay

**The Breakers.** 1 South County Road; (561) 655-6611 or (800) 833-3141; www.thebreakers.com. A posh old dame of a resort on the beach, with complete amenities. If your bank account can take it, you may want to check into its summer kids' camps. Year-round it holds youth programs. $$$–$$$$

## For More Information

**Palm Beach County Convention and Visitors Bureau.** 1555 Palm Beach Lakes Boulevard, Suite 800, West Palm Beach 33401; (561) 471-3995 or (800) 833-5733; www.palmbeachfl.com. Open 8:30 a.m. to 5:30 p.m. Monday through Friday.

# West Palm Beach

Downtown West Palm Beach is a happening place for shoppers and diners, especially in the stylish Clematis Shopping and Entertainment District along Clematis Street (between Flagler Drive and Rosemary Avenue).

Drift and wreck diving attracts the scuba crowd to these parts. You'll have no problems finding outfitting and certification operations throughout the Palm Beach area.

### SunFest (ages 5 to 13)

**Flagler Drive between Banyan Street and Lakeview Avenue (mailing address: 525 Clematis Street, West Palm Beach 33401); (561) 659-5980 or (800) SUN-FEST; www.sunfest.org. Admission at the gate is $23 per person over age 12; children ages 12 and under are admitted free with an adult. Multiday and other options are available online only.**

Begun as a jazz festival in 1982, it has grown into a well-known, well-attended extravaganza of music in all genres, plus an art and crafts show, a youth park, food, and fireworks. It takes place late April through early May.

### Palm Beach Zoo at Dreher Park (all ages)

**1301 Summit Boulevard; between Southern and Forest Hills Boulevards; (561) 547-WILD; www.palmbeachzoo.org. Open 9:00 a.m. to 5:00 p.m. daily. Admission is $12.95 for adults, $9.95 for seniors, $8.95 for children ages 3 to 12.**

The twenty-three-acre zoo provides home to more than 900 animals of native and exotic species, some of which are endangered. The reptile exhibit and petting zoo fascinate kids. Enjoy the new Tropics of the Americas exhibit.

### South Florida Science Museum (ages 6 to 13)

**In Dreher Park at 4801 Dreher Trail North; (561) 832-1988. Open 10:00 a.m. to 5:00 p.m. Monday through Friday, 10:00 a.m. to 6:00 p.m. Saturday, and noon to 6:00 p.m. Sunday. Admission is $9.00 for adults, $7.50 for seniors, and $6.00 for children ages 3 to 12. Call for planetarium and science theater hours. Planetarium admission is $4 extra per adult, $2 extra per child.**

Family oriented, the museum has the usual bubble, electricity, sound, energy, and hand-manipulative gadgets found in today's interactive science museums, but with more extensive aquariums. They hold marine life from the Pacific, Atlantic, coral reefs, and mangroves. The jawbone of a sperm whale reaches floor to ceiling.

## Hibel Museum of Art (ages 6 to 13)

**1910 Seventh Avenue North, Lake Worth; (561) 622-5560; www.hibel.org. Open 11:00 a.m. to 4:00 p.m. Monday through Saturday. Admission to the museum and festival is free.**

Amid the community's renowned art scene, you'll find the Hibel, dedicated to the paintings, lithographs, porcelains, and sculptures of American artist Edna Hibel. In March, your kids will enjoy the Doll Festival and Tea Party. The artist herself is on hand to autograph her doll creations.

## Rapids Water Park (ages 4 to 13)

**6566 North Military Trail; (561) 842–8756 or (561) 848–6272. Open daily 10:00 a.m. to 7:00 p.m. mid-May through August. Admission is $31.95 plus tax for ages 2 and older.**

Cool off and splash down at Rapids Water Park. It soothes summer swelter with giant water slides, a wave pool, a lazy river, and a rain forest. Separate pools are designed for kids and adults.

## Palm Beach Polo & Country Club (ages 9 to 13)

**Forest Hill and South Shore Boulevards, west of Highway 441 South, 11199 Polo Club Road, Wellington; (561) 204-5687; www.palmbeachpolo.com. Public matches begin 3:00 p.m. Sunday, January through mid-April. Admission is $15.**

Polo and croquet are two trademark Palm Beach–area sports. To catch a polo match, attend Palm Beach Polo & Country Club's Sunday events. At halftime, join the stompers, who go onto the field to stamp down divots made by the horses' hooves.

## Lion Country Safari (all ages)

**Off Southern Boulevard (Highway 441/98), west of Highway 1 about 20 miles; 2003 Lion Country Safari Road, Loxahatchee; (561) 793-1084; www.lioncountrysafari.com. Open 9:30 a.m. to 5:30 p.m. daily (no admissions after 4:30 p.m.). Admission is $21.99 plus tax for adults, $19.99 for seniors, and $16.99 for children ages 3 to 9.**

One of the best wildlife experiences your child can have in Florida: Your car becomes a safari jeep as you leisurely wend your way past lions lolling on the roadside, as well as giraffes, rhinoceroses, zebras, chimps, bison, elephants, ostriches, and wildebeest, through 500 acres of animals large and larger. At the end of the ride, Safari World entertains with rides, a petting zoo, miniature golf, dinosaur models, a free-flight feeding aviary, and other adventures. It's definitely worth the trip from the beach. Your car must have a hard-top roof or you must trade it in for a rental. Ask about the weeklong summer day camps for kids ages six to thirteen.

**KOA Kampground** (ages 5 to 13) (△)
Next door to Lion Country Safari; 2000 Lion Country Safari Road, Loxahatchee; (561) 793-9797 or (800) 562-9115. RV sites for two persons range from $38 to $47 per night, depending on the season. Tent sites are $33; less for extra nights.

A full-service campground, it has a swimming pool, playground, sports facilities, and general store. Campers receive a discount to Safari World. Cabins are also available.

# Weekend Jaunt: Lake Okeechobee

Continue heading west on Highway 98/441 to escape the metropolis for the rural. Turn north on Highway 98 to reach the town of Okeechobee on Lake Okeechobee's north shore, or north on Highway 27 to get to Clewiston on the south shore.

As distant as ritzy Palm Beach County may seem from the lifestyles and wilderness of the Florida Everglades, it is tied into the same ecosystem, which includes Lake Okeechobee some 20 miles to the west.

Lake Okeechobee, known also as Florida's Inland Sea, is the second-largest freshwater lake entirely within U.S. boundaries. Problem is, you can't see it unless you are in or atop it. That's because in 1928, following a devastating hurricane flood, President Herbert Hoover mandated the construction of a 35-foot-high dike now bearing his name.

If you want to show the kids how sugar grows, drive around the south end of the lake to Clewiston, site of the annual Sugar Festival in April.

## On a **Budget**

- **Hoffman's Chocolate Shoppe,** Greenacres City, free admission
- **Gumbo Limbo Environmental Complex,** Boca Raton, free admission
- **Holocaust Memorial,** Miami Beach, free admission
- **Miami Museum of Science and Planetarium,** Miami, free planetarium show first Friday of the month
- **National Key Deer Refuge,** Big Pine Key, free admission

### Arthur R. Marshall Loxahatchee National Wildlife Refuge

(ages 8 to 13)

A couple of minutes west of Lion Country Safari, 10216 Lee Road, Boynton Beach; (561) 734-8303. The visitor center is open 9:00 a.m. to 4:00 p.m. weekdays, 9:00 a.m. to 4:30 p.m. weekends, except in summer (May through October), when it closes Monday and Tuesday. The park is open sunrise to sunset daily. Admission is $5 per vehicle.

This is the nearest access to the raw, wet nature that Florida struggles to keep in its grasp. Vast and often forbidding, the 146,000-acre preserve is best seen by guided tour. Stop first at the visitor center at the refuge's south end and experience its audiovisual programs. Walking and canoe trails introduce you to its rare ecology.

### Lake Okeechobee Scenic Trail (ages 8 to 10)

(800) 871-4403.

You can walk along the lake's dike. Bike riding is a great way to get an elevated view of the waters, the surrounding landscape, and its abundant wildlife. You can enter this hiking-biking trail, 100 miles long, from any major highway.

### Lake Okeechobee Guide Association (ages 6 to 13)

(863) 763-2248 or (800) 284-BIG-O. Cost for a full day is $325, which includes tackle. Bait is extra. Freshwater fishing license may be required.

Bass and speckled perch fishing is Lake Okeechobee's lure. For a charter, contact this association.

### Okeechobee Airboat Rides (ages 5 to 13)

Intersection of Routes 441 and 78; 220 Highway 78; (863) 763-2700. Open 7:00 a.m. to 5:00 p.m. daily.

Catch an airboat or pontoon tour of the "Big O." You can also rent your own pontoon.

### Hoffman's Chocolate Shoppe (ages 2 to 10)

5190 Lake Worth Road (Route 802), Greenacres; south of Highway 98 via Highway 441; (561) 967-2213. Open 9:00 a.m. to 8:00 p.m. Monday through Saturday, 9:00 a.m. to 6:00 p.m. Sunday. Admission is free.

On the return trip to the coast, watch the modern-day candy-making process at Hoffman's, seated in a Bavarian Tudor building within a quiet botanical garden setting. A model Candyland Railroad train runs through the grounds. You can watch the kitchen through a glass wall. Everyone gets a free sample. During the holidays (beginning the weekend before Thanksgiving), the site turns magical with lights, music, Santa, and performances by local artists and schools.

## Where to Eat

**Clewiston Inn.** 108 Royal Palm Avenue, Clewiston; (863) 983-8151 or (800) 749-4466. This historic setting may seem like a formal place to take the kids, but it's quite family friendly and affordable. Home-cooked Southern-style fare is served in a colonial setting. Breakfast, lunch, and dinner Tuesday through Saturday; open only for breakfast and lunch Sunday; dinner only on Monday. Luncheon buffets on Friday and Sunday. $–$$

## Where to Stay

**Roland Martin's Marina and Resort.** 920 East Del Monte Avenue (off Highway 27), Clewiston; (863) 983-3151. Tailor-made for fishing fanatics. Pool, marina store, cafe, and full-service marina. Rooms, efficiencies, and bungalows. $–$$

## For More Information

**Clewiston Chamber of Commerce.** P.O. Box 275, Clewiston 33440; (863) 983-7979; www.clewiston.org.

**Okeechobee County Chamber of Commerce.** 55 South Parrott Avenue, Okeechobee 34972; (863) 763-6464.

# Boca Raton

Take Route 802 east to I-95 and head south to exits 48, 45, or 44.

Back to the coast, and on to another of southeast Florida's most chichi neighborhoods: Boca Raton has nice beaches and assorted attractions to offer families.

### South Beach Park (all ages)

**400 North Ocean Boulevard (Route A1A); (561) 393-7973. Open 8:00 a.m. to sunset. Parking costs $17 weekends and holidays, $15 weekdays.**

A series of well-maintained, nicely landscaped public beach accesses with paid parking stretch along Route A1A. This one is a favorite and provides lifeguards and showers.

### Gumbo Limbo Environmental Complex (all ages)

**1801 North Ocean Boulevard (Route A1A), across from Red Reef Park; (561) 338-1473. Open 9:00 a.m. to 4:00 p.m. Monday through Saturday and noon to 4:00 p.m. Sunday. Admission is free.**

It educates children through nature trails, interpretive displays, aquariums, an observation tower, seminars, field trips, and other programs. Outdoor marine tanks hold baby loggerhead turtles, local fish, tide pool inhabitants, and touchables. Visitors can often observe rare and endangered species—such as manatees, ospreys, sea turtles, and brown pelicans—in the wilds.

### Morikami Museum and Japanese Gardens (ages 6 and up)
**4000 Morikami Park Road, Delray Beach; (561) 495-0233; www.morikami.org. Museum open 10:00 a.m. to 5:00 p.m. Tuesday through Sunday, gardens open 10:00 a.m. to 5:00 p.m. Tuesday through Saturday. Admission is $10 for adults, $9 for seniors, and $6 for college students and children ages 6 to 18.**

The museum houses 5,000 Japanese art objects and artifacts. The 200-acre gardens reflect major periods of Japanese garden design, from the eighth to the twentieth centuries.

### Children's Museum (ages 2 to 10)
**498 Crawford Boulevard; (561) 368-6875. Open noon to 4:00 p.m. Tuesday through Saturday. Admission is $3 per person.**

Hands-on permanent exhibits here include a mini-mart, bank, Dr. Dig's Backporch, a pioneer kitchen, and Faces: A Celebration of Florida Cultures. It hosts workshops, story times, and special events such as KidsFest every April.

### Boomer's Family Recreation Center (ages 4 to 13)
**3100 Airport Road; (561) 347-1888; www.boomersparks.com. Indoor play is open 10:00 a.m. to 10:00 p.m. Sunday through Thursday, 10:00 a.m. to midnight Friday and Saturday. Outdoor activities are open 1:00 to 10:00 p.m. Monday through Thursday, 10:00 a.m. to midnight Friday and Saturday, 10:00 a.m. to 10:00 p.m. Sunday. Major attractions cost $3.49 to $24.49. Family packages available.**

Games, bumper boats and cars, laser tag, a rock-climbing wall, miniature golf, go-karts, junior (under age ten) play area, and a play center all have an Australian theme.

### Butterfly World (all ages)
**Tradewinds Park South, 3600 West Sample Road, Coconut Creek; (954) 977-4400. Open Monday through Saturday 9:00 a.m. to 5:00 p.m. and 1:00 to 5:00 p.m. Sunday (ticket sales end at 4:00 p.m.). Admission is $19.95 for adults, $14.95 for children ages 3 to 11.**

Watch their eyes light up with the natural magic of three acres of waterfalls and gardens all aflutter with beautiful butterflies. You'll also see other insects, plus fish and birds, including lorikeets.

## Where to Eat

**Tom's Place.** 1225 Palm Beach Lake Boulevard, West Palm Beach; (561) 997-0920. The food is down-home and good for the soul (if not the heart). Lunch and dinner Tuesday through Saturday. $$–$$$

## Where to Stay

**Boca Raton Resort & Club.** 501 East Camino Real; (561) 395-3000 or (800) 327-0101. Historic landmark on the Intracoastal Waterway, with a marina, sports facilities, shops, and several restaurants. Boca Baby takes care of guests age two and under;

Boca Tots ages three to five; Boca Bunch ages six to eleven; and tweens and teens ages twelve to seventeen. Parents can order gourmet baby food from the restaurant's menu. Security gates. $$$$

## For More Information

**Greater Boca Raton Chamber of Commerce.** 1800 North Dixie Highway, Boca Raton 33432-1892; (561) 395-4433; www.bocaratonchamber.com.

# Fort Lauderdale

About 15 miles south of Boca Raton along Route A1A or Highway 41.

Fort Lauderdale has outgrown its *Where the Boys Are* reputation to become a mecca for families instead of party animals. Its attractions sample history, nature, science, and sports.

One of the world's most famous beaches, Fort Lauderdale Beach is also one of the most developed. It has been restyled with a wavy wall that separates beach from a paver-brick walk for strollers, bikers, and in-line skaters. Across the street, sidewalk cafes line up with shops, bars, and motels. The central hub of the beach lies at the intersection of Las Olas and Ocean Boulevards. You'll find water-sports rentals on the beach and in nearby shops.

### South Beach Park (all ages)
**South of the Route A1A (Southeast Seventeenth Street) Causeway.**

Here the crowds are thinner and the development less intrusive. For families, there are picnic tables and a playground. Street parking is metered. Lifeguards supervise.

### Hugh Taylor Birch State Park (ages 5 to 13)
**Off Ocean Boulevard at 3109 East Sunrise Boulevard; (954) 564-4521. Park is open 8:00 a.m. to sunset daily. Beach gate is open 9:00 a.m. to 5:00 p.m. Park entrance is $4 per vehicle of eight persons or fewer, $1 per extra passenger, cyclist, or pedestrian.**

It accommodates four biological habitats as well as recreationers. Within its 180 acres between ocean and Intracoastal, it has canoe rentals and a 1.7-mile exercise course for hikers and runners. The beach lies across the street from the entrance.

# Florida **Trivia**

**Stately Butterfly** Most states have a state tree and flower. But did you know Florida has a state butterfly? In 1996 the zebra long wing—named for its black stripes—was so declared.

## Bonnet House Museum & Gardens (ages 5 to 13)

900 North Birch Road, (954) 563-5393; www.bonnethouse.org. From December to April, tours are 10:00 a.m. to 4:00 p.m. Tuesday through Saturday, last tour at 2:30 p.m.; from May to November, tours are 10:00 a.m. to 3:00 p.m. Wednesday through Friday; Sunday, tours are noon to 4:00 p.m. with the last one at 2:30 p.m. The museum is closed Monday. Tours are $20 for adults, $18 for seniors, $16 for children ages 6 to 12; children 5 and under free. Admission to grounds only, $10.

It's more than a historic attraction. Built by two artists in the 1920s between the sea and a small lake, the ninety-five-acre estate holds lush grounds beautified by swans, orchids, and monkeys. Its beach is located across the street. Visitors can see the house by seventy-five-minute tour only but can walk the nature trail on their own. In April, the property is the site of Bonnet House Jazzfest on the Green.

## Water Taxi (all ages)

651 Seabreeze Boulevard; (954) 467-6677. Taxis run 9:00 a.m. until midnight daily, sometimes later. An all-day pass costs $5, $4 for a one-way fare anywhere on the route ($11 round-trip).

Getting around by boat is the best way to go in Fort Lauderdale. If you don't have one, you can jump aboard the Water Taxi and get a lift to shopping, restaurants, and other attractions. Reserve in advance or wait (for up to thirty minutes) at a scheduled stop.

## Winterfest (ages 4 to 13)

(954) 767-0686.

Lighted boat processions are common throughout Florida at Christmastime. One of the first and grandest illuminates the waterway during a monthlong celebration.

## Fort Lauderdale Stadium (ages 6 to 13)

1301 Northwest Fifty-fifth Street, off Commercial Boulevard; (954) 776-1921. Tickets cost $5 to $20.

The excitement of major league baseball visits Fort Lauderdale each March when the Baltimore Orioles train preseason here.

### Everglades Day Safari (ages 4 to 18)

**Call (239) 472-1559 or (800) 472-3069 for reservations and to arrange pickup location; www.ecosafari.com. Departs Fort Lauderdale each morning at 7:45 a.m. and returns about 5:30 p.m. Fee is $135 for adults and $99 for children under 12.**

This guided trip through the Everglades includes a jungle cruise, nature walk, lunch, wildlife drive, and an airboat ride.

### Parker Playhouse (ages 3 to 13)

**707 Northeast Eighth Street; off Highway 1; (954) 763-8813; box office (954) 462-0222. Ticket prices vary.**

It brings children's classics to the stage. Professional performances are run daily October through April.

### Stranahan House (ages 7 to 13)

**335 Southeast Sixth Avenue at Las Olas Boulevard; (954) 524-4736. Open 10:00 a.m. to 3:00 p.m. Wednesday through Saturday and 1:00 to 3:00 p.m. Sunday. Tours are on the hour. Admission is $10 for adults, $9 for seniors, and $5 for children under age 12.**

The area's oldest home, circa 1901, is lavishly furnished with period antiques. Docents gear the tour toward any children in the group.

### Museum of Discovery and Science (all ages)

**401 Southwest Second Street; (954) 467-6637 or (954) 463-IMAX; www.mods.org. Open 10:00 a.m. to 5:00 p.m. Monday through Saturday, noon to 6:00 p.m. Sunday. Admission to the museum, including one IMAX film, is $15 for adults, $14 for seniors and students, and $12 for children ages 2 to 12. Ramp parking across the street costs $3 to $7.**

The best the city has to offer families occupies two floors packed with exciting curiosity sparkers. Kids love Virtual Volleyball, the space flight simulator, and the nature section with its fascinating aquariums, spiders, snakes, and enchanted Florida forest. Games slyly teach about fitness, health, physics, and other scientific phenomena. Stop in the gift shop for learning tools of the painless variety. Ecofloat environmental boat tours showcase the beaches, barrier islands, mangrove estuaries, sinkholes, and other diverse local habitat during the summer. Part of the complex, Blockbuster 3-D IMAX Theater shows sky-high discovery films about nature and science.

### Riverwalk Park (all ages)

**20 North New River Drive; (954) 828-5346.**

Across the street from the museum, this linear recreational area prettily follows New River to Las Olas Boulevard and features educational stations like the one that lets you play with marine navigational instruments. Sunday jazz brunches feature top artists.

## Smart **Travel**

- Big cities call for big precautions. Always keep car doors locked and drive on main thoroughfares.

- Getting lost in Miami can mean speaking a different language to get directions back on track. It wouldn't hurt to brush up on your Spanish and bring along a phrase book.

- You cannot fully enjoy the Florida Keys without getting into the water. The best way to understand its treasures is by snorkeling. Children can snorkel as early as age four. If they're afraid of the water, have them stand at the beach's edge and just stick their head in the water with you holding the mask to their eyes. Chances are they'll be fascinated.

- For your own safety and the health of the reefs, never touch or stand on coral.

### Old Dillard Museum (ages 5 to 13)
**1009 Northwest Fourth Street; (954) 765-6952. Open noon to 4:00 p.m. Tuesday through Saturday. Admission is free.**

Housed in what was the first local public school for African Americans, it today holds three permanent displays: a hands-on, minds-on exhibit; the Jazz Gallery; and a replica of the 1920s classroom.

### Brian Piccolo Park (ages 6 to 12)
**9501 Sheridan Street, Cooper City; (954) 437-2626. Admission to the skate park is $7 per person for two hours; velodrome admission is $2 to $4 per person. Park entrance fee on weekends only. Hours for skate park and velodrome vary.**

Pack a picnic lunch and head out of town to Brian Piccolo Park—or eat at its Snack Attack stand. Just don't forget your wheels. The best parts of Brian Piccolo are its skate park and velodrome (bike racing track). You can rent skates, skateboards, and race bikes. The facilities stay open in the evening. Lessons and classes are available.

## Where to Eat

**Mai-Kai.** 3599 North Federal Highway; (954) 563-3272. Polynesian decor and dance performance. Special kids' performance Sunday (kids under age twelve admitted to show free every night). Dinner only. Show is extra. $$–$$$

## Where to Stay

**Embassy Suites Fort Lauderdale.**
1100 Southeast Seventeenth Street; (954) 527-2700 or (800) EMBASSY for reservations; www.embassysuitesftl.com. Close to the beach and local attractions. Great pool with splashy waterfalls and lush tropical setting; **free** breakfast buffet. $$–$$$$

**Harbor Beach Marriott Resort & Spa.**
3030 Holiday Drive; (954) 525-4000 or (800) 228-9290; www.marriottharborbeach.com. A beach, water-sports rentals, a large free-form pool, and a kids' recreational program give families all they need in a Fort Lauderdale resort; away from the beach crowds. Mom and Dad will appreciate the $8 million, 20,000-square-foot spa. $$–$$$$

## For More Information

**Greater Fort Lauderdale Convention and Visitors Bureau.** 100 East Broward Boulevard, Suite 200, Fort Lauderdale 33301; (954) 765-4466; www.sunny.org.

# Weekend Jaunt: Miccosukee Country

Follow Interstate 595 west to Interstate 75 (Alligator Alley). Detours off the interstates take you to the natural and other attractions on Fort Lauderdale's other side.

### Sawgrass Recreation Park (ages 4 to 13)
**2 miles north of I-75 at 5400 North Highway 27 (P.O. Box 291620), Fort Lauderdale 33329; (954) 389-0202 or (800) 457-0788. Open 6:00 a.m. to 6:00 p.m. seven days, year-round. Admission to thirty-minute airboat tour and exhibits is $19.50 for adults and $10.00 for children ages 4 to 12. Tax is additional.**

An eighteenth-century Indian village is the main attraction here. Spend the day exploring, airboating, and fishing. Spend the night camping. You'll also find alligator and reptile shows, fishing boat rentals, a birds of prey exhibit, a gift shop, picnic tables, airboat tours, and a barbecue cookhouse.

### Young at Art Children's Museum (ages 2 to 13)
**11584 West Route 84, Davie; (954) 424-0085; www.youngatart museum.org. Open 10:00 a.m. to 5:00 p.m. Monday through Saturday and noon to 5:00 p.m. Sunday. Admission is $8.00 for anyone older than 2; $7.50 for seniors.**

The museum invites kids to participate in its interactive galleries, special exhibitions, workshops, classes, and special events.

### Flamingo Gardens and Arboretum (ages 5 to 12)

3750 South Flamingo Road, Davie; 3 miles south of I-595; (954) 473-2955; www
.flamingogardens.org. Open 9:30 a.m. to 5:30 p.m. daily. Closed Monday June through
September. Admission is $17.00 for adults, $8.50 for children ages 4 to 11. Twenty
percent discount for seniors and students. Optional tram tour $4.00 for adults, $3.00
for children.

A tram takes you through the sixty acres of citrus groves, botanical gardens, free-
flight aviary, and habitat for flamingos, alligators, hummingbirds, and other fauna.
Centerpiece is the 1933 Wray estate, framed by 200-year-old oaks. The gardens spe-
cialize in the cultivation of endangered heliconia plants and the protection of wood
storks and roseate spoonbills.

### Billie Swamp Safari & Camping Village (ages 3 to 13)

19 miles north of I-75 off exit 49; 12261 Southwest 251st Street, Princeton; (800) 949-
6101; www.seminoletribe.com. Open 9:30 a.m. to 2:00 p.m. daily for complete day
package; gift shop open 8:30 a.m. to 6:00 p.m. Tours begin at $25 for adults and $15
for children ages 4 to 12.

To see the Everglades through the eyes of a Native American, stop here. There is
also a gift shop, wildlife shows, and the Swamp Water Cafe. Tours include the
wildlife show and an hour-and-a-half swamp buggy tour into the wetlands of the
Everglades. Guided hikes and night swamp buggy safaris are also available. Ask
about family and overnight packages.

# Dania and Hollywood

Just south of Fort Lauderdale along Highway 1.

### Boomer's (ages 5 to 13)

1801 Northwest First Street, west of Highway 1, Dania; (954) 921-1411; www.boomers
parks.com. Open 10:00 a.m. to midnight Sunday through Thursday, 10:00 a.m. to 2:00
a.m. Friday and Saturday; one arcade stays open twenty-four hours. Miniature golf
admission is $7.49; under 5 free. Go-kart rides cost $6.49.

Have a harrowing adventure on the Sky Coaster, which simulates a bungee jump.
Tamer rides include bumper cars, a roller coaster, and Naskart racing. There's also
miniature golf, batting cages, and video arcades.

### IGFA Fishing Hall of Fame & Museum (ages 2 to 12)

300 Gulf Stream Way, Dania Beach; (954) 922-4212; fax (954) 924-4220; www.igfa.org.
Open 10:00 a.m. to 6:00 p.m. daily. Admission is $5 for children ages 3 to 16, $6 for
persons 17 and older.

Toddlers to teens will love the hands-on stuff—especially the virtual marlin or tarpon
they reel in. Play the computerized "Name That Fish" game. Kids ages two to seven

can make fish prints and go pretend-boating in the Discovery Room. Ask about the Junior Angler Club and educational youth programs. Suave and state of the art, the museum features a school of prize fish hanging from the ceiling with plaques set into the floor to identify their world-record winners. Across the parking lot, visit Outdoor World, a football-field size sports store with a huge aquarium and Florida-style shooting range.

### Dania Jai-Alai (ages 5 to 18)

**301 East Dania Beach Boulevard, Dania Beach; (954) 920-1511. Matinees at noon on Tuesday, Saturday, and Sunday; nightly at 7:00 p.m. Tuesday through Saturday. Minors not admitted after 3:00 p.m. for matinees or 9:00 p.m. for evening performances. Reserved seats, $2 to $7. A child must be accompanied by an adult, and both must use reserved seating. Children must be 39 inches or taller and persons under 18 years of age may not place bets but may watch.**

Jai-alai is a thrilling game of handball, invented in the Basque region of Spain. The *Guinness Book of World Records* says it is the fastest ballgame, with the rock-hard *pelota* traveling at speeds up to 180 mph. Players use three walls and *cuestas,* or handheld baskets. It's fast and dangerous (for the players) and is a pari-mutuel sport, meaning that adults may bet on the outcomes of games. The Dania Jai-Alai *fronton* is the largest in Florida.

### John U. Lloyd State Park (ages 6 to 13)

**6503 North Ocean Drive, Dania Beach; (954) 923-2833. Open 8:00 a.m. to sunset daily. Park entrance is $5 per vehicle with up to eight passengers, $3 for a single passenger, and $1 for extra passengers, bicyclists, and pedestrians.**

Watch the big ships coming in and out of Port Everglades from the beach. Rock jetties and a boat ramp ($5 fee) serve sportsmen, plus there are canoeing and picnic facilities at the dunes-edged park. The south end feels entirely set apart from nearby urban pressures.

## Top Family **Beaches and Parks**

1. **Crandon Park,** Key Biscayne

2. **John D. MacArthur State Park,** North Palm Beach

3. **Loggerhead Beach Park,** Juno Beach

4. **Bahia Honda State Park,** Bahia Honda Key

5. **South Pointe Park,** Miami Beach

6. **Carlin Park,** Jupiter Beach

# Top Family **Resorts**

1. **Doral Golf Resort and Spa,** Miami

2. **Hawk's Cay,** Marathon

3. **Holiday Isle Resort & Marina,** Islamorada

4. **Cheeca Lodge,** Islamorada

5. **Sonesta Key Biscayne,** Miami

6. **Palm Beach Shores Resort,** Palm Beach Shores

### Anne Kolb Nature Center (ages 5 to 13)

**751 Sheridan Street, Hollywood; between Highway 1 and Route A1A; (954) 926-2480. Park hours vary according to daylight; open daily. Exhibit hall is open 8:00 a.m. to 6:00 p.m. daily. Admission to parts of the park is free; $1 per person over age 5 at the park's west entrance and recreation area (1200 Sheridan Street) on weekends and holidays. Admission to the exhibit hall is $1 for adults and children. Boat tour is $5 for adults, $3 for children.**

It provides more than 1,500 acres for hiking, biking, birding, canoeing, kayaking (rentals available), pier fishing, picnicking, and family recreation. Narrated boat tours, a five-story observation tower, and environmental exhibits teach about the local wildlife. It's located at the lovely oasis known as West Lake Park.

### Hollywood Beach Broadwalk (all ages)

**Park around Johnson Street (off of Route A1A) to get closest to the restaurants and shops. Parking is metered.**

Strolling the Hollywood Beach Broadwalk, you're likely to hear French accents drifting from open-air cafes. French Canadians arrive here *en groupe* to winter. Year-round, enjoy a Riviera ambience under an awning at one of the French-style cafes, reasonably priced. The beach is family oriented and perfect for cycling, in-line skating, and water sports.

## Where to Eat

Dining on the water is practically required when in the area. The Intracoastal Waterway provides a scenic venue for spying on passing yachts and humbler watercraft.

**Le Tub.** 1100 North Ocean Drive (Route A1A), Hollywood; (954) 921-9425. Small, out of the way, and casual. It was built from flotsam and jetsam. Burgers, seafood, and ribs. Lunch and dinner daily. $

## Where to Stay

See Fort Lauderdale listings for lodging suggestions.

## For More Information

**Greater Hollywood Chamber of Commerce.** 330 North Federal Highway, Hollywood 33020; (954) 923-4000 or (800) 231-5562, fax (954) 923-8737; www.hollywoodchamber.org.

# Miami

About twenty minutes south of Hollywood along Route A1A, Highway 1, or I-95.

Cosmopolitan Miami sparks adventures of the ethnic and cultural variety, but it has its natural gifts to offer as well. Explore the various ethnic neighborhoods settled throughout the years by Jews and immigrants from the Bahamas, Cuba, Haiti, Jamaica, Nicaragua, and elsewhere. They combine to give Miami its own saucy style, fashion, music, and cuisine. Streets and cafes are alive with the chatter of foreign tongues.

Miami Beach is the hot spot for vacationers, especially fashionable South Beach, but other, more family-oriented attractions are scattered throughout the city, particularly south of downtown.

### Jai-Alai Fronton (ages 8 to 13)
**3500 Northwest Thirty-seventh Avenue; (305) 633-6400. Admission is $1.**

A game actually originated by the Basque people of Spain, jai-alai has become synonymous with Miami and its environs. Sample the complicated, fast-paced betting game here.

### Pro Player Stadium (ages 6 to 13)
**2269 Dan Marino Boulevard; (305) 626-7400 for Marlin tickets, www.flamarlins.com; Marlin tickets cost $9 to $55; (305) 452-7000 for Dolphin tickets; (305) 620-2578 for Dolphin information, www.miamidolphins.com. Dolphin ticket prices vary.**

It is home to two professional sports teams: the Florida Marlins and the Miami Dolphins. The Florida Marlins baseball team plays April through October. August through December, watch the Miami Dolphins kick off.

### Enchanted Forest Elaine Gordon Park (ages 2 to 9) 🧗 🏇
**1725 Northeast 135th Street, North Miami; (305) 895-1119. Admission is free.**

Just like the name says, this place is enchanted: A park where swans, storybook thickets, nature trails with wood bridges, a tot lot, and horseback riding stir magic.

One expects Robin Hood to come charging in at any minute. Bring carrots and apples to feed the horses.

### Haulover Park (all ages)

10800 Collins Avenue, North Miami Beach; (305) 947-3525. Cost for all-day parking is $5 per car, $10 per recreational vehicle.

This is a huge center for recreation, with a pretty beach, picnic shelters, grills, food concessions, trails, bike path, lifeguards, tennis, golf, and a marina with boat rentals. The 1,103-foot pier sells bait and rents tackle. A portion of the beach is designated clothing optional, Florida's only legit nude beach. It is patrolled to discourage oglers.

### THERAPY-IV (ages 5 to 13)

Haulover Park Marina, 10800 Collins Avenue, Miami Beach; (305) 945-1578; www .therapy4.com. Open daily. Half-day fishing costs $150 per person.

Go deep-sea fishing for a half or full day. Catch shark, sailfish, marlin, and other game species.

### Holocaust Memorial (ages 8 to 13)

1933–1945 Meridian Avenue, Miami Beach; (305) 538-1663. Open 9:00 a.m. and 9:00 p.m. daily. Admission is **free.**

See an inspirational monument to Jewish victims of the Holocaust in a park setting marked by a dramatic sculpture.

### South Beach

This erstwhile bastion of winter-sun tourism has risen to its former glory, thanks to the redemption of South Beach's Art Deco district.

SoBe, as it's known in shorthand, is a place most suitable for adults. It makes for a fun morning drive (come late afternoon, Ocean Drive traffic stops to a crawl and parking is near impossible), and Lummus Beach provides a lot of action for older children with its water-sports rentals and sidewalks perfect for biking and in-line skating (rentals are available on the beach). There are two playgrounds for the younger kids. Topless sunbathing occurs with frequency.

# Little **Haiti**

Bounded roughly by Northeast Second Avenue and Forty-first and Eighty-third Streets, the neighborhood designated Little Haiti bursts with the color and spirit that is Haiti.

# Orange **Blossom**

Miami owes its existence, legend has it, to an orange blossom. In the winter of 1894–95, freezing temperatures in Palm Beach had developer Henry Flagler all aquiver. Guests at his posh resort were complaining, while oranges were dying on the tree. Miami pioneer Julia Tuttle, interested in putting her backwoods town on the map, sent a bouquet of fragrant orange blossoms to Flagler's Palm Beach home. The ploy worked. By 1896, work had begun on Miami's Royal Palm Hotel.

### Art Deco District Welcome Center (ages 10 to 13)

**1001 Ocean Drive, Miami Beach; (305) 531-3484. Walking tours at 10:30 a.m. Saturday and 6:30 p.m. Thursday. Price is $20 for adults, $15 for seniors and students with ID; under 5 free. Tape rental for the self-guided tour is $15 for adults, $10 for seniors and students with ID. Available daily 10:00 a.m. to 7:30 p.m.**

The center conducts ninety-minute guided and audio self-guided walking tours of South Beach's Art Deco District, 1 square mile of 800 classic buildings—the largest collection of Art Deco architecture in the world.

### Parrot Jungle Island (ages 2 to 18)

**1111 Parrot Jungle Trail; (305) 400-7000; www.parrotjungle.com. Open 10:00 a.m. to 6:00 p.m. daily. Admission is $27.95 for adults, $25.95 for seniors, $22.95 for children 3 to 10; under 3 free.**

Parrot Jungle Island opened in June 2003 as an animal attraction, featuring trained birds, a serpentarium, Manu Encounters in its aviary with 200 free-flying birds, dance and musical presentations in the Jungle Theater, a flock of real pink flamingos glamorizing Flamingo Lake, a rare plant nursery, a petting barn, and a kids' area called Monkey Bars.

### Bayside Marketplace (ages 4 to 13)

**Off the island via MacArthur Causeway, turn south on Biscayne Boulevard (Highway 1); 401 Biscayne Boulevard, R-106; (305) 577-3344; www.baysidemarketplace.com. Open 10:00 a.m. to 10:00 p.m. Monday through Friday, 10:00 a.m. to 11:00 p.m. Saturday, and 11:00 a.m. to 9:00 p.m. Sunday (extended hours at some restaurants and bars). A parking ramp charges $2.00 to $2.50 per hour, $10.00 maximum.**

For dining and shopping, head to this open-air, festive waterside mall. It is also a good place to find a boat tour of the glamorous homes of Star Island, where celebrities of all kinds have homes. Two popular boats are the *Island Queen* (305-379-5119;

www.islandqueencruises.com) and *Schooner Heritage of Miami,* a tall sailing ship (305-442-9697). Both do daily tours; *Schooner Heritage* operates only September through May.

## American Airlines Arena (ages 6 to 13)
**601 Biscayne Boulevard; (786) 777-1000; www.heat.com. Tickets cost $9 to $165.**

The Miami Heat National Basketball Association team plays at this state-of-the-art arena, connected to Bayside Marketplace by bridge.

## Historical Museum of Southern Florida
**101 West Flagler Street; (305) 375-1492; www.hmsf.org. Open 10:00 a.m. to 5:00 p.m. Monday through Saturday, 10:00 a.m. to 9:00 p.m. on the third Thursday of each month, and noon to 5:00 p.m. Sunday. Admission is $5 for adults, $2 for children ages 6 to 12.**

Hands-on displays and changing exhibits trot you along the local time line. Children can try on pirate costumes, play with pioneer toys, and hop aboard an old-fashioned streetcar.

## Little Havana

Miami's Cuban culture, strong as a *café con leche,* centers along Southwest Eighth Street (Highway 41), known locally as Calle Ocho, site of the annual whopper Carnaval Miami each March. Calle Ocho, one of the festival events, is billed as the world's largest block party with the world's longest conga line.

## Key Biscayne
**South of downtown and east off Highway 1 onto Rickenbacker Causeway (toll $1.25).**

South of downtown Miami, take a turn for the more natural, upscale Miami when you veer toward Key Biscayne. The island attracts families with its lovely parks and other attractions. Along the causeway, windsurfers congregate at sands known as Hobie Beach. You can usually rent equipment there from mobile vendors.

# Miami in the **Movies**

Movies filmed in Miami: *Stuck on You* (Matt Damon), *Bad Boys II* (Will Smith), *Heartbreakers* (Sigourney Weaver), *Any Given Sunday* (Al Pacino), *Random Hearts* (Harrison Ford), *Analyze This* (Billy Crystal), *There's Something About Mary* (Cameron Diaz), *Wild Things* (Kevin Bacon), and *Miami Vice* (Jamie Foxx).

# Southeastern **Climes**

Temperatures average 77 degrees year-round. January is the coldest month, with an average low of around 66 degrees. August and September are the hottest, when daytime temperatures reach into the mid-90s. The east coast benefits from breezes off the ocean, which keep things cooler and less buggy than the west coast.

The Keys are as tropical as it gets in the continental United States. You'll never see freezing here, yet summer breezes manage to keep it climate controlled.

## Key Biscayne Boat Rentals (ages 7 to 13)

3301 Rickenbacker Causeway, Key Biscayne; (305) 361-7368.

Stop here for power and jet boats and Wave Runners, rentable by the hour or for half and full days. All-inclusive packages are available for fishing, waterskiing, snorkeling, diving, and sightseeing.

## Miami Seaquarium (all ages)

4400 Rickenbacker Causeway, Key Biscayne; (305) 361-5705; www.miamiseaquarium .com. Open 9:30 a.m. to 6:00 p.m. daily (ticket sales end at 4:30 p.m.). Admission is $31.95 plus tax for adults, $24.95 plus tax for children ages 3 to 9. Parking is $7. Swim with Dolphins program is $188 per swimmer and $40 for observers and includes tour of aquarium.

See Flipper the dolphin, along with Lolita the killer whale, Salty the sea lion, lovable manatees, and feeding sharks. The killer whale show is the most impressive. Tour the alligator exhibit, reef aquarium, and rain forest habitat. Swim with Flipper (must be 52 inches or taller).

## Crandon Park (all ages)

4000 Crandon Boulevard, Key Biscayne; (305) 361-5421. Open 8:00 a.m. to sunset daily. Parking is $4 a day ($10 for recreational vehicles and buses).

This is Miami's best outdoor venue for families. The causeway toll limits crime, the view of cruise ships coming and going is great, and the vast recreational area contains a variety of activity arenas—a wide beach, an amusement center, a golf course, tennis courts, baseball fields, soccer fields, a bike path, volleyball courts, a playground, and a marina. Families spend their weekends here, barbecuing, beaching, and relaxing, with lifeguards on duty.

### The Tennis Center at Crandon Park (ages 8 to 13)

**7300 Crandon Boulevard, Key Biscayne; (305) 365-2300. Open daily 8:00 a.m. to 9:00 p.m. Per-hour use fee is $3 for adults, $2 for children.**

It hosts the NASDAQ 100 in March. The public can use its courts (seventeen hard, eight clay, and two grass).

### Aquatic Rental Center and Sailing School (ages 9 to 13)

**1275 Northeast Seventy-ninth Street, Pelican Harbor Marina; (305) 751-7514. Open daily. Rentals run $80 for two hours, $135 for a half day, $195 for a full day.**

It rents sailboats and teaches certification classes.

### Bill Baggs Cape Florida State Park (all ages)

**1200 South Crandon Boulevard, Key Biscayne; (305) 361-5811; www.floridastateparks .org. Open 8:00 a.m. to sunset daily. Park entrance is $5 per vehicle with up to eight passengers, $3 for a single passenger, and $1 for extra passengers, bicyclists, and pedestrians. Lighthouse tours take place at 10:00 a.m. and 1:00 p.m. Thursday through Monday. Limit is twenty people; register at the gate. Must be 8 years or older to climb the tower.**

South of the island's commercial area, you'll find another beach and picnic spot that families love. Bring your own food or eat at the Cuban-style restaurant. The park holds the added attraction of a historic site—Cape Florida Lighthouse, south Florida's oldest structure, built in 1825, which you can climb by tour only.

### Coral Gables

**Lies south of Highway 41 and east of Route 959 (Southwest Fifty-seventh Street).**

Coral Gables is a special place, a respite from the anonymity of city life. One of the nation's first planned cities, it was built in Mediterranean Revival style back in the 1920s. It is known for its art galleries, theaters, and fine restaurants. To get a taste of the town's Old European flavor, follow the scenic route along Old Cutler Road north to Riviera Drive, then west on Anastasia Avenue, looping back south along Granada Boulevard. A bike path follows most of the route. For a more detailed map, call Coral Gables Development Department (305-460-5311).

## Venetian Pool (ages 5 to 13)

**2701 DeSoto Boulevard, Coral Gables; (305) 460-5356. Opens 11:00 a.m. Monday through Friday, 10:00 a.m. Saturday and Sunday. Closing time varies with the season. Admission is $10.00 for adults, $6.75 for children ages 3 to 12, April through October; $5.50 for adults, $3.50 for children ages 3 to 12, November through March.**

Why take 'em to any old swimming pool when they can splash around the Venetian Pool? Carved from a coral rock quarry, this 1923 landmark features caves, lush foliage, stone bridges, and waterfalls.

## Actors' Playhouse at the Miracle Theatre

**280 Miracle Mile, Coral Gables; (305) 444-9293; www.actorsplayhouse.org. Children's theater performances Saturday at 2:00 p.m. Tickets for children's shows are $12.**

It presents award-winning children's musical theater, among other offerings.

## Coconut Grove

**East of Coral Gables at the south end of Bayshore Drive.**

If South Beach is the free-spirited youth of the family, then Coconut Grove is the matured ex-hippie. With its chic shopping arenas and burgeoning arts scene, it is one of Miami's more fashionable neighborhoods. Try to visit during its Coconut Grove Arts Festival in February, zany Bed Race in May, or colorful Goombay Festival in June. The Goombay festival is the largest African-American festival in the United States, featuring Bahamian Junkanoo bands and a sailing regatta. It recalls the district's roots as a community for migrating Bahamian seafarers. On Charles Avenue, you can see many of their early homes, circa 1890.

"The Grove's" shopping district takes on a holiday atmosphere around Grand Avenue. (Take McFarlane Road off Bayshore Boulevard.)

## Miami Museum of Science and Planetarium (ages 4 to 13)

**3280 South Miami Avenue; south of Rickenbacker Causeway; (305) 646-4200; www .miamisci.org. Open 10:00 a.m. to 6:00 p.m. daily; the box office and wildlife park close at 5:00 p.m. Admission to the museum and planetarium daytime shows is $20 for adults, $18 for seniors and students with identification, $13 for children ages 3 to 12. Free planetarium show presented the first Friday of the month.**

Birds of prey are one of the specialties of this modest but popular facility. Known for its work rehabilitating predatory birds, it keeps more than 175 live animals and features permanent and special natural history exhibits. Indoors, see the Smithsonian's Latin America–Caribbean exploration exhibit, play virtual basketball, and surf the Internet. The planetarium hosts astronomy and laser shows.

## Vizcaya Museum and Gardens (ages 7 to 13)

**3251 South Miami Avenue; across the street from the science museum; (305) 250-9133; www.vizcayamuseum.com. Ticket office is open 9:30 a.m. to 4:30 p.m. daily; the house closes at 5:00 p.m., the gardens at 5:30 p.m. Admission is $12 for adults, $5 for children ages 6 to 12; 5 and under free.**

It allows the curious a peek at the lifestyles of Miami's early rich and famous. Chicago industrialist James Deering built this Italian palace and its gardens in 1916. Its thirty-four rooms of richly ornate furnishings and artwork date from the fifteenth to the nineteenth centuries. Guests can wander the home's second floor and gardens on their own.

## Barnacle Historic State Park (ages 6 to 13)

**3485 Main Highway; off McFarlane Road; (305) 442-6866. Open 9:00 a.m. to 4:00 p.m. Friday through Monday, with tours at 10:00 and 11:30 a.m. and 1:00 and 2:30 p.m. Admission is $1 for persons age 6 and older.**

Tour the unusual cone-shaped home built in 1891 by Coconut Grove's founding father, Commo. Ralph Middleton Munroe.

## Wings Over Miami Museum (ages 6 to 13)

**14710 Southwest 128th Street; in Tamiami Airport; (305) 233-5197; www.wingsovermiami.com. Open 10:00 a.m. to 5:30 p.m. Thursday to Sunday. Admission is $9.95 for adults, $5.95 for seniors and children under 12 years of age.**

Immerse yourself in wartime aircraft. It features planes from the world wars and keeps a video collection for your perusal.

## Matheson Hammock Park (ages 2 to 8)

**9610 Old Cutler Road; (305) 665–5475. Parking is $4.**

Families with small tots like this little-known park for its calm, protected Atoll Pool Beach. It also provides picnic facilities, lifeguards, showers, dressing rooms, concessions, a marina, and a nature trail.

## Miami Metrozoo (all ages)

**12400 Southwest 152nd Street; (305) 251-0400; www.zsf.org. Open 9:30 a.m. to 5:30 p.m. daily (ticket booth closes at 4:00 p.m.). Admission is $11.50 for adults, $10.50 for seniors, $6.75 for children ages 3 through 12.**

Komodo dragons, koalas, wallabies, white Bengal tigers, and Himalayan black bears are among the 225 species of animals that call this 300-acre habitat home. To hold the interest of the tiny, there is a playground, rides, a petting zoo, and a meerkat exhibit. Ecology and wildlife shows take place all day long. An air-conditioned monorail helps you get around the vast grounds.

## Monkey Jungle (ages 2 to 8)

**14805 Southwest 216th Street; off Highway 1; (305) 235-1611. Open 9:30 a.m. to 5:00 p.m. daily. Admission is $25.95 plus tax for adults, $23.95 for seniors, $19.95 for children ages 3 to 9.**

You're in the cage and the animals run free in an Amazon rain forest and other settings. Kids love dropping food in their cups and watching them pull it up from overhead.

## Where to Eat

You'll find a wide selection of restaurants in Miami, which has developed its own rising style of local cuisine, known popularly as Floribbean or Miami New World—a fusion of Florida, Caribbean, and global styles. Legends in dining are created here, but many are not for families. Try these.

**Allen's Drugs.** 4000 Red Road, South Miami; (305) 665-6964. Sandwiches, homemade meals, banana splits at the thirty-year-old soda fountain. Breakfast, lunch, and dinner weekdays; breakfast and lunch weekends. $–$$

**Cafe Tu Tu Tango.** CocoWalk complex at 3015 Grand Avenue, Coconut Grove; (305) 529-2222. Starving-artist theme; eclectic appetizer-style foods known as tapas (for adventurous palates only). Overlooks Coconut Grove's bustling street scene. Lunch and dinner daily. $–$$$

**Mambo Cafe.** 3105 Commodore Plaza, Coconut Grove; (305) 448-2768. New Cuban cuisine in a sidewalk-cafe setting under awnings or umbrellas, with bakery-takeout counter. Kids' selections. Open daily for lunch and dinner. $$–$$$

**Sundays on the Bay.** 5420 Crandon Boulevard, Key Biscayne; (305) 361-6777. Bright murals, aquariums, and a marina view make this a cheerful place to dine on pasta, seafood, sandwiches, and steak. It opens daily for lunch and dinner and for Sunday brunch. $$$

**Tap Tap Haitian Restaurant.** 819 Fifth Street; (305) 672-2898. Wholesome, inexpensive, authentic Haitian stews and fish in a bright setting off Ocean Drive. Open daily for dinner. $–$$

## Where to Stay

**Doral Golf Resort and Spa.** 4400 Northwest Eighty-seventh Avenue; (305) 592-2000 or (800) 71-DORAL; www.doral resort.com. Known for its great golf, spa, and Blue Lagoon Recreation Park. Kids' program teaches golf and undertakes other creative endeavors. Eleven hard and clay tennis courts and stadium, kiddie pool, security gate. $$–$$$$

**Sheraton Bal Harbour.** 9701 Collins Avenue, Bal Harbour; (305) 865-7511 or (800) 325-3535; www.sheraton.com. Fantasy swimming pool, beachfront, watersports rentals, tennis, workout gym, restaurants, 645 rooms and suites, and kids' program. $$–$$$$

**Silver Sands Beach Resort.** 301 Ocean Drive, Key Biscayne; (305) 361-5441. Mini-suites and cottages with kitchenettes looking out onto the pool or beach. $$–$$$$

## For More Information

**Greater Miami Convention and Visitors Bureau.** 701 Brickell Avenue, Suite 2700, Miami 33131; (305) 539-3000 or (888) 766-4264; www.miamiand beaches.com.

# Homestead

About 25 miles south of Coral Gables–Coconut Grove area. To avoid city congestion, take the Florida Turnpike (toll) from Cutler Ridge to Homestead.

## Fruit and Spice Park (ages 6 to 13) 🏕️

**24801 Southwest 187th Avenue; (305) 247-5727. Open 9:00 a.m. to 5:00 p.m. daily. Admission is $6.00 for adults, $1.50 for children under age 12.**

Homestead is known as Florida's capital of exotic fruits. Here you can see more than 500 varieties of rare fruit, herb, nut, and spice trees and plants in the setting of a historic farm community known as Redland. Visit the gift shop and have a picnic while you're there.

## Homestead-Miami Speedway (ages 6 to 13) 🏁

**Off Canal Drive (Southwest 328th Street); 1 Speedway Boulevard; (305) 230-5000.**

It is home to NASCAR and Indy Car events.

## For More Information

**Greater Homestead–Florida City Chamber of Commerce.** 43 North Krome Avenue, Homestead 33030; (305) 247-2332.

# Weekend Jaunt: Biscayne National Underwater Park and Everglades National Park

Primal wilderness lies less than an hour away from the skyscrapers and bright lights of Miami. Homestead is the threshold between two unique federal parks. At the juncture of Palm Drive, head in one direction for Biscayne's marine life, another for the wetlands and hammocks of the Everglades.

### Biscayne National Underwater Park (ages 5 to 13)

**9 miles east of Homestead on North Canal Road; 9710 Southwest 328th Street/Route 9336, Homestead; (305) 230-1100 for park information and (305) 230-7275 for tour reservations; www.nps.gov/bisc. Open 9:00 a.m. to 5:00 p.m. daily. The three-hour family snorkeling tour departs at 1:30 p.m. daily. Tour fare is $35.00 for adults, $29.95 for children under 12; snorkel equipment is included. The three-hour glass-bottom boat tour departs at 10:00 a.m. Admission is $24.45 for adults, $19.45 for seniors, $16.45 for children under 12. Round-trip transportation for island camping is $35.95 November through May. Camping permit is $10. Canoe rentals are $12 per hour, $31 for a half day, $62 for a full day. Kayak rental is $16 per hour, $43 for a half day, $70 for a full day. Diving trips (available Saturday and Sunday at 8:30 a.m. and 1:00 p.m.) cost $54; equipment rental extra. Call for reservations.**

For a truly remarkable day that is full of experiences unique to Florida, head for Biscayne National Underwater Park. The park comprises 181,500 acres, 95 percent of which is underwater. The remaining acreage dots the seas with a cluster of keys that form a chain, which heads the Florida Keys. Mangrove and magnificent coral habitat make up the underwater portion. A variety of excursions range from the tame to the adventuresome: glass-bottom boating, canoeing, snorkeling, and scuba diving. Advance reservations are recommended. You can see much of the same marine life here as you would in the Keys, Bahamas, and Caribbean. The beautiful Convoy Point Visitors Center provides exhibits, breezy picnic grounds, and a nature trail. For primitive overnights, you can camp on Elliott or Boca Chica Key, which are part of Biscayne National Park and are accessible only by boat. Facilities include showers, restrooms, and drinking water on Elliott Key only. You must haul your own trash off the island.

### Everglades Alligator Farm (ages 4 to 13)

**40351 Southwest 192nd Avenue, Florida City; en route to Everglades National Park; (305) 247-2628; www.everglades.com. Open 9:00 a.m. to 6:00 p.m. daily. Admission is $13.50 for adults, $8.50 for children ages 4 to 11. With airboat ride included, cost is $19.00 and $12.00.**

If you spend time in the Everglades, you'll have no problem spotting alligators. Here, you can see how they are farmed and handled. Snakes add to the creepy crawliness

## Florida **Trivia**

**Extent of the Everglades** First called River Glades by early intimidated explorers who penetrated no farther than the open saw grass expanses, *Everglades* refers generically to a wetland ecology that spreads far to the north of park boundaries.

Everglades National Park encompasses 2,100 square miles and contains the largest mangrove forest and the slowest-moving river in the world.

of the place. A thirty-minute airboat ride provides opportunity to observe hawks, ospreys, roseate spoonbills, and, of course, alligators in their natural habitat. The farm also introduces you to caged bobcats, cougars, and an American black bear and presents alligator and hourly wildlife shows.

### Everglades National Park (ages 6 to 13)
**About 15 miles south and west of Homestead on Route 9336; 40001 Route 9336; (305) 242-7700. Admission is $10 per car (good for seven days), $5 for pedestrians or cyclists.**

The Everglades' main visitor center lies outside the park's entrance gate and provides a thorough and state-of-the-art examination of 'Glades critters and the factors that influence them. One exhibit that kids like identifies the calls of cricket frogs, limpkins, and other noisy park residents. A map directs visitors to trails and other facilities along the 40-mile road on the park's east access (for western access, see Southwest Florida chapter).

Two short interpretative trails depart from the Royal Palm Visitors Center, 4 miles inside the park. Anhinga Trail is best in the park for wildlife—lots of gators and birds. Others penetrate slash pine, hammock mahogany, saw grass prairie, and cypress environment. At Pa-hay-okee Overlook, 13 miles inside the park, a boardwalk leads to an observation tower. Eco Pond on Flamingo Road is another good place to spy wildlife—alligators, otters, roseate spoonbills, egrets, and other wading birds.

The Flamingo Visitors Center and Marina features natural history exhibits and information on camping, sightseeing cruises, charter fishing, canoeing, and boat, houseboat, and bicycle rentals. (Some services are limited after the high season ends.) The park hosts interpretive programs, including a weekend family session, in season.

# Glades **Critters**

The alligator and Florida panther are the stars of the Everglades critter show. Snakes, river otters, manatees, mosquitoes, and more than 600 types of fish and 300 bird species inhabit the teeming wetlands.

Legend discloses one other Everglades creature. Some Glades residents swear to the existence of the Everglades skunk ape—smelly, hairy, and Bigfoot-league. Others sneer it off as a hoax.

## Shark Valley (ages 7 to 13)

**From Homestead, follow Krome Avenue (Route 997) 20 miles north to Tamiami Trail and head west for about 20 miles (mailing address: P.O. Box 1739, Tamiami Station, Miami 33144); (305) 221–8776. Open 9:15 a.m. to 5:15 p.m. daily. Admission is $10 per car. Bike rentals are available from 8:30 a.m. to 3:00 p.m. for $6.25 per hour. Two-hour tram tour costs $14.50 for adults, $13.50 for seniors, $8.75 for children ages 12 and under.**

Other east-end access to the Everglades National Park lies along Highway 41. From here, you can catch a tram tour, rent a bike, or begin a hike to explore the quiet natural infrastructure of the Florida Everglades via a paved 15-mile loop road into the Shark Valley Slough. Watch for alligators (lots of them, often quite close to the path), roseate spoonbills, wood storks, snail kites, panthers, and other rare inhabitants of the saw grass marshes and hardwood hammocks. An observation tower gives you a heightened view. It's best to try the hike or bike trip in cool weather, when mosquitoes are less likely to carry off the little ones.

## Miccosukee Indian Village and Airboat Rides (ages 5 to 13)

**About a quarter of a mile west of Shark Valley Information Center; (P.O. Box 440021), Miami 33144; (305) 552-8365. Open 9:00 a.m. to 5:00 p.m. daily. Admission is $10 for adults, $5 for children ages 5 to 12. Airboat tours cost $10 per person.**

Alligator wrestling gets top billing at the Miccosukee village. Tribesfolk also sell their crafts and host thirty-minute airboat tours. The Miccosukee Restaurant offers a taste of local ethnic cuisine, including fry bread and alligator tail, as well as family favorites.

# Upper Keys

About 45 minutes south of Homestead along Highway 1.

You are now leaving Florida and the United States as you know it and entering the world of the Florida Keys—part Bahamian, part Caribbean, and part plain unclassifiable. This becomes especially apparent the farther south you travel, the farther you range from what dictates and concerns life on the mainland.

Incidentally, the farther south you drive, the smaller the numbers become on green markers alongside the road. These mile markers (MM) are the Keys' answer to street addresses along Highway 1, also referred to as the Overseas Highway. The numbers tell you how far you are from Key West, which lies at the end of the road.

Since all waters surrounding the keys were designated as the Florida Keys National Marine Sanctuary in 1990, they are protected, making them a diver's paradise where angelfish, barracuda, octopuses, conch, and lobsters hang out at the local coral bar. (*NOTE:* Conch collecting is not allowed in Florida.)

Fish are prime tourist bait in the Keys. The area is particularly noted for its bonefish, tarpon, dolphinfish, grouper, sailfish, and marlin. Fishing charters and party boats are found at most large resorts and marinas. Party boats charge about $30 per person for a day on the high seas; small charter boats charge about $550 per day for four to six persons.

### John Pennekamp Coral Reef State Park (ages 6 to 13)

**Mile marker 102.5 (P.O. Box 1560), Key Largo 33037; (305) 451-1202 for park information; (305) 451-6300 for concession information and tour reservations. Open 8:00 a.m. to sunset daily. Park entrance is $5.00 per vehicle with up to eight passengers, $3.50 for a single passenger, and $1.50 for bicyclists and pedestrians. Glass-bottom boat tours cost $22 for adults, $15 for children under age 12.**

First stop for underwater enthusiasts: Its most popular sea-bottom sight is the 4,000-pound bronze statue called *Christ of the Deep*. Besides snorkeling and diving charters, you can keep busy canoeing, hiking, sailing, motorboating, and setting up camp in the campground. A concession rents all the necessary water-sports equipment and operates a glass-bottom boat tour three times daily. Stop by the visitor center to see the 30,000-gallon aquarium 9:00 a.m. to 5:00 p.m. daily. **Free.**

### Theater of the Sea (all ages)

**Mile marker 84.5, Islamorada; (305) 664-2431. Shows run continuously 9:30 a.m. to 4:00 p.m. daily. Admission is $23.95 for adults, $15.95 for children ages 3 to 12, including a guided tour and bottomless boat ride. Cost for swimming with dolphins is $165 per person; for swimming with a sea lion, $125; for swimming with stingrays, $50.**

A longtime sea critter attraction, it will delight little ones with dolphin, sea lion, and shark shows. Anyone age five or older can arrange to swim with a dolphin, sea lion, or stingrays if you call in advance. Snorkeling tours and other programs are also available.

## Cheeca Lodge and Spa

Mile marker 82 (P.O. Box 527), Islamorada 33036; (305) 664-4651 or (800) 327-2888; www.cheeca.com.

If you're looking for lodging where all of your needs are met on-property, you'll like this. It's a classy place, but its reputation is built primarily on its environmental awareness. Kids do outdoors stuff, such as snorkeling and fishing, and learn how to be environmentally responsible. Even the restaurant menus are benevolent to the environment. The resort has a nice private beach; a historic cemetery; swimming, tennis, a spa, boat charters, golf; and all the makings of a self-contained vacation. Ask about family packages. $$$$

## Long Key State Park (all ages)

Mile marker 67.5; 67500 Overseas Highway, Long Key; (305) 664-4815. Open 8:00 a.m. to sunset daily. Park entrance is $3.50 for vehicles with a single passenger, $6.00 for two passengers, and 50 cents for each additional passenger. Camping fees are $31.49, tax included, per night.

You can camp or picnic right on the beach here. The lanky key hosts abundant birdlife, which you can observe on nature trails and canoe trips. Reservations are accepted for campsites.

## Where to Eat

**Manny and Isa's.** Mile marker 81.6 (P.O. Box 826), Islamorada 33036; (305) 664-5019. Home-cooked Cuban food, great conch chowder, and Key lime pie. Lunch and dinner Wednesday through Monday. Closed October to November 15. $–$$$

**Papa Joe's.** Mile marker 79.7 (P.O. Box 109), Islamorada 33036; (305) 664-8109. Fresh seafood at the edge of a marina. Lunch and dinner daily (closed Tuesday during slow periods). $$–$$$

## Where to Stay

Lodging is plentiful and varied in the Keys, with options in every price range. See also Cheeca Lodge and Spa.

**Holiday Isle Resort and Marina.** Mile marker 84, 84001 Overseas Highway, Islamorada; (305) 664-2321 or (800) 327-7070; www.holidayisle.com. Marina with rental boats and fishing and diving charters, pools, restaurants, shops, playgrounds, and endless entertainment. Rooms, efficiencies, cottages, and suites are available. $–$$$$

**Key Largo Bay Marriott Beach Resort.** Mile marker 103.8, 103800 Overseas Highway, Key Largo; (305) 453-0000 or (800) 932-9332; www.marriottkeylargo.com. Lush resort with 153 rooms overlooking the bay. Man-made beach, pool, restaurants, tiki bar, dive shop, kids' club, and fitness room. $$–$$$$

## For More Information

**Key Largo Chamber of Commerce.**
106000 Overseas Highway, Key Largo
33037; (305) 451-1414 or (800) 822-1088;
www.keylargo.org.

**The Florida Keys and Key West.** P.O.
Box 866, Key West 33041-0866; (800) FLA-
KEYS; www.fla-keys.com.

# Marathon

About a half hour south of Long Key on Highway 1.

### Hawk's Cay Resort and Dolphin Connection (all ages)

**Mile marker 61, north of Marathon; 61 Hawk's Cay Boulevard, Duck Key; (305) 743-7000 or (888) 443-6393; www.hawkscay.com. Swim with the dolphins, $150 per person. Call for times and reservations.**

One of its finest assets is the Dolphin Connection, a facility that enables families to observe dolphins from the dock for **free** and participate in more extensive interaction and encounter sessions for a fee. Four pools (one with an interactive pirate ship run aground), a sheltered beach lagoon, a tree-house playground with climbing wall, and an adventure kids' program get high marks from young guests. Older ones can take advantage of the resort's fly-fishing and offshore sailing schools. The Dolphin Connection is open to the public. $$$$

### Crane Point Museum & Nature Center (ages 2 to 10)

**5550 Overseas Highway (bayside at mile marker 50); (305) 743-9100; www.cranepoint .net. Open 9:00 a.m. to 5:00 p.m. Monday through Saturday and noon to 5:00 p.m. Sunday, with shortened hours in summer. Admission is $9.50 for adults, $8.00 for seniors, $6.00 for students; 6 and under free.**

Small and homey, this is a must-stop, free of the commercialism of a lot of other attractions. Be sure to see the simulated coral reef. Children may dress up as pirates and play on the pirate ship. Nature trails lead to more discovery, including an aviary for bird rehabilitation.

## Florida **Trivia**

**Seven Mile Bridge** The Seven Mile Bridge that connects Marathon and the Lower Keys, also known as the Eighth Wonder of the World, affords a magnificent view and is the longest segmental bridge in the world. It was built in 1982 in pieces in Tampa and shipped to the Keys to be assembled.

## Pigeon Key (ages 6 to 13) 🏛

**Visitors Center at mile marker 48 (1 Knight's Key Boulevard), oceanside right before the Seven Mile Bridge on Marathon; (305) 743-5999. Tours depart from the center hourly 10:00 a.m. to 4:00 p.m. daily. Admission and shuttle is $11.00 for adults, $8.50 for ages 6 to 13; under 6 free.**

Still in its developmental stages, it makes for a most interesting historical attraction that you can reach by bike or foot, or via a tram from the Visitors Center, housed in a vintage railroad car. You can see the tiny key as you cross the bridge, but you can reach it only by the old bridge, which allows no car traffic. The key is significant for the role it played during the building of the railroad in 1905 and for its surviving Bahamian architecture. The museum, occupying the assistant bridge tender's house, holds old postcards, paintings, photographs, and memorabilia.

## Where to Eat

**Herbies.** Mile marker 50.5, 6350 Overseas Highway; (305) 743-6373. Casual, picnic-table atmosphere. Choice seafood and beef. Lunch and dinner Tuesday through Saturday. $$

## Where to Stay

See also Hawk's Cay.

**Conch Key Cottages.** Mile marker 62.3 oceanside, 62250 Overseas Highway, Walker's Island; (305) 289-1377 or (800) 330-1577; www.conchkeycottages.com. Twelve oceanside self-sufficient cottages with small beach, pool, and boat docks. $$–$$$

## For More Information

**Greater Marathon Chamber of Commerce.** 12222 Overseas Highway, Marathon 33050; (305) 743-5417 or (800) 842-9580; www.floridakeysmarathon.com.

# Lower Keys

Continue south along Highway 1.

South of the Seven Mile Bridge, the temperament changes. Activity level drops a notch. Wildlife and vegetation heighten.

The second largest of the Keys, Big Pine Key remains one of the most undeveloped, gratifying adventures with its abundant opportunities for fishing and nature exploration.

Offshore of Big Pine Key, diving hits its spectacular peak at Looe Key National Marine Sanctuary. Technicolor reefs attract tropical fish of sheer dazzle, mostly in less than 30 feet of aquarium-clear water. Summer is the favorite time for divers. The waters are warm, and the season is open for lobster. No spear or lobster fishing is allowed within the sanctuary, however.

## Bahia Honda State Park (all ages)

Mile marker 37, south of the Seven Mile Bridge, north of Big Pine Key; 36850 Overseas Highway, Big Pine Key; (305) 872-2353; www.floridastateparks.org/bahiahonda. Open 8:00 a.m. to sunset daily. Park entrance is $5 per vehicle with up to eight passengers, $3 for a single passenger, and $1 for extra passengers, bicyclists, and pedestrians, plus a county surcharge of 50 cents per person 6 years and older.

If you're craving a nice beach, something you don't find much of in the Keys, head to Bahia Honda for a day, overnight, or as long as you can get away with it. It has two beaches, actually, one on the ocean side, another bayside. The bayside beach is favored by families because of its calm waters and extensive facilities, including shaded picnic tables with grills, food concessions, and a nearby marina and concessions that rent kayaks, sailboards, and snorkeling equipment and offer snorkel boat excursions. Off the beach, you can stake a tent or rent a cabin, go on a fishing charter, or hike a nature trail that leads over an old railroad bridge.

## National Key Deer Refuge (ages 4 to 13)

Entrance on Key Deer Boulevard (Route 940), off Route A1A at mile marker 30.5; (305) 872-2239. The visitor center is off to the right in the Big Pine Key Shopping Plaza (P.O. Box 430510, Big Pine Key 33043); it conducts tours in the winter. The center is open 9:00 a.m. to 4:00 p.m. Monday through Friday. The refuge is open sunrise to sunset daily. Admission is free.

The tiny Key deer, a subspecies of the white-tailed deer, survives in the far-off reaches of Big Pine Key and is protected at the 8,000-acre refuge. Best times to spot one of the 800 or so deer is on a slow drive during the morning or evening hours. Visit the refuge's Blue Hole (a lake formed by quarry digging) to see alligators, turtles, and fish in the see-through waters and hike two self-guided nature trails.

## Reflections Nature Tours (ages 7 to 13)

P.O. Box 431373, Big Pine Key 33043; (305) 872-4668; www.floridakeyskayaktours.com. Open daily. Cost is $50 per person for three-hour guided tour. Tours at 9:00 a.m. and 1:00 p.m.

Explore National Key Deer Refuge, the Everglades, and other wilderness areas by kayak. Half- and full-day tours and rentals with backcountry ferry are available.

## Underseas Inc. (ages 10 to 13)

Oceanside at mile marker 30.5 (P.O. Box 430319, Big Pine Key 33043); (305) 872-2700 or (800) 446-5663. Open daily. Snorkeling charter cost is $29.95 per person, including gear.

Conducts snorkeling and scuba charters and instruction (ages twelve and older) and rents equipment. Half-day charters take you to two different sites.

## Where to Eat

**Mangrove Mama's.** Mile marker 20, 19991 Overseas Highway, Sugarloaf Key; (305) 745-3030. Stop for a typically Keys casual bite hidden among the banana trees. Ribs, steak, fresh shrimp and fish, and legendary Key lime pie in an atmosphere of color-splashed fun. Lunch and dinner daily. $$–$$$

## Where to Stay

**Big Pine Fishing Lodge.** Oceanside at mile marker 33 (P.O. Box 430513, Big Pine Key 33043); (305) 872-2351. Well-maintained park with campground and mobile home, motel, efficiency units, complete marina, boat rentals, fishing charters, a pool, and bait and tackle shop. $

## For More Information

**Big Pine and Lower Keys Chamber of Commerce.** P.O. Box 430511, Big Pine Key 33043-0511; 31020 Overseas Highway (mile marker 31); (305) 872-2411 or (800) 872-3722; www.lowerkeyschamber.com.

# Key West

At the end of the road.

In 1982, Key West symbolically seceded from the Union, dubbing itself the Conch Republic in honor of its Bahamian background (residents of Bahamian heritage are known as Conchs). Though the act was not official, Key West remains a land with its own rules and free-spirited attitude. Expect somewhere totally different. You won't be disappointed.

Old Town is the center of activity and attractions. Look for a copy of *Walking & Biking Guide* for a historic self-guided tour. Plan to stay for sunset to get a taste of what the town is all about. Each evening at Mallory Square, sword swallowers, human statues, tightrope walkers, other street performers, food vendors, tourists, and residents gather to celebrate the day's finale.

### Conch Tour Train (all ages)

**Departs from station at 303 Front Street; (305) 294-5161; www.conchtourtrain.com. Open 9:00 a.m. to 4:30 p.m. daily. Admission is $27 for adults, $13 for children ages 4 to 12. A $43 for adults and $21 for kids combination ticket includes admission to the Key West Aquarium and Shipwreck Historeum for adults.**

To get to know the town and its history in short order, take the Conch Tour Train ninety-minute tour. Learn how Key West became the richest city in the United States from salvaging ships wrecked on yonder reefs. **Free** reboarding is allowed.

### Key West Aquarium (all ages)

**1 Whitehead Street; (305) 296-2051. Tours at 11:00 a.m. and at 1:00, 3:00, and 4:30 p.m. daily. Admission for a two-day pass is $10 for adults, $5 for children ages 4 to 12.**

On the waterfront near Mallory Square, this is a small, open-air, Key West–style aquarium, meaning it's kind of funky, nothing plastic or dressed up. You can watch shark and turtle feedings and feel around the touch tank.

### Key West Shipwreck Historeum (ages 4 to 13)

**Across the street from the aquarium at 1 Whitehead Street; (305) 292-8990; www.shipwreckhistoreum.com. Guided tours with a show commence every half hour 9:15 a.m. to 4:45 p.m. daily. Admission is $11 for adults, $5 for children ages 4 to 12.**

It will thrill young adventurers with tales of salvaging, using actors, films, and lasers. The kids can even climb the 65-foot captain's observatory to watch for reefs and wrecks and get a feel for the danger and excitement involved in Key West's most prosperous industry of yore.

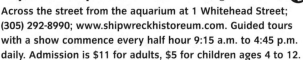

### Key West Lighthouse Museum (ages 7 to 13)

**938 Whitehead Street; (305) 294-0012; www.kwahs.com. Open 9:30 a.m. to 4:30 p.m. daily. Admission is $10 for adults, $9 for seniors, $4 for children and students.**

Climb the 150-year-old, 90-foot, 88-step structure, walk inside a 12-foot prism lens, and have a look at the photos and memorabilia inside the reconstructed Keepers Quarters.

### Mel Fisher's Maritime Museum (ages 4 to 13)

**200 Greene Street; (305) 294-2633. Open 9:30 a.m. to 5:00 p.m. daily. Admission is $11 for adults, $6 for children.**

One of Key West's most recent finds was a spectacular trove of treasure aboard the sunken seventeenth-century *Atocha,* displayed here.

### Fantasy Fest (ages 8 and up)

**(800) FLA-KEYS; www.fla-keys.com.**

Key West takes Halloween dress-up seriously, with ten days of costumed carnival, including a Children's Day and Pet Masquerade. Be prepared to see partial nudity (usually covered with body paint) on the street at any time.

**Fort Zachary Taylor State Historic Park** (all ages)
End of Southard Street on Truman Annex (P.O. Box 6560) Key West 33041; (305) 292-6713. Open 8:00 a.m. to sunset daily. Park entrance is $6.00 per vehicle with up to eight passengers, $3.50 for a single passenger, and 50 cents for extra passengers, bicyclists, and pedestrians, plus a 50 cent county surcharge per person 6 years and older. Bicycle rental $1.50.

Beaches are not Key West's strong suit. This one is man-made and fringed with shade trees. When it's time to get out of the sun, a history refreshment awaits in the form of a fort that was built before the Civil War. Living-history tours are conducted the last weekend of the month during winter season. Join a ranger-guided tour of the fort at noon or 2:00 p.m. daily year-round.

# More Things to See and Do
# in Southeast Florida

- **Fun Depot,** Lake Worth; (561) 547-0817
- **Children's Museum of Boca Raton,** Boca Raton; (561) 368-6875
- **International Swimming Hall of Fame,** Fort Lauderdale; (954) 462-6536
- **Everglades Holiday Park,** Fort Lauderdale; (954) 434-8111
- **Ancient Spanish Monastery,** North Miami Beach; (305) 945-1462
- **Scott Rakow Youth Center Ice Rink,** Miami Beach; (305) 673-7767
- **Environmental Center,** Miami; (305) 237-2600
- **Fairchild Tropical Gardens,** Miami; (305) 667-1651
- **Everglades Safari Park,** Miami; (305) 226-6923
- **Indian Key State Historic Site,** Long Key; (305) 664-9814
- **Perky Bat Tower,** Sugarloaf Key
- **Dolphins Plus,** Key Largo; (305) 451-1993
- **Audubon House,** Key West; (305) 294-2116
- **Cayo Hueso y Havana,** Key West; (305) 293-7260
- **Wreckers' Museum and Oldest House,** Key West; (305) 294-9502
- **Little White House Museum,** Key West; (305) 294-9911
- **Ernest Hemingway Home and Museum,** Key West; (305) 294-1575
- **East Martello Museum & Gallery,** Key West; (305) 296-3913

### Fort Jefferson (ages 5 to 13)

Garden Key, Dry Tortugas; (305) 294-7009 or (800) 634-0939; www.yankeefreedom.com. The Yankee Fleet ferry service from Key West (at 240 Margaret Street) will take you there and back for $129 for adults, $119 for seniors, $89 for children ages 4 to 16 (includes breakfast, picnic lunch, tour, and snorkel gear). Park entrance is $5 for ages 17 and up; $3 camping fee.

Now, to really get away from it all, plan a trip from Key West to Dry Tortugas, where you can snorkel and explore Fort Jefferson, which once served as a prison that held Dr. Mudd, the physician who patched up Lincoln assassin John Wilkes Booth. Restrooms are the only facilities.

## Where to Eat

**El Meson de Pepe.** 410 Wall Street; (305) 295-2620. Indoor-outdoor traditional Cuban restaurant. Lunch and dinner daily. $–$$

**Kelly's Caribbean Bar and Grill.** 301 Whitehead Street; (305) 293-8484. Owned by Kelly McGillis (of *Top Gun* fame), in the historic Pan Am building and its courtyard. Island atmosphere and cuisine, home-brewed beer. Lunch and dinner daily. $$–$$$

## Where to Stay

Key West is known for its intimate guest houses, but many of them do not accommodate children. Families should try the larger hotels and resorts.

**Hyatt Key West Resort & Marina.** 601 Front Street; (305) 296-9900 or (800) 233-1234. Close to the action at Mallory Square and Duval Street, but safely removed and gated, Hyatt Key West offers families water-sports rentals and charters, an on-site restaurant, and pool in a compact 120-room complex. $$$–$$$$

## For More Information

**Greater Key West Chamber of Commerce.** 402 Wall Street, Key West 33040; (305) 294-2587 or (800) LAST-KEY.

## Annual Events

**Children's Theatre Festival.** Miami; (305) 444-9293. Three-weeks-plus of events in January, including Festival Family Fun Day.

**Homestead Rodeo.** Homestead; (305) 247-2332. Rodeo events, parade, food, and arts and crafts the latter part of January.

**Old Island Days.** Key West; (305) 294-9501. A celebration of Key West's multifaceted past and architecture with activities for the whole family. **Free.**

**Carnaval Miami.** Miami; (305) 644-8888. Miami's most lively celebration at Mardi Gras time. Ten days of sports, concerts and Latin food, music, and dance at the world's largest block party.

**SunFest.** West Palm Beach; (561) 659-6980. Late April or early May, its For Kid's Sake Park features an art show and fireworks during this four-day event.

**Fantasy Fest.** Key West; (800) FLA-KEYS; www.fla-keys.com. A live street fest in October that lasts for ten days and includes a costumed carnival, Children's Day, and a Pet Masquerade.

**Junior Orange Bowl International Youth Festival.** Coral Gables; (305) 662-1210. Youth athletic and fine art competitions and parade, October through January.

**Miccosukee Indian Arts Festival.** Miccosukee Indian Village; (305) 223-8380. Representatives from about twenty tribes perform in December and January.

# Index

# F

# G

# H

# About the Authors

**Chelle Koster Walton** combined her career as travel writer with her calling as a parent upon the birth of her son, Aaron, who immediately became her traveling companion. From her home on Sanibel Island, Florida, the author has written or contributed to numerous guidebooks—two of which won Lowell Thomas Awards—and magazine articles for *FamilyFun, Caribbean Travel & Life, National Geographic Traveler, Arthur Frommer's Budget Travel, Endless Vacation*, the *New York Post,* and other print and electronic media. Walton is cofounder of www.guidebookwriters.com and a member of the Society of American Travel Writers.

**Sara Kennedy** is a longtime journalist and traveler. She began travel writing at *Flying* magazine in New York City and departed occasionally from news editing and reporting to write travel stories for various newspapers, including the *Tampa Times* and the *Philadelphia Inquirer.* For more than a decade, as her children grew up, she operated a Tampa freelance business, writing for the *New York Times, FamilyFun* magazine, *Cooking Light, Hemispheres,* Michelin's *Green Guide to Florida,* and Tampabay.City search.com. She has edited a cookbook entitled *Clarita's Cooking Lighter* and contributed to the *New York Times What's Doing Around the World.*

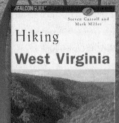
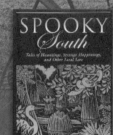
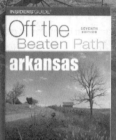

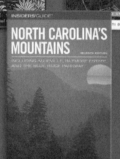